THE GREAT
BACKPACKING
ADVENTURE

Chris Townsend

 The Oxford Illustrated Press

© Chris Townsend, 1987

Printed in England by J.H. Haynes and Co. Limited, Sparkford, Nr. Yeovil, Somerset.

ISBN 0 946609 29 2

Published by:
The Oxford Illustrated Press, Sparkford, Nr. Yeovil, Somerset.

Haynes Publications Inc., 861 Lawrence Drive, Newbury Park, California 91320, USA.

British Library Cataloguing in Publication Data
  Townsend, Chris
  The great backpacking adventure.
  —(The Great adventure series)
  1. Backpacking
  I. Title. II. Series
  796.5'1'0924   GV199.6
ISBN 0–946609–29–2

Library of Congress Catalog Card Number 86-83214

CONTENTS

Introduction

DEDICATION

For my Mother

ACKNOWLEDGEMENTS

Many people have been involved in one way or another with the journeys described in this book. I would like to thank Denise Thorn for typing the original drafts of chapters two and three and accompanying me to the start of the End to End Walk; all my companions on these and other adventures plus those friends who wrote to me on the American treks and whose letters from home helped keep me going — especially Fran Townsend, Denise Thorn, Rachel O'Neill, Graham Huntington, Alain Kahan, Scott Steiner, Mark Edgington, Chris Ainsworth, Andy Hicks, Al Micklethwaite and Steve Twaites; the following people and companies for their help and encouragement — Paul and Sarah Howcroft of Rohan, Peter and Kate Lumley, publishers of *Footloose*, Mike Parsons of Karrimor International, Ben and Marion Wintringham, Tony Pearson, Brian Spencer of YHA Services, Rod Pashley and John Hinde and the rest of the staff at Outward Bound Loch Eil, Nigel Gifford of Camera Care Systems, Charlie and Terry Lingard of MOAC, Ian Gundle of Field & Trek, John Traynor, Freddy Markham of Survival Aids, Cameron McNeish, Roger Smith, Tom Waghorn, Hamish Brown, Warren Rogers, Jim Wolf, *Ultimate Equipment, Berghaus, Optimus, New Balance* and finally all the people I met along the, way whose help and kindness made all my treks so much more enjoyable and successful. I hope you enjoy the book, folks!

INTRODUCTION

This book tells the story of seven backpacking treks I made during the years 1976-86, treks that vary from two six-month-long ones in the wildernesses of the western USA to one of just a week in the rugged interior of Iceland. All have one thing in common: they are all journeys where I carried all I needed on my back and moved on from day to day, a definition, if one is needed, for the term 'backpacking'. They were also all done with a purpose whether it was to walk from Mexico to Canada along the Pacific Crest Trail, climb as many peaks as possible on the Corrour to Ullapool Scottish trek or just progress as far as possible in three days as on the Iceland venture. But I hope the stories of these adventures show that these pragmatic explanations are only superficial, and do not touch the real essence of why I go backpacking. After all what possible reason can there be to walk cross-country from Land's End to John O'Groats or stubbornly staying as close as possible to the watershed of the United States despite appalling weather conditions? Enjoyment is, of course, the motivating factor. These days pleasure is often seen purely in terms of passivity, of being entertained, and many people find it hard to believe that something which requires physical exertion, that may even result in some measure of discomfort and danger, can be fun — but it is so. I'd rather fight my way through the thawing spring snows of Iceland or risk encounters with grizzly bears in the Rocky Mountains than watch the best television programme ever made. Backpacking, travelling in remote places carrying all you need in a rucksack, is a means to freedom, the freedom of the wilderness, a freedom which I have relished over the years and the experience of which I hope to portray here.

But enough of definitions and explanations, if the stories of my backpacking adventures cannot put across the excitement and intensity of the activity and perhaps give some inkling of why I keep returning to the wilderness with a pack on my back then no words of introduction will do so. On to the trails then. I hope you enjoy what is to be seen and done along the way.

I

England

THE PENNINE WAY

As I left Leicéster station early on 6 April 1976 aboard the train for Sheffield I felt more tense and nervous than on any walk before or since. I was setting off to walk England's most famous, oldest, and most walked long distance path, the Pennine Way. As this was my first ever long distance walk I did not know how I would react to being alone and walking every day for two or more weeks whilst coping with adverse conditions and sleeping in a tent every night.

I'd been backpacking for a couple of years but had done no more than undertake weekends away with companions or a week or so's day-walking, with backpacking used to travel between valley bases. As my ambition was to undertake a Land's End to John O'Groats walk I had to progress at some point from casual, weekend backpacking to serious long distance walking. I chose the Pennine Way as my first long distance route because it seemed to have the right balance between safety and commitment. I wanted to do both a high-level route and a linear one and as at this time I had yet to discover the Scottish Highlands, the Pennine Way seemed the ideal route. That it was walked in its entirety by around 4,000 people a year mattered not a bit to me. The challenge was in whether I personally could walk it, a challenge common to everyone who tries it.

Another aim of the walk, if it can be called an aim, was simply to spend a long enough period of time in the hills to feel part of them, to feel as though living in them was a way of life in itself and not just a short escape from another, apparently more real, existence. This last aim has become, I think, the real reason why I continue to go on long backpacking treks as only on such trips, where I'm completely self-sufficient for weeks on end and am staying in the wilderness every night, can I really find that identification with nature that I am seeking. Walking a line

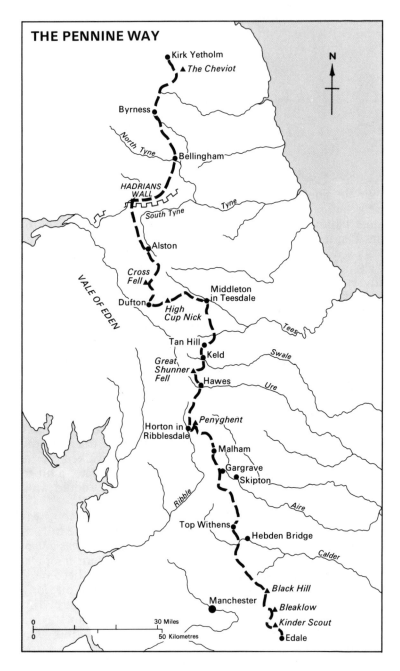

THE PENNINE WAY

N

Kirk Yetholm
▲ The Cheviot

Byrness

North Tyne

Bellingham

HADRIANS WALL

South Tyne

Tyne

Alston

Cross Fell ▲

VALE OF EDEN

Dufton

Middleton in Teesdale

High Cup Nick

Tees

Tan Hill

Keld

Swale

Great Shunner Fell ▲

Hawes

Ure

Horton in Ribblesdale

Penyghent ▲

Malham

Gargrave

Skipton

Ribble

Aire

Top Withens

Hebden Bridge

Calder

Black Hill ▲

Manchester

Bleaklow

Kinder Scout ▲

Edale

0   30 Miles
0   50 Kilometres

2

from A to B has become an excuse, a rationalisation, an easy explanation of why I make these long trips. It satisfies the part of my mind that requires an apparently logical reason for taking part in such an activity. I find that if I set off to go backpacking in an area with no clear plan, no peaks to climb, no long route to walk, then I frequently feel aimless and even dissatisfied. I need my backpacking trips to have a clear goal even if I no longer believe that achieving that goal is the real reason for going on them.

But to return to that train to Sheffield. On it we find a young man with a huge rucksack perusing a guidebook and a pile of maps, feeling nervous and excited whilst trying to appear cool and experienced. At Sheffield I changed to the train for Edale, the tiny hamlet that lies under the shadow of the great peat moorland of Kinder Scout where the Pennine Way starts. The valley looked tranquil in the calm dusk; its skyline of Win Hill, Lose Hill, Mam Tor, Rushup Edge, Brown Knoll and, to the north, the long line of Kinder Scout, outlined softly against the pale grey night sky. High up a thin mixture of cirrus and stratus clouds gave the lie to the apparently settled nature of the weather. Change was on the way. I was glad of the gentle quiet of this first night as it helped quell my excitement and anticipation though it must be admitted that this was assisted by a few pints of bitter in the Nag's Head. Before ambling over to the pub I'd pitched my tent on Cooper's, a popular farm site with only a dozen tents on it as the Easter holiday and the start of the summer season were still a week or so away. Under the light of a quarter moon, it took me forty minutes to set up that first camp of my long distance backpacking career.

The Pennine Way runs from Edale in the Peak District National Park, up the spine of the Pennines through the Yorkshire Dales National Park and the Northumberland National Park, to Kirk Yetholm just across the border in Scotland. Much of the route crosses bleak moorland between 1,000 and 2,000 feet above sea level rising to a high point of 2,930 feet on Cross Fell, the highest peak in the Pennine chain. Peat moorland overlying gritstone rocks makes up much of the terrain but in the Yorkshire Dales very different limestone country is crossed and, although still covered with peat bog, the Cheviot Hills near the northern end are granite based. In between the blocks of high country the path threads its way through the upland

3

pastures of sheep farms, along the winding, silvery river valleys of the Aire, the Tees and the South Tyne, eastwards along Hadrian's Wall and through the dark conifers of the Border Forest Park.

First conceived of in 1936 by Tom Stephenson of the Ramblers Association, the Pennine Way is a route that is both challenging and varied, a worthwhile route and one whose creation opened up vast tracts of country hitherto closed to hillwalkers. This was one of the main reasons why Tom Stephenson fought for the creation of the Pennine Way. He wanted to see a day when a walker could travel up the length of the Pennines to Scotland without hindrance, impossible in the thirties and forties when grouse moors were closed year round and guarded by keepers as were the lands of the Water Boards, although in theory they were publicly owned. In these circumstances the proposed Pennine Way was an imaginative and radical idea and this ought to be remembered now it has become fashionable to decry the walk, mainly it seems because so many people use it. It is far better known than any other long distance path and this in itself ensures its continuing popularity. People like to tell others what they have done and there is still a cachet in being able to say, especially to non-walkers, 'Oh, yes, I've walked the Pennine Way'.

And it's not that easy either. Most people who set out each year intending to complete the whole route fail in their aim. The going can be tough with deep bogs, featureless terrain and days of constant rain and low mist to contend with even at the height of summer. Though the 270 miles have been completed in astonishingly fast times by top fell runners (Mike Cudahy currently holds the record with his 1984 run, which took just 2 days 54 minutes and 30 seconds), most people take from two to three weeks. Youth hostels, 'Bed and Breakfasts', guest houses and hotels are accessible enough, lying either on or near the route at convenient distances, so that the Way can be walked using accommodation every night. The advantage in using these is that you need only carry a light rucksack, but the disadvantages are that each day's destination has to be reached regardless of the weather or any feelings of tiredness or laziness.

My own feeling is that the only way to really appreciate the Pennine Way is to backpack; to travel with all that is

4

needed to spend one's nights out under the stars far from the warmth and comforts of hostels or hotels. This way the walk becomes a total experience, one that last twenty-four hours every day, and is not just a series of day walks starting from a different base each day. The backpacker is free to stop when and where desired, to walk through the night and to sleep all day, to stomp thirty miles one day but amble five the next, to camp in wild and beautiful locations with only the lonely cry of the curlew, the rustle of the wind in the grass and the noises of night creatures for company, to wake with the morning sun bathing the hillsides with its cool light and sparkling on the dew-covered tent whilst high above the skylark welcomes the new day. Of course against that the backpacker must carry a heavy pack and be prepared for the nights when the sounds will be of driving rain on the flysheet and the roar of a gusting wind rushing up the valley or across the hillside to rattle the flimsy shelter that is his only protection against the elements. But I'd rather that than a night in a bed in a warm room, cut off from the world I've come to be part of, a night that then requires a whole day to restore that contact only to lose it again in another return to civilisation. That desire to experience the wilderness to the full, night and day, is what distinguishes the backpacker from the walker.

My initiation into long distance backpacking began in the rain and mist of a typical Pennine day. I had been, unfortunately, right in my weather prediction and conditions had deteriorated with the wind veering to the north east. Waking at 6.30, I turned over and went back to sleep until 9.30. Sometimes this delaying tactic works and one wakes later to a nice day but on this occasion it didn't and it was still overcast and drizzling. My second ruse was to try the prolonged breakfast tactic. I was partially rewarded this time for when I finally set off at 11.45 there were some sunny periods and it had stopped raining.

The Pennine Way throws the backpacker in at the deep end immediately. After a short walk across Edale Meadows towards the dark bulk of Kinder Scout the path, well-worn here, starts to climb up the rugged and rocky Grindsbrook Clough, a v-shaped ravine cut by its stream deep into the flat 2,000-foot plateau that is Kinder Scout. As I ascended the track towards the plateau edge I thought I'd never make it, the pack felt so heavy, and at that point I just couldn't imagine how I was going to carry this load the full 270 miles. But, as always, the top was reached and soon, in mist and occasional bursts of sunlight, I was following a compass bearing across the heart of Kinder, where the deep, steep-sided peat groughs covered with tussocks of vegetation, made walking quite difficult. Underfoot it was, as usual on Kinder, very wet and I went in up to the knee a couple of times. At the waterfall of Kinder Downfall, where the River Kinder leaves its youthful meanderings across the plateau to tumble over broken cliffs to Hayfield Reservoir, I stopped for lunch. The journey was underway.

The desolate moors of Mill Hill, Moss Castle and Featherbed Moss led, wetly, to the Snake Road (A57) where I climbed gently up to the high peat bog plateau of the Bleaklow, crossing en route Doctor's Gate. Doctor's Gate is thought by some to be the remnants of a Roman road that once linked the forts of Navio near Castleton and Ardotalia near Glossop though others consider it to date only as far back as the Middle Ages. Either way it is a recent intrusion in the landscape when compared with the ancient, worn down, gritstone boulders and outcrops that occur on Bleaklow and which provide welcome focal points for navigation. I needed to take a compass bearing in the middle of the plateau to ensure finding the route down to Longdendale by Torside Clough. Once down in this heavily industrialised valley (two roads, a chain of reservoirs, power lines and a railway) I crossed over and headed quickly up the valley of Crowden Great Brook to camp by a little stream below the dark crags of Rakes Rocks high on the valley's side above me. I had walked about $16^1/2$ miles in about 8 hours but more importantly I'd completed the first day of the Pennine Way and the first day of my long distance walking career. The great backpacking adventure had begun.

After a frosty night when I was glad of my borrowed down-filled sleeping bag (I'd guessed, correctly, that my old threadbare feather-filled one would not be warm enough in the Pennines in early spring) I woke to a calm, sunny day which, as often happens, had changed to an overcast one with a strong north-west wind by the time I was ready to start walking. The dark peat bog country I'd been in the day before continued with the same combination of gritstone outcrops above stream-cut cloughs and featureless plateaus

6

sticky with mud. Laddow Rocks, a traditional rock climbing crag (though these days neglected for ones more accessible by car), gave some views down into the valleys but Kinder, Bleaklow and, ahead, Black Hill were mist-shrouded. Crossing Black Hill in thin swirls of mist it felt very mysterious and other-worldy. Sides of groughs and lumps of peat would loom up out of the mist like great black cliffs or fortresses only to dwindle into minor if slippery obstacles on being approached.

The bogs continued and I had my worst scare on Featherbed Moss when I went in up to my knees and had to crawl out to firmer ground. It took me a few minutes to recover before I felt ready to continue on into the mist. Moor and mountain mists like this can be quite frightening until you are used to them as your world shrinks to a small circle that moves with you and navigation depends solely on compass bearings. On this occasion I was glad to reach Standedge, where a road cuts through the moors, for my guidebook told me that a cafe should be there. Unfortunately all I found was a heap of burnt timbers for the cafe had been destroyed by fire several years previously. This was very demoralising! The only thing to do when faced with a disappointment like this is to walk it off and to make up for it, I was determined to reach the White House Inn where I hoped to spend a few hours out of the clinging, wet mist and enjoy a decent meal. But, I hear you say, what was all that stuff about wanting to escape civilisation and preferring the wilderness even in bad weather? Half a day in a bit of mist and all he can think about is finding a pub! Well, this was my first ever long distance backpack and sinking in the bog had given me a bit of a fright. On all walks (on all my walks at any rate) there are points when warmth and shelter are very welcome if available and sometimes only the knowledge that they lie ahead keeps one going. On the Pennine Way the need for such comfort simply occurred very early in the walk.

The White Horse was not all I hoped for anyway as there was no food available except peanuts. And I don't like peanuts! So my evening meal, instead of a good three course pub dinner, was Batchelors Savoury Tomato Rice with a curry flavour Oxo cube and some dried mixed vegetables stirred in. My camp was in an old quarry on the edge of the pub car park, not the most salubrious of sites but at least it was out of the peat bogs. I hoped I would have easier walking ahead. The first 34 miles had been quite tough. The misty weather continued. Visibility the next morning was fifty yards at most as I walked along a track beside several reservoirs with many pied wagtails fluttering about all around me. Halfway round Warlands Reservoir I suddenly walked out of the mist, a quite eerie occurrence. I looked back and there a few yards away was the wall of white. To check this wasn't some form of illusion I walked in and out of the mist a few times. No, it was quite real. Out of the mist it was drier and warmer and I was glad to shed the clammy feeling that had accompanied me since I had left Edale. I climbed up to Stoodley Pike and its monument which was originally built in 1814 to commemorate the Peace of Ghent and Napoleon's downfall but has been rebuilt twice since after it collapsed. The Pike commands a view over the Calder valley and the mill towns of Hebden Bridge and its neighbours with their houses looking as though they are stacked on top of each other on the steep hill sides. Although the Way crosses the valley a mile above Hebden the town was my goal as I needed to stock up on food and fuel.

Leaving Calderdale involves the negotiation of a complex network of small fields, hedges, paths and farms. Here I was very glad of my guidebook, Wainwright's *Pennine Way Companion,* which showed every feature and gave enough detail to show me which side of a hedge the path ran. I took one detour at Long High Top Farm when, on passing through a gate, I was chased by a large number of pigs. With the words of Ted Hughes' poem 'View of a Pig' springing to mind ('Their bite is worse than a horse's/They chop a half-moon clean out.') I surprised myself at how fast I could move with a heavy pack on my back and made a rapid exit!

Back on the moors and in Brontë country I camped at Top Withens, a ruin that may have been the inspiration for the Earnshaw's home in Wuthering Heights though a plaque on the wall, erected by the Brontë Society, points out that the buildings, before their deterioration, bore no resemblance to the house described by Emily Brontë though the situation of them may have been in her mind when writing the book. Certainly the images of desolation, bleakness and life on the edge of civilisation conjured up by the book fit these grim and colourless moors where sunlight seems an intrusion into a world that is by its very nature drab and grey. It reflected my mood too as I arrived after a nineteen-mile day with sore feet, two blisters and all my socks wet. Not a good way to end a day, especially as the next day I hoped to leave the low moors and farmland behind by walking the twenty-five miles to Malham and the start of the Yorkshire Dales section of the Pennine Way.

I wanted to push on because I was becoming a little bored with what I described in my journal as 'very ordinary undulating farmland' and was looking forward to some bigger hills. I had my first, inspiring, view of them from Ickornshaw Moor and Pinhaw Beacon with Ingleborough and Penyghent prominent in the view ahead. The sight of them kept me going for the twelve hours it took to reach Malham, a walk finished in the dark alongside the infant River Aire. I found I had added another blister to my collection and my feet ached even more. A prosaic journal entry points out that I 'must wash out and thoroughly dry my socks'! En route to Malham I stopped to read a sign put up by an enterprising farmer through whose yard the route passes. It directed me into the house with the promise of food and drink. I duly turned left and lunched on poached eggs on toast. Lower Summer House Farm was very welcome as was the cafe in Gargrave where I had fish and chips. Two cooked meals in a day was most unusual but very morale boosting! Even though it was only my fourth day out I was finding my diet inadequate for the effort involved in carrying a heavy load up and down hills for many miles every day. I'd only planned on snacks for lunch — mintcake, chocolate, biscuits, muesli bars and similar — and dried meals for supper. I suspect that I was not getting enough calories as I know now just how many calories are needed for backpacking.

I never intended to walk the Pennine Way as a fixed line from which I was not to deviate since there were various sights and places near the official route I wanted to visit. One of these was Gordale Scar so instead of staying in Malham I walked out of the village to camp on a farm site opposite the entrance to the Scar. The view out of the tent door was one of the best of the walk even though I was on a commercial camp site (twenty pence a night!) and this has become one of my favourite sites in the Yorkshire Dales though in the summer season it tends to become very

9

crowded (as indeed do both Malham and Gordale). Viewing the overhanging cliffs and complex rock sculpure of Gordale Scar the next morning I was reluctant to leave but I had to if I was to see Malham Cove and cross both Fountains Fell and Penyghent before nightfall, as planned. After the gritstone scenery further south, the limestone country of the Dales came as a welcome change and after Gordale I spent some time at the great curving cliff of Malham Cove and followed the nature trail round Malham Tarn, one of the few natural lakes on the whole Pennine Way.

Peat bogs returned on the ascent of the 2,100-foot Fountains Fell as did the rain and mist so that after a brief glimpse of Penyghent, one of the finest Pennine summits, I was back to coping with limited visibility. This time though the rain was heavy and constant and for the first time on the walk I changed my cotton windproof jacket, adequate in the light showers and drizzle I had experienced so far, for my proofed nylon jacket, a garment I hated wearing because of the build-up of condensation that occurred inside and left me feeling hot and clammy. I laboured stickily up and down the invisible Penyghent and into the hamlet of Horton-in-Ribblesdale where I went straight into the Penyghent Cafe for a large meal and a pint of coffee plus a chance to dry out. Here I met three teenagers walking the Dales section of the way and we walked a brief way out of Horton to camp together at Sell Gill Hole. As I was not sure whether we should camp there or not without permission I was a little concerned about the tent my three temporary companions had as it was both large and bright orange unlike my tiny sludge brown one which was indistinguishable from its surroundings from a short distance away. Having fellow backpackers to talk to for the first time on the trip I went back into Horton with them for a drink at the Crown Inn. I'd hoped for a meal too but again the only food was peanuts!

Our camp site proved to be an exposed one when the wind veered to the north east and increased in strength, and the rattling of the flysheet meant I had a disturbed night's sleep. Breakfast consisted of instant soup, as I was running out of food again, and after attending to my blisters, I struck camp and moved off. A good, fairly level track leads for the sixteen miles from Horton to the Wensleydale market town of

Hawes and I set off briskly intending to reach there before the shops shut. I was stopped briefly after a half mile or so by a farmer in a tractor who wanted to pass the time of day. After a chat mostly about the weather he said he'd be getting on as he wanted a word with someone who was camping illegally on his land. I looked, I hoped, both innocent and puzzled. 'How do you know?' I asked. The farmer pointed back the way I had come. I looked round and there standing out clearly against the dark hillside could be seen the bright orange tent of my companions.

The route to Hawes passed by several interesting pot holes and gave good views of the Three Peaks: Penyghent, Ingleborough and Whernside, as well as Wensleydale and the fells overlooking it. In Hawes I stocked up on food, remembering this time to buy more than I thought I needed, and ate a hearty meal. Camped on the Brown Moor Farm Site I had my first shower of the trip for six days, and caught up on some necessary washing — two little things that are nevertheless important morale boosters on a long walk.

A pattern had been set for the walk now. After a week I was into the middle of it, into the heart, the point where I thought neither of the beginning nor the end but simply of the next hill, the next campsite, the next day. I was usually off by 9.30 and camped again by 5.30 after a day of around 17 miles with a couple of brief snack stops. Drizzle and cloud accompanied me up Great Shunner Fell as I left the limestone lightness to return to the dark scenery of peat moorland. The 2,300-foot summit was reached in thick mist, heavy rain and a strong wind. I was having problems staying comfortable in this weather. My cotton jacket was sodden and I was cold without my waterproof jacket on but with it on I was too hot. I was wet either way. Despite the weather I enjoyed the terrace walk in Swaledale between Thwaite and Keld. The day's waterfalls — Hardrow Force at Hawes and Kidron Force at Keld — were magnificent. There are compensations in any kind of weather.

Beyond Keld I plodded across storm-swept moorland to camp on very rough ground behind Tan Hill Inn, at 1,732 feet the highest public house in England. My journal for the day tells me that I spent it thinking about how to solve the problems of sore, blistered feet and constantly damp clothing. I partly alleviated the former by removing one of my two pairs of socks which allowed my feet to spread more. The latter I decided could only be changed by using synthetic clothing rather than wool and cotton. I also realised that I needed many more plastic bags as my rucksack was far from waterproof. Some items I dried out in the pub bar which I shared for the evening with a dozen others including three backpackers walking the Pennine Way from north to south in two journeys. This was their second and final trek and they were hoping to reach Edale in five days, two days less than it had taken me to reach here. I wished them luck! Despite the warmth of the bar I felt chilly as I crawled into my damp sleeping bag and was sure the temperature was much lower than on previous nights.

Waking to find the tent partially collapsed onto my sleeping bag I unzipped the door and looked out to find it covered with snow! It certainly had become colder. By the time I set off the snow had changed to sleet which later turned to heavy rain backed by a gale force wind. In these adverse conditions I waded down the path to Sleightholme then across seemingly endless boggy moors to Middleton-in-Teesdale. Lunch was taken in the damp but sheltered cover of an old lime kiln opposite the natural arch of God's Bridge which spans the River Greta. Wanting to reach Middleton before the post office shut as I had, or hoped I had, some money awaiting me (I was down to my last seventeen pence), I didn't stop often. I walked fast only to find, on arriving in the town that it was half day closing and the post office had been shut since midday. The old railway station and yard had been turned into a caravan site and here I camped for the sum of sixty pence which I agreed to pay the next day. The two other tents on the site were ones I'd seen at Hawes but on talking to their occupants, I discovered that, fed up with the wet weather, they'd hitch-hiked from Thwaite. We took all our wet gear into the site washroom to try and dry it out and created a warm if damp atmosphere by doing our cooking in there too. As it seemed preferable to damp tents we slept on the site's TV and reading room floor, it was nice and dry, enabling me to wake with a dry sleeping bag; quite a luxury on this walk.

A dry morning had me spreading my gear out on the grass to finish drying whilst I stocked up on food. Leaving at 1 pm I found walking up beautiful Teesdale in dry weather a relief after all the rain and I was able to enjoy the scenery and to note that despite the weather, spring was well under way. Celandines on the banks and catkins in the trees gave a splash of yellow to the fresh green of the new leaves. On the Tees dippers sped up and down, bobbing on the rocks and running into the water, presumably after some food. High Force was powerful and dramatic but overshadowed by a helicopter and new car parked nearby and a camera crew swarming all over the place; I gathered a TV advertisement was being filmed there. Cauldron Snout was a roaring torrent too but the initial wild impact was spoilt by the gradual appearance, as I climbed the natural staircase of dolerite rocks beside it, of the Cow Green dam and reservoir constructed to supply pure water to ICI because lower down, the Tees was too polluted for the water to be used. So instead of cleaning up the river they came here to destroy the beauty of the Upper Tees. A walker coming the other way told me that Cross Fell (a day or more away) was covered in snow. I camped that night by a feeder of Maize Beck on the side of Rasp Hill, a bleak but satisfyingly remote site.

High Cup Nick, a huge defile in the hills, was passed en route to the little hamlet of Dufton on the western edge of the Pennines where I found myself actually farther from Kirk Yetholm at the end of the Pennine Way than I had been in Middleton! I realised later that in fact there is no need to descend to Dufton unless supplies or accommodation are needed and it would have been simpler and quicker to head north from High Cup Nick to Cross Fell. As it was I had to climb all the way back up to the roof of the Pennines arriving on snow-covered Cross Fell at 7.30 pm. Above 2,000 feet I was again in thick mist. On my way up two day-walkers on Knock Fell had told me of a hut on Cross Fell which was usable for an overnight stay and I worked out this was both the old mine cottage mentioned by Wainwright and Greg's Hut marked on the O.S. map.

Greg's Hut was my first introduction to bothies (and the Mountain Bothies Association) and the start of a great love affair with remote, simple shelters in the hills. Bothies are unlocked shelters, often old shepherd's or gamekeeper's cottages, that are renovated by the MBA, which is a voluntary organisation. The properties do not change hands and the MBA negotiates with owners for permission to renovate and maintain shelters, usually with success. Greg's

Hut is an old mine building as Wainwright says, but in the years 1968-72 it was rebuilt by the MBA in memory of John Gregory who was killed skiing in the Alps in 1968. Only tiny, the hut has one 'living' room and one storage room. Once I entered it I knew I wanted to spend the night there. Coal and wood were present so I lit a small fire with the aid of some solid fuel I was carrying, the remainder of which I left in the bothy for others to use. By the light of a Tilley lamp I found in the hut I read the bothy book, a visitors' book in which people put their comments and views. One of the attractions of bothying for me is the bothy books. I love seeing who has been to a bothy, what they were doing and what they thought, and how often it is visited. My bed for the night was a real one though it was so damp that I put my plastic survival bag and Karrimat on top of it.

The hut was warm overnight but that was because another warm front was passing through; I woke to mist and wind through which I wandered down to Garrigill to leave behind the Pennine chain. For, despite its name, from Cross Fell the Pennine Way drops down out of the Pennines to follow the valley of the South Tyne before turning east along Hadrian's Wall then north again through the Border Forest to climb back up into the Cheviot Hills, a pleasant route but not a Pennine one. A true Pennine Way would continue on from Cross Fell to Cold Fell, the true end to the Pennine chain, and terminate there. The walk up the South Tyne valley was an obstacle course of stiles, gates, farms and lanes. 'Thank God for Wainwright' I wrote in my journal. Alston was a pleasant lunch stop. The town claims to be the highest market town in the UK and certainly has some of the steepest streets amongst its attractive, delightfully un-planned buildings. It was packed with visitors but then it was, as I discovered, the Saturday of the Easter weekend.

A camp at Glendue Burn, just out of sight of the road, followed by more plodding up the valley led to the dull moor of Wain Rigg where in the latest bout of mist and drizzle the hipbelt on my pack ripped out and I had to sit in the mud stitching it back up again. As the pack, an expensive American packframe model, was new at the start of the trip I wasn't very pleased. Still it provided a diversion. I noted the occurrence in my journal as the 'most interesting bit' of the walk to Hadrian's Wall from Glendue Burn! Once on the Wall though, life improved with excellent views and an excellent path. Smooth turf! I walked it with two others who were staying in B&Bs and reckoned on completing the walk in eleven days. With half the weight or less I thought I could probably do it in that time too. I camped below the Wall on a farm site near the Twice Brewed Inn where I ate supper. I had three days left to complete the walk and about 65 miles to go so a hard push was needed, especially as I still had the Cheviots to cross.

Up on Winshields Crag I met a father and son team also doing the Pennine Way but in a rather different way to me. By the time they'd described their method to me I felt amateurish and disorganised. This was their eleventh day out (it was my thirteenth) and they had walked to a strict schedule of ten hours and twenty miles a day with no deviations. This meant they hadn't seen Gordale Scar or Hardrow Force amongst other sights but they felt that taking deviations was not really 'Walking The Pennine Way' a phrase they spoke as if in capitals. The father had a swollen tendon and looked exhausted and the son was wearing his proofed nylon overtrousers which seemed unusual as it was a dry day and the terrain wasn't muddy. The reason, he told me meaningfully, was because of his experiences on the Lyke Wake Walk. I didn't delve into these but whatever they were they must have been awful to make someone go through the unpleasantness of wearing overtrousers on a dry day. Because they didn't trust water from streams the father was carrying a gallon of water and they had fresh foodstuffs including items like jars of jam. Overall their packs were far heavier than mine and I'd been complaining about the weight I was carrying. Whilst I couldn't imagine treating backpacking the way they did, I hope they completed it because it seemed that that was the only joy they would gain from the trek.

I left my companions at Rapishaw Gap — having walked with them along the Wall over Highshields Crag — past reed fringed Crag Lough with its swans and coots and because I wanted to detour to see Housesteads Fort half a mile further along the Wall. As it was Easter Monday there were many people wandering round the Roman ruins and the museum but it was still worth the visit because it put the Wall in perspective for me. What Southern Europeans thought of this cold, wet, northern outpost of an empire based on the Mediterranean it's hard to imagine. Back at

Rapishaw I left the Wall to head north into the vast coniferous forests that have been planted on the bleak moorland here, a forest that covers over three hundred square miles and is known as the Border Forest Park. The Pennine Way touches the eastern edge of this huge plantation and passes through two of its six constituent forests: Wark and Redesdale. After the dismal and featureless scenery immediately south of the Roman Wall I found myself enjoying the forest walking and this is one of the few places in the British hills where I can see no objection to the planting of such woodlands though it would still be an improvement to have more varied planting and less serried ranks of conifers.

Certainly the forest was preferable to the farmland that led to the village of Bellingham on the North Tyne and the moorland beyond on which I camped just below the indistinct summit of Lough Shaw. Moorland birds had been a feature of the walk throughout but here I had a host of them calling round the tent to make it a memorable site. A snipe drummed, curlews bubbled and whistled, lapwings and oystercatchers called; together their sounds summed up the wild loneliness of the moorland sections of the Pennine Way. It was what made the wild sites like this on Lough Shaw so much more part of the Pennine Way than the organised camp sites with their facilities and people. I'd never done much wild camping before. Now I knew that I wanted to do much more, wilderness backpacking was the future for me.

Forty miles to go gave an edge of urgency to the last few days and I was glad of the best weather so far for the trek from Lough Shaw to Rennies Burn in the Cheviots. For just this one day it was gloriously sunny and clear with not a cloud in the sky. And for once I had a companion for the whole day. Crossing the Gib Shiel Road an hour after setting off I had met another walker called Roland. A veteran walker at sixty-two years old he'd been walking the Pennine Way in sections for ten years with back-up support provided by his wife who drove a Dormobile between sections. Today Roland was about to set off to walk to Byrness so we walked together. As we went to he told me of previous walking adventures. A Yorkshireman, he'd been a hillwalker all his life and recollected doing all 14 3,000-foot peaks in Snowdonia in 16 hours in the 1930s. He'd climbed all the 2,500-foot summits in England and many hills in Scotland especially in the Cairngorms, his favourite area. Stories of the Scottish mountains, an area I knew nothing about, gave me my first desire to walk in these hills that were to become such an important part of my life in just a few more years. As we crossed Padon Hill and Brownrigg Head (both gave excellent views) and entered Redesdale Forest, he told me of World War II in which he was a despatch rider being present at Dunkirk and then serving in the Sahara and Yugoslavia.

After afternoon tea in the Dormobile I left Roland and his wife at Byrness as I wanted to push on to give myself the best chance of finishing on the morrow. I continued over the foothills of the Cheviots to the Roman Camp at Chew Green which has a fascinating outline when seen from above, much clearer than is apparent when you're actually there. But what caught my eye as I descended was a very familiar looking Dormobile. My new friends had decided to come here to spend the night and I had a welcome if unexpected supper offered me before I travelled on a few more miles to camp on the rough slopes adjacent to Rennies Burn. It has become the norm on my long walks at the end of a long section to throw all my remaining food into a pan and cook and eat it all. On this occasion the combination of savoury rice, dried mixed vegetables, two chicken soups, a mushroom soup and a curry Oxo cube was filling if not exactly the most appetising of meals. This was my sixth wild camp but the first I shared with other backpackers: the father and son team I'd last seen on the Roman Wall.

My efficient companions woke me at seven o'clock as they were about to leave, too early for me. The weather was cold and windy and the tent was shrouded in a dense mist. My crossing of the Cheviots was carried out in mist throughout as were my ascents of every section of the Pennine Way over 2,000 feet high. Sheltering behind the tumulus on Windy Gyle I met three women backpackers who'd spent the night there and were having breakfast. It was so cold in the wind that as well as all my clothes I was wearing my woollen balaclava helmet. My mind was now on the finish so I sped on stopping only once more, in the old railway wagon that sits near the summit of Auchope Cairn and is labelled Auchope Refuge Hut. Here I ate my last Mars Bar before descending to Kirk Yetholm which I reached at four o'clock, despite nearly going astray for the first time on the walk by wandering down the wrong valley a short way and having to climb back up. I camped on a caravan site in Town Yetholm where the warden brought me a bowl of thick lentil broth which she thought I needed.

So I had completed the Pennine Way. And how did I feel? Pleased of course but also disappointed. Disappointed because it was over. I didn't want to return to college. I wanted to go on walking, to see what lay over the hill, to experience the oneness with nature I'd never felt so strongly before, to recapture those times when walking was effortless and I forgot I existed and just flowed along with the land. I'd found a way of life that suitedme and knew that I would soon return to the hills and to long distance backpacking. But as I noted in my journal, this was the most important walk of all for this was the one that showed me I could actually manage a long walk, that I enjoyed travelling every day and living out of a rucksack. I had learnt much about myself. Now I had to put into practice what I'd learnt by going on a much longer walk.

2

Britain

LAND'S END TO JOHN O'GROATS

I can trace my backpacking career back to one book: John Hillaby's *Journey Through Britain*. Until I read that book I didn't know that such adventures were possible for ordinary mortals. Basically a loner, I belonged to no walking or mountaineering clubs and had no contact with other hillgoers. That whole world was unknown to me and was to remain so for many years. Once I had read Hillaby's book I wanted to know more but found information hard to come by. Backpacking was new to the British outdoor scene — or at least the word, imported from the USA, was — of course walkers had been making long treks on which they camped out for decades. In the early 1970s the outdoor activity boom was only just beginning and the only specialist magazines *(Climber & Rambler* and *Mountain Life)* then available were basically concerned with rock climbing and mountaineering and after glancing at these I put them aside as they did not seem to have much to offer the aspiring Land's End to John O'Groats walker.

However some campers and walkers in the south of England, also not in the outdoor mainstream, wanted to promote backpacking in the UK so they set up the Backpackers Club which was initially advertised through the pages of *Practical Camper,* a magazine mostly to do with family camping on organised sites, edited by Peter Lumley who became one of the club's founders. He used his position to promote lightweight camping and backpacking in the magazine so that it became essential reading for followers of the new activity. Once I had discovered *Practical Camper* and the Backpackers Club I became a regular reader of the first and a member of the second and all my initial knowledge of backpacking was gleaned from these two sources. I began to practice the techniques they outlined and as the outdoor boom gathered strength I bought the

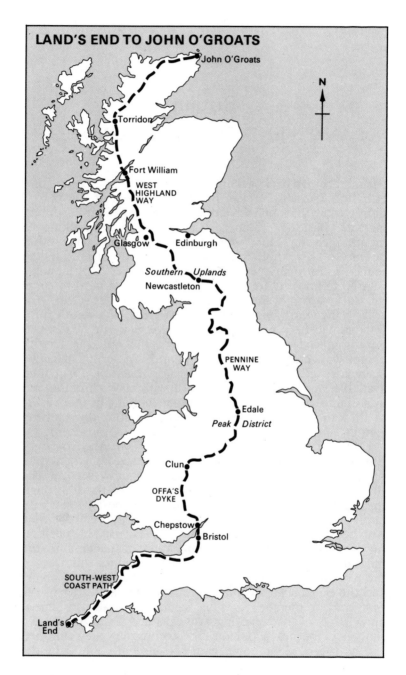

LAND'S END TO JOHN O'GROATS

- John O'Groats
- Torridon
- Fort William
- WEST HIGHLAND WAY
- Glasgow
- Edinburgh
- *Southern Uplands*
- Newcastleton
- PENNINE WAY
- Edale
- *Peak District*
- Clun
- OFFA'S DYKE
- Chepstow
- Bristol
- SOUTH-WEST COAST PATH
- Land's End

N

books these first writers on backpacking in the UK wrote: *Teach Yourself Backpacking* by Peter Lumley, *The Backpacker's Handbook* by Derrick Booth, who wrote a column on the subject for *Practical Camper*, and *Backpacking In Britain* by Robin Adshead who wrote a backpacking column for the magazine *Camping* which had soon followed its rival in taking up the new pursuit. Through the club, the magazines and the books I learnt about backpacking and began to think of myself as a backpacker.

But what has all this to do with walking from Land's End to John O'Groats? Well, it describes the context in which the walk and my 'career' in backpacking came about. Until the 1970s I doubt if any prospective outdoor person wanted to be a backpacker. A mountaineer probably, or a fell walker, perhaps a climber, but not a backpacker. There was resistance to the word from some quarters too with a feeling that this imported word was unnecessary to describe an activity people did anyway. But for me it crystallised that aspect of outdoor activity I was interested in. So all my reading and walks in the 1970s, including my Pennine Way walk, were a build-up to the time when I felt capable of backpacking from Land's End to John O'Groats.

That time came in 1978. The Pennine Way walk in 1976 had shown me I was capable of a long solo backpacking trip and my employers, YHA Shops (where I learnt much about equipment), were prepared to give me unpaid leave to do my new walk. So, over the winter of 1977-8, the planning went ahead. I didn't want to follow Hillaby's route exactly and so I mapped out one of my own, which took in places I particularly wanted to see. The result was a 1,250-mile route that I hoped I could walk in ten weeks. The route planning was not detailed which left room for some spontaneous decision making as I went along. The decision where to camp and how far to walk was made each day and not preplanned. At times I even changed the route due to bad weather or just a desire to see somewhere not on my original route. Physically I did no training, mainly because I didn't have the time. I went away backpacking for the occasional weekend as normal, and I tested some of my equipment in Snowdonia over the Easter weekend before the walk began so I was reasonably fit anyway. Extra fitness would come as the walk progressed. I don't believe you can prepare for a long walk except by doing a long walk.

Mentally I did not know what to expect and I was prepared to take things as they came. I knew from the Pennine Way walk that I could spend at least a fortnight walking on my own with no problems. If I found difficulties attempting ten weeks solo I would deal with them as they arose.

As the weeks passed and my starting date drew nearer, a suppressed excitement grew in me and the events of daily life became remote. I wanted to be walking. Nothing else really mattered. Three and a half months elapsed between deciding to attempt the walk and boarding the train for Penzance, from where I would catch a bus to Land's End. It was long enough. Longer and I think I would have lost some of the impetus for the walk. Spring had been chosen to see the changes unfold as I walked and to avoid the heat and the crowds of summer. I began in the south so as to benefit from the longer hours of daylight and to better my chances of having good weather in the mountains of the north; also I thought the walking would be easier in the south.

On April 16th I left the campsite at Land's End, said farewell to the friend who had accompanied me to the start, and walked off through the tourists, outwardly calm but inside agitated and nervous. After all the planning and waiting the long walk had begun. Past the Last House I joined the South West Way, the coastal path I was to follow for 230 miles. It was a clear, sunny spring day and a good day to begin something new. I admired the massive granite cliffs and noted the many flowers: stitchwort, celandine, violets and primrose, that lined the path and watched the myriads of screeching seabirds plus the less noisy stonechat, wheatear and kestrel that sang, bobbed and hunted in the gorse bushes.

I used a guidebook for the South West Way section and found this made route finding for the first fortnight simple, even though I had to use it backwards, (it began at Minehead towards which I was walking), leaving me to concentrate on the walking and the finding of campsites, the latter not being so easy for although the coast is wild, the land here is mostly farmland and wild pitches are not so frequent as they are in the mountains. I camped where I could, usually at dusk, and often wondering if I'd be thrown off in the morning. I never was, though I never went quite as far as John Hillaby who camped on waste ground in the middle of St Ives only to be evicted by the local police who actually escorted him to the town boundary. Occasionally I used official sites in order to take advantage of their facilities such as hot water and showers but I preferred not to do this. Water was a problem. Camping by streams gave me a source, but it had already been through farms and villages, so a combination of sterilising tablets and fierce boiling were necessary to purify it.

I am basically a mountain walker not a coastal one but I enjoyed the trek along the South West Way. In Cornwall I found the mixture of little fishing villages, now mainly dependent for a living on tourists, and really wild cliff scenery interspersed with the remains of the once-flourishing mining industry, an attractive combination. Remnants left by early inhabitants give added interest to this section of coast and I detoured to see Carn Gloose, a chambered cairn that is possibly neolithic. I found this odd structure fascinating and spent some time clambering on its four-foot thick walls and in its deep chambers. Originally it was covered and archaeologists think it may have been a religious shrine. This is not certain though, and an air of mystery surrounds the place. Feeling akin to the nature worship of the Neolithic peoples I silently requested the blessings of them and their deities for my walk. It was that sort of place.

My guidebook was general enough to cover pubs and other places of refreshment and the first day being hot I finished it with a pint in the Tinner's Arms in Zennor, an interesting little hamlet with two ninth-century crossheads in the churchyard. As darkness fell I wandered out onto Zennor Head and camped on an exposed but superbly situated site. I'd walked seventeen miles, which was in fact to be my daily average for the first 500 miles of the walk. That first evening I lay in the tent feeling very contented. I had actually begun.

The walk soon fell into a pattern, as all walks do, though on a long walk like this one there tend to be several patterns corresponding to the different sections of the walk. On the coastal part of the walk I usually started walking between 8.30 and 10.30 am after a small breakfast, small because on most days I would arrive in a village within a few hours where I would buy a newspaper and settle into a cafe or pub for a second breakfast or early lunch, depending on the time. Then I'd continue walking, often stopping for afternoon tea or an early dinner at another village before camping at dusk. This was a luxurious way of walking which I enjoyed because I knew it wouldn't last and that for much of the walk cafes and pubs would be days not hours apart.

One aspect of the coastal walk I found infuriating was that of crossing the many estuaries. The first road slog of the walk was around the Hayle estuary, a trek relieved only by the bird life: shelduck, mute swans, redshank, and a merganser amongst others. The industrial sadness of Hayle itself lay only a few hundred impassable yards away and I wished fervently for a bridge, especially along the last unpleasant mile which lay on the busy A30. As I reached the other side of the estuary the weather changed, becoming windier and cloudier. Rain was on the way and as I wound my way through the soft sand and wooden chalets of the Towans it began to drizzle. On the beach the first object in sight was a dead seal with its face slightly decayed to show some bone. It seemed drearily appropriate. The trudge along the beach was fairly heavy going in the soft wet sand but was improved by some unexpected (that is, not mentioned in the guidebook), and impressive convoluted cliffs with caves and separate squat stacks of rock at the far end. An attempt to ford the Red River at the next estuary ended in failure when I lost my nerve at the point where it was over knee deep and I wasn't halfway across. This stream really is red in colour and stains the sea for quite a distance around. The colour comes from waste out of the mines at Redruth. I crossed safely by a bridge in a nearby sand quarry and decided I ought to have a tide table. I noted it down on my shopping list but never did buy one. It would have been useful. I suspect the Red River and other streams are easily fordable at low tide.

By the afternoon of this, my second day out, it was raining steadily and my polycotton windproof jacket was soon soaked. Feeling chilly I donned my waterproofs, a pair of proofed nylon leggings and a jacket made of the then new 'breathable' waterproof material called Goretex. After a few hours it stopped raining but the wind blew hard so I kept my waterproofs on. I was astonished when I finally removed my jacket to discover that my wet clothes had dried out through the Goretex. I was impressed, so much so in fact that I've used Goretex clothing on every long walk I've done since.

Ramsons, herb robert, yarrow and mayblossom decorated the steep bank as I descended into a deep combe to camp just above Porth-cadiak Cove after a twenty-one mile day. The heavy overnight rain had faded into a fine misty drizzle by the time I set off the next day for Portreath, breakfast number two, and an easy, ominous path alongside the high fences of Nancekuke Defence Area, a place I was glad to get away from as quickly as possible. I stopped for a pint and a sandwich in Porthtowan and watched the rain begin again and the mist roll in. I had a strong desire to stop but felt that if a little rain halted me after five miles I might as well give up so out I went. The thick mist reduced visibility to about ten yards so that the disused mines around St. Agnes Head loomed up like Gothic castles in a Hammer horror film. I was surrounded by invisible shrieking seabirds; St. Agnes Head has the largest breeding colony of kittiwakes in the area.

In St. Agnes I took refuge in a seaside shelter high above the bay where I sat munching dates and Edam cheese, a combination that tastes remarkably like chocolate, and watching wet-suit-clad surfers charging into the turbulent sea. Then the rain eased off, the waterproofs dried and soon I was back on the very impressive wind and wave lashed cliffs watching white foam bursting over the intricate, tortured rock shapes. A dramatic scene and one that left me feeling quite heady with elation, a mood that evaporated in Perranporth, yet another sad little empty out-of-season resort where everything was shut bar one fish and chip shop. A solemn notice on the wall asked regulars to place orders for good pasties as in the madness of the next six months cheaper varieties were to be provided for the tourists. It was hard to imagine the transformation of this forlorn shut-up wet place into a brash August resort. The thought left me glad I'd started the walk early in the year. It was distracting enough to come down to a village every four or five miles anyway without the added confusion of crowds and noise.

Beyond Perranporth I left the cliffs behind for a while and crossed the wide and shifting Gear and Penhale Sands, an area of major significance in the early history of Christianity in this country. Here the remains of an eighth-century chapel, St. Piran's Oratory, lie encased in a drab military-green building shrouded in barbed wire and warning notices. More interesting is a granite cross standing nearby which dates back at least as far as the tenth century. Behind it, framed against a savage red and yellow sunset as the day fought to the last flicker of light, stood a modern concrete cross set on a high sand dune. As an image it was very powerful. Ironically I noticed that on one side of this Christian enclave stood a holiday camp and on the other a Ministry of Defence training area. Avoiding the latter, I pitched camp on nearby heathland. The area felt familiar. Formby, where I was brought up, has a coastline just like this. Lying fifteen miles north of Liverpool it has a barrier of sand dunes backed by lowland heath and pinewoods to keep the sea out as it is below sea level. It was in this area that I discovered a love for the countryside and exploration. Sand dunes were the first hills I ever climbed and I knew that area of heath and wood better than any area I've known since. I drifted to sleep wrapped in boyhood memories. The connection between the dreams of an eleven-year-old playing explorer in the local woods and this older man walking to John O'Groats felt very strong indeed.

The stormy weather continued the next day, starting with cloud, intermittent drizzle and the sound of skylarks. I was sitting on a bench in impersonal Newquay feeding crumbs to the gulls when the rain began. I left the town in a heavy downpour, strong winds and poor visibility. It grew colder as I slogged along the cliffs between Watergate and St. Mawgan where I cowered in a bus shelter for a snack. Apart from full waterproofs I was also wearing my balaclava and mittens. Back on the cliffs the scene was savage with the wind-driven rising tide smashing against the impressive eroded granite stumps of Bedruthan Steps and Diggory Island. Battered by the storm and feeling the effects of 71 miles in four days with a heavy pack, I headed for Treyarnon and a night in the youth hostel. It was one of the low points of the walk. I felt defeated and small.

I woke determined to walk all day and feeling vaguely ashamed of the previous night's low. With another 1,100 miles to walk I couldn't afford to be put off by a bit of rain. In contrast to the day before I seemed to cover the distance without effort and ended up walking 21 miles. Padstow, reached early on, helped improve my mood. Unlike other resorts it felt like a genuine fishing village that just happened to attract tourists. A friendly place, it was the opposite of Newquay. I finished the day in Port Isaac and my journal tells the story of the evening succinctly: "Spent evening in Golden Lion supping St. Austell Special Bitter — excellent — then staggered off up cliff to camp here — wherever I am! Will find out tomorrow no doubt."

Arriving in Trebarwith meant arriving for the first time at a place I'd visited before. I settled into the Port William pub for lunch with reminiscences. A van-load of us had come down from Leicester in June 1975 after exams were over and camped on the cliffs just above this pub. It had been very, very hot and we'd all been sunburnt after a week of long lazy days lying on the cliff tops in the shimmering haze overwhelmed by the rich scent of the luxurious vegetation. Now it was grey and damp-looking but the rain held off as I tramped to Tintagel, a romantic name from my childhood as I'd always been fascinated by the Arthurian myths. There is still a magic feel here, in the castle and the caves if not in the crude commercialisation of the village where I dined on beans on toast in King Arthur's Cafe. To me the Arthurian Romances are very real; musing on this over lunch I realised that the stories are as real to me as most recorded history; more real than some. Symbols hold an emotional power and the Arthurian ones are significant for me. Especially the Grail Quest, an eternal idea, the search for the other. Yet in the end the Questor and the Quest are the same. Through any activity one learns about oneself and therefore about what one is doing. This walk was a challenge to my identity. Dreaming about doing it was easy but now I was trying to realise my dreams, a dangerous task.

These thoughts left me feeling very fond of Tintagel and, feeling more confident than I had for a few days, I really enjoyed the cliff top walk to Boscastle, a favourite place of previous visits. On the way there I passed the Rocky Valley which, although interesting, hardly lived up to the claims that it was Cornwall's Grand Canyon! The sixteenth-century pub in Boscastle was very friendly, finding me some food an hour before they usually provided meals. The sky was just darkening as I rounded Boscastle's narrow and spectacular harbour. A high tide was blasting through the slot of the entrance watched by crowds of people entranced by the endless fascination of the sea.

At Upton the next day I met a 78-year-old American sitting on a bench looking out to sea, back towards his homeland. A retired outdoor pursuits instructor, he told me of his plans to celebrate his 80th birthday by climbing a peak in the Catskill Mountains in the USA. I hope he succeeded. I was approaching Devon now and my camp that night, in a combe near Morwenstow, was to be my last in Cornwall. It had been a hot day for once and my feet felt like they were on fire. They were still glowing an hour after I removed my boots and socks. The boots themselves just stood and steamed.

A strong south-west wind set me off up the coast into Devon and to Hartland Point, a brisk walk delayed only by a detour inland to Morwenstow to see the church and vicarage of the eccentric poet, the Reverend R.S. Hawker. I didn't find them very exciting but I did get stuck in dense bramble undergrowth trying to find my way back to the path and spent an hour extricating myself. Back on the cliffs I visited the much more interesting 'Hawker's Hut', a small driftwood shelter built by the parson himself in the seventeenth century as a place to sit and write in solitude. The hut is a few yards below the cliff top, perched right above the sea with spectacular views, which must have been a distraction though perhaps also an inspiration to writing.

The day ended with a steep descent into Clovelly, a carefully preserved pre-automobile fishing village built up the sides of steep cliffs. No cars are allowed in the old village but a taxi service ferries tourists up and down the steep road outside the preserved area. Clovelly with its cobbled streets and old shops is pleasant but very museum-like. The pubs, unfortunately, were very modern with soft lights, piped muzak and extortionately priced fizzy 'beer'. An overriding problem was that there was clearly nowhere to camp here so cutting my visit short I headed back up into the steep woods in search of a discreet pitch. I couldn't find one as I wandered through the woods known as The Hobby. The ground was far too steep. Nearing the road I decided I had to risk a totally illegal camp and nipped over a fence into a lush meadow and put up the tent. I could see no farm buildings and it was far too late at night to seek permission.

To avoid detection of my little indiscretion I arose at 5.30 and packed up immediately. As I downed the tent two badgers ambled across the field in the half light oblivious of my presence, a nice reward for an unusually early start. Back on the path I wandered through the old gnarled and moss-covered woods looking at the flowers and birds. White stars in the grey-green undergrowth turned out to be wood anemones whilst white campion lined the path. I put up a jay which chattered angrily, and at the same time startling some magpies and jackdaws into flight.

Hot and thirsty road walking took me from Westward Ho! to Barnstaple. I reflected on how much richer and more prosperous Devon seemed compared with Cornwall. Lush meadows of plump contented cattle replaced the sparse, neglected Cornish pastures. Woodland stretched down to the sea and I realised how few trees, especially large mature hardwoods, I'd seen in Cornwall. A much more indolent county this.

Roads close to the coast meant I had to pound tarmac for too many miles especially between Westward Ho! and Braunton, with Barnstaple passed through en route: a muzzy, hazy atmosphere thick with lifelessness where everything looked insubstantial and the view gradually faded into nothing, made for hot, dusty walking. The main road to Braunton had no footpath or verges and the stream of fast traffic meant I was literally in fear of my life. Angry drivers repeatedly tooted at me to get out of their way. Where I was supposed to go I don't know. Tense aggressive faces rushed past. When I finally regained the coast path at Saunton I felt quite fed up and for the first time wondered why I was doing this walk. Pessimism cleared as I returned to the sanity of a good cliff-top path followed by a long beach walk across Woolacombe Sands, a dull tan colour in the afternoon's grey light. The highlight of the day was sinister and malevolent Morte Point where jagged vertical knife-edge rocks stretch far out to sea creating a spectacular tidal race where many ships have been wrecked. The path here is almost at sea level; behind it rises a serrated ridge of rock spires reminiscent of the armour plating of a stegosaurus or the dorsal fin of a perch. The grey thin light was just right for this place. Spots of rain fell and the wind rose as I raced the storm to camp just beyond Bull Point.

Minehead, now only two days away, marked the end of the coastal section of the walk. This final bit of the South West Way was accompanied by the usual rain and wind, and a steep climb up the 1,044-foot high Great Hangman, a dark and sinister mound with low cloud swirling round it. A magnificent camp site was found in the Valley of the Rocks:

I perched the tent halfway down the cliff amongst a jumbled riot of rocks, new bracken fronds and gorse, with the sea crashing below and the spires of the valley rising above, decorated by some wild looking goats. Minehead itself was an opportunity for a washing, posting, shopping, domestic day. A laundrette was most welcome and I washed everything in stages using the public toilet opposite as a changing room.

Clean and restocked I was ready for the second stage of the walk, the crossing of Somerset to Bristol wher I would head for the Severn Bridge, Chepstow, Wales and Offa's Dyke. Caravan sites at night and road walking by day made much of this section tedious but the Quantock Hills were pleasant though very crowded with both off-road motorcyclists and the unpleasantness of a fox hunt with dozens of people on horses, packs of dogs and attendant voyeurs with their cars. I lost them only when I descended to the Somerset plain through large conifer plantations where the felled areas made progress awkward.

'Welcome to Historic Bridgwater' the signs read but there was nowhere to pitch a tent so I ended up outside the town on a transit site sandwiched between the M5 motorway and a mainline railway. I was charged £1 for this, my most unpleasant camp yet. The discovery that the next Monday, when I'd planned on being in Bristol to collect my next batch of maps and other mail from the post office, was a Bank Holiday, meant I had an extra day in Somerset so instead of going via Cheddar Gorge as orignally intended I decided to visit Glastonbury and Wells, places I'd not been to before. May Eve, the old Celtic fire festival of Beltane, when the Spirit of Summer fights and defeats the Spirit of Winter, releasing the land from the latter's iron grip, was an appropriate time to visit Glastonbury, claimed by some as the Avalon of the Arthurian myths and thus Arthur's burial place. I was especially looking forward to visiting the magic hill of Glastonbury Tor with which many varied mystical beliefs are connected. I was in the right mood for all this as I was reading T.H. White's marvellous retelling of the Arthurian legends *The Once And Future King*. Remembering White's attack on the 'iconoclasts' who destroyed the myth by attempting to 'prove' the historical reality of Arthur, I was quite happy to let my imagination wander and believe anything.

An inquisitive and friendly boy on a bicycle from the local hamlet of Chedzoy accompanied me for several miles along country lanes as I approached Glastonbury. A boy scout, he told me about camps he'd been on and about bivvying in a survival bag in Scotland. I realised he was the first person I'd spoken to for more than a few minutes since I'd started the walk two weeks previously.

I left my companion and plunged optimistically down an overgrown and muddy cow-track marked on my map as a public footpath. Its negotiation involved crawling under brambles and climbing over locked gates topped with barbed wire whilst underfoot thick mud clung to my boots. An hour and two miles later I emerged back on the road much more bedraggled and dirty than I'd left it. I was learning that in flat farm country like this footpaths were really an optimistic myth and that if I wanted to make progress I'd have to stick to the roads.

By the time I reached the top of Glastonbury Tor the rain and cloud that had been around all day had cleared to leave a perfect spring evening that gave marvellous views of Brent Knoll away towards the coast, the gash of Cheddar Gorge and in particular Wells Cathedral, all standing out sharp and clear across the Somerset plain. It was easy to see the dominance in this area of the Tor and of its importance when all the land around was marshland. By the time I reached a farm campsite just outside Wells it was raining again but I'd enjoyed my little bit of magic from Glastonbury: a clear sunny period of three hours centred on the Tor.

Now it was back to the hard reality of road pounding in the rain. Only the few hours spent looking round magnificent Wells Cathedral broke the monotony of the walk to Bristol along with the bird life at Chew Lake where I saw mute swans, mallard, tufted duck, coots, great crested grebes and grey wagtails as I passed. I ended up on the outskirts of Bristol in a pub on Dundry Hill drying out before a welcome wood fire, having pitched the tent in thick mist on some common land near rusting car frames and other junk. An appropriate place to start an urban day.

I headed into Bristol in mist and drizzle and became confused by the noise of the traffic and the road signs and was soon lost, for the first time on the walk. Foolishly I followed signs for the centre that were meant for motorists not walkers. They took me in a huge circle right round the centre before I managed to enter it. Even then I had difficulty finding the shops and the right post office to collect my mail from. A phone call confirmed that a friend was travelling down from Manchester to join me on Offa's Dyke and I arranged to meet him on the campsite in Chepstow the following evening. Leaving Bristol to camp at Severn Beach right on the estuary, I sat in the tent reading letters from friends. I was glad to receive them but the world they wrote about seemed most unreal and distant.

Along the Severn Beach seawalls and salt marshes I went on, through a misty morning, with the outline of the Severn Bridge gradually hardening ahead. In the early morning light it looked very graceful yet powerful too. The crossing, at least on foot, is deceptive for it looks far shorter than it is. Below, far below, lies the swirling, eddying muddy river. The bridge shakes constantly from the traffic and when I left it the pavement felt like it was moving, as though I'd been on a boat. It crosses the River Wye too and really is a marvel of engineering. Surveyed and designed between 1945 and 1949 it was begun in 1961 and finished in 1966 though not in time for John Hillaby who had to use the ferry. The main Severn Bridge has a main span of 3,240 feet with two side spans of 1,000 feet each. Linked to it is the smaller Wye Bridge with side spans of 285 feet and a main one of 770 feet. So at well over a mile in length it was no surprise that it felt a long way to walk.

Wandering round the gaunt impressive castle in Chepstow I remembered that T.H. White had written how castles, when first built, were bright and colourful inside rather than just grim grey shells. It was hard to imagine. From Chepstow I traced the line of Offa's Dyke back to the river. The Offa's Dyke Path only follows the actual dyke in part and from the Severn to Highbury Plain, a distance of fourteen miles, is one such section. The dyke vanishes at Highbury and the path takes a diversion over the easternmost ridge of the Black Mountains, rejoining the dyke 55 miles further on where it reappears on Rushock Hill above Knighton. An overgrown ditch past a sewage works and through a housing estate with roads named Mercian Way and Offa's Close was not a promising beginning.

Offa's Dyke was a boundary, probably a defensive barrier, between the lands of the Anglo-Saxons and those of the

Celts, lands that became England and Wales. Offa, King of Mercia from 757 to 796 AD, built the dyke and had it constructed to give unimpeded views and access to the Celtic lands of the west. The dyke lies therefore on the western slope of the hills and gives excellent views into Wales. I was to follow Offa's Dyke Path to Spoad Hill, a distance of 86 miles of which 31 are actually on the Dyke.

Morning dawned in Chepstow but there was no sign of my companion-to-be, Graham Huntington. I phoned his home and discovered that he'd phoned the previous evening to say he was in Chepstow. So where was he? A hasty enquiry led to the discovery that Chepstow had two campsites, a possibility that hadn't occurred to me. I rushed off to the other site where sensibly Graham had left a message. He'd set off along the Dyke two hours previously. I set off in pursuit. The walk through the woods was enjoyable if rushed although I did stop to look over the Wye from Wintour's Leap where limestone cliffs jut out above the river providing a good viewpoint. A similar view down to Tintern Abbey from the Devil's Point left me with a dilemma. I wanted to visit Tintern, which was not on the route, but would Graham have done so? A new direction arrow made of twigs lay in the path at the fork pointing down to Tintern. I guessed it was Graham's. At the bottom of the steep and treacherously muddy path I met him starting back up. He returned with me for a brief look at the ruined abbey which I decided looked better from the cliffs above the Wye.

After the rains of the previous days the dry, warm weather made it feel like spring again. Birch, horse chestnut and larch were in leaf and the buds on the beech were just opening. The patterns made by the tree foliage across the Wye were beautiful as was the woodland floor, carpeted with wood anemones, violets and the first bluebells. Cherry blossom was out and the sharp garlic smell of ramsons betrayed the whereabouts of the spiky white flowers.

On the two days to Pandy I was glad of company as pleasant woodland walking, enlivened by the panoramic view down the Wye over Redbrook to Monmouth from Highbury, gave way to farmland walking over what seemed like a million stiles, mostly of the leaning fence variety. White Castle, a grim, austere moated ruin of a fortress, was a point of interest. It was built by the Norman Marcher

Lords as a defense against the Celts. We had free admission as the gatekeeper, although he saw us enter, was too engrossed in the television to come out and collect any money. He was watching the Cup Final.

Pandy was my eighth night on a campsite in a row and I longed for a wild camp. A broken camera and the realisation that I'd only been averaging $13^{1}/_{2}$ miles a day for the last six days and had now taken three weeks to walk 361 miles didn't do much for my morale either. However a glorious day on the Black Mountains above the fields, stiles, roads, houses and other restrictions of the civilised valleys changed my mood totally. For thirteen miles Offa's Dyke Path followed the eastern ridge of the Black Mountains with a high point of 2,306 feet, the highest on the walk so far. The space and freedom of the open moorland felt wonderful despite the haze which meant we could only just see the other mountain ridges fading into the west. Pen-y-Beacon, the abrupt end of the ridge, gave good views down to Hay-on-Wye. Small cars and tiny people dotted the common below whilst hang-gliders soared from the ridge. In Hay an ancient, gnarled but excellent pub called the Three Tuns served beer from the wood. It was a good place for a farewell drink as Graham was leaving the next day and I would be on my own again.

After Graham's departure I had two more days on Offa's Dyke, following it from Hay-on-Wye to the Clun Valley. This part of the country is very empty (except for the sheep) with few villages, the sparse population thinly scattered in isolated farms or else gathered together in the few small towns built at stragetic points along the river valleys. I enoyed the silence and revelled finally in a wild camp 1,000 feet up on the dyke between Rushock Hill and Herrock Hill where I watched hares from the tent door and listened to an owl in the nearby pines. No noise, no cars, no people. It was very restful.

The view from the dyke was superb as I stormed across the rolling border hills that rejoice in the names of Bradnor, Rushock, Herrock, Evenjobb, Furrow, Hawthorn, Ffridd, Panpunton, Cwm-Sanahan, Llanfair and Spoad, broken by the gaps of the Hindwell, Fugg, Teme and Clun, all fast flowing hill streams in rich vales. The walking was on wide grassy uplands and the clear weather just right for Offa's Dyke. Most of the pleasure is in the wide panoramas for there is nothing of much interest close at hand. The Dyke is more significant too when you can see the line of it rolling and tumbling over a series of hills commanding the view into Wales. The town of Knighton is where the official opening of Offa's Dyke Path took place on 10 July 1971 in the Offa's Dyke Park, a creation of a local amenity group at Tref-y-clawd. I lunched at a picnic table. The opening was by Sir John Hunt (now Lord Hunt) with other dignitaries in attendance. Such a formal affair seemed a long way away to a lone and scruffy backpacker eating chocolate at the same spot.

After crossing the dyke's highest point at 1,400 feet I left it behind to descend into Clun, one of A.E. Houseman's 'quietest places under the sun'. In the little village I located a small meadow called Tom Priest's Field where I'd been told people could camp. Allowing me to pitch my tent unfortunately meant turning a poor pony out of the field and into a small stable. I felt quite mean but rationalised that perhaps the pony was stabled there at night anyway. I was charged fifty pence for my stay with the explanation that that was the charge per tent regardless of size or number of occupants; very cheap for the twenty scouts who'd stayed there in two tents two years previously, the farmer told me. Through the tent door I could see the ruined outline of Clun Castle against the darkening sky.

Plantation covered hills and country lanes led me onto the Long Mynd as I turned east towards the Midland plain which I had to cross to reach the Peak District. The long whaleback ridge of the Mynd, in view long before I reached it, was to be my last taste of the high country for some time. On the cropped grass ridge the dominant features, visually and aurally, were the gliders. They rushed and soared close above my head, thrown into the air by a tension wire and an engine. One failed to make it and bumped clumsily across the ground like an albatross landing, to be towed away by a tractor. To the west scattered hills stretch away into Wales but the best features of the Long Mynd are the long, deep, twisting valleys on the dip slope to the east. Cardingmill, a well known local beauty spot, is particularly impressive with its sudden view down to Church Stretton, nestled in the bottom like an Alpine village.

As I reached the flat Midlands plain a serious problem arose. My right ankle swelled up and became more and more painful until I was hobbling badly. The walking, on minor roads mostly, was nondescript except for one memorable moment. In Willeypark Wood at dusk I stopped and rested by a tree. An open hedged ride was nearby and I watched a totally silent and ghostly white barn owl hunting up and down by the hedge, flying just above ground and passing only a few yards from me. I stood spellbound for some moments and the enchantment continued for some time afterwards. It is one of the few events from this section of the walk, apart from my hurt leg, that still lives in my mind. During the next few days my leg became worse and I decided it must have attention so I hobbled to Stafford and limped into the Infirmary, pack and all. A badly bruised ankle was diagnosed, requiring two weeks' rest. How it had happened I did not know but for now the trek was over. Reluctantly I broke the walk and went to stay with my parents whilst my ankle healed. I sat in an armchair with my leg up for four long frustrating days. After that time the need to continue the journey overcame worry about the ankle which certainly felt better and I returned to Stafford.

I left Stafford station at 2.30 pm, walked nineteen miles and my ankle felt fine. I was overjoyed and the feeling of being back on the road again was incredible. As I walked I noted the scenery changing, growing more hilly and more wooded. The fields were smaller whilst hedges and the first few dry stone walls began to replace the wire fences. I was approaching the Pennines. The going became more rugged as I crossed a series of south-east running river valleys, those of the Trent, Blithe, Tean and Churnet. More trees were in leaf now and I especially noted the delicate almost transparent green of the beech trees standing out against the darker more solid greens of the other trees.

At Tean I stopped at the Dog and Partridge for a pint and, strangers with large rucksacks and big boots being a rarity hereabouts, was questioned as to my activities. My reward for telling them was a free pint. I'd been wary about mentioning the true goal of my walk but was now feeling more confident and with 500 miles done prepared to admit my purpose. I left the pub with four sets of directions to campsites or youth hostels. It was very confusing and three sets were wrong. The fourth was right and produced a caravan site at 10.30 pm.

Beyond the pleasant market town of Ashbourne I entered the Peak District National park by the Tissington Trail and left tarmac for the first time since the Long Mynd. The Tissington Trail follows the line of the old London and North Western Railway from Ashbourne to Buxton joining the High Peak Trail at Parsley Hay after thirteen miles. The line itself was opened to passengers in 1899 and the final section closed in 1967 so it did not last long as a railway. Let us hope that the footpath and cycleway, opened in two sections (Ashbourne to Hartington in 1971 and Hartington to Parsley Hay in 1972), lasts longer. The Peak Park Planning Board and Derbyshire County Council operate a cycle hire service on the trails between them.

I only stayed with the Tissington Trail for three miles, leaving it for Dovedale, a beauty spot I wanted to see. As the field path to it topped a rise I saw Thorpe Cloud rising ahead, the first real hill since the Long Mynd. I felt relief. The flat lands were behind me now. This part of the Peak District is scenically very different from the Shropshire hills, being limestone country. The appearance of every landscape is determined by the underlying rock structure but limestone is the one rock above any other that visibly determines its surroundings. A light airy feeling pervades limestone country and to me it always has a spring-like air to it. Botanically it makes for a very rich flora giving a luxurious setting to the dry watercourses, disappearing streams, pot holes, caves, scars and tottering pinnacles typical of limestone scenery.

Thorpe is a remarkably unspoilt hamlet considering it lies at the mouth of Dovedale, one of the country's three most famous and popular limestone beauty spots, the others being Cheddar Gorge and Malham Cove. The pressures on Dovedale can be clearly seen in the state of the paths and the amount of litter but despite this it is both beautiful and spectacular. Steep wooded slopes, sheer cliffs towering above the trees, caves, springs and jagged spires of naked rock make it a place to worship nature and the power of creation. Dippers bobbed on the rocks in the delightful tumbling stream whilst either side spread the variegated pattern of mixed woodland in spring. I wound my way slowly up the dale as darkness fell, indulging in the sheer glory of it all. Camp was a few fields away behind the George Inn in Alstonefield.

Edale was 25 miles away, my next map pick-up point and the start of Pennine Way. I reached it in one day. It was

37

hard to realise that only a week before I had limped out of Stafford Infirmary feeling that the walk might be over. More limestone dales were linked to reach Edale and gritstone country; Wolfscote Dale, Beresford Dale, Horseshoe Dale, Deep Dale (with its steep cliffs dotted with caves in which traces of prehistoric peoples have been found towering above the narrow valley), Wye Dale and Chee Dale. I found the closed-in and densely wooded Wye valley just as attractive as Dovedale though clearly much less frequented. Nodding cowslips lined the path, bright against the dark green of most of the vegetation. Continuing my dales walk I followed Peter, Hay and Dam Dales to Peak Forest and a very welcome though unexpected, pub. Unexpected because it was not on the map. It would, I thought, be a shame if the Ordnance Survey were so perfect that there were never any surprises round the next corner.

Over the moors from Peak Forest the silhouette of the Mam Tor and Lose Hill ridge suddenly appeared in the dusk looking far larger than life. I raced the darkness over Mam Nick, a v-shaped notch between Mam Tor and Rushup Edge, and down the track to Edale, arriving at 10 pm to camp on a site crowded and noisy with the Saturday night visitors from Manchester and Sheffield, both less than twenty miles away. For once I didn't care. I was too tired.

Sunday was an enforced day of rest as I had to wait for the post office to open before I could leave Edale. I felt so restless that after wandering round Edale all morning visiting the shop and the cafe in turn a couple of times I stormed over to Castleton via Hollins Cross in forty-five minutes to sit in a different cafe and visit different shops amongst a different crowd of people. I had walked 62 miles in three days and did not feel like stopping. In the evening a friend, Steve Twaites, turned up to walk the first few days of the Pennine Way with me.

So there I was ready to set off on the Pennine Way again just over two years since I'd first walked it. I hoped this time for better weather but I wouldn't have dared hope for the weather that actually occurred. Six and a half hours saw us over Kinder and Bleaklow in clear conditions and down to Crowden. Even in good weather these gritstone moorlands are always bleak. The soil is so acid that very little grows here. The common plant is the white wispy cotton-sedge that gives way to billberry on the slopes of the plateaux. The area is a total contrast to the luxuriant limestone areas which had been left behind when I crossed the Mam Tor–Lose Hill ridge, the shale dividing line between limestone and gritstone; the White Peak and the Dark Peak. Limestone is porous whilst gritstone is not, which is why the great beds of peat have built up over the millenia. Kinder was dry underfoot for once but Mill Hill, Moss Castle, Featherbed Moss and Bleaklow required the wearing of gaiters for the first time on the walk. Since I'd last been at Crowden a special camp site had been set up to accommodate backpackers and here we camped. An hour in a phone booth failed to locate a colleague from the YHA Shop, Brian Cropper, who was supposed to come out and meet me here. We did eventually effect a rendezvous — in Glencoe!

Black Hill and the other peat bogs seemed tamer without the swirling mist of two years previously and the ground was firmer. Steve only went in up to his knees twice. To make up for last time's disappointment Standedge had an unexpected snack van where we dined on coffees, soft drinks and cheese butties and alleviated our chronic dehydration, not a problem I'd considered in relation to the Pennine Way but it was extremely hot! The closed White House Inn had an ominous 'no boots inside' notice over the door but this time we weren't stopping anyway. In fact we didn't stop until Hebden Bridge where we spent a fruitless evening trying to find a friend who lived there but who was in fact in Manchester that day. Unfortunately she lived at the top of a steep hill, an unwelcome climb after 27 miles. Back in Hebdon we got lost trying to find Hardcastle Crags in the dark. When we did reach the woods I was so tired I couldn't be bothered with the tent and just lay my sleeping bag on the ground and climbed in. I lay on my back and tree-gazed. It was very magical, quiet and peaceful. Finally, relaxed, I drifted off to sleep.

The large red and brown wood ants crawling over us when we woke up seemed harmless so we ignored them. Saying good morning to four surprised hikers we realised that Steve was sleeping across the path! Two days was all the time he had so back in Hebden I saw him on the bus and headed off alone again for Brontë country. Top Withens passed, I lunched in Ponden Hall, bypassed on my first Pennine Way walk. The massive seventeenth-century farmhouse is quite fascinating inside with its huge blackened beams, varnished furniture and bizarre trappings. The food was good, plentiful and cheap and I was reluctant to leave. The place had a nice feel to it. So many of the eating places I used were modern, slick and totally without character either in appearance or food.

I shared a field in Thornton-in-Craven with another backpacker, the first other long distance walker I'd met on the whole walk. This was his third day out and he was hoping to complete the Way in a fortnight. I was to meet Derek several times in the next few days but not to walk with him as he was usually off and walking whilst I was still sound asleep. I entered the Yorkshire Dales National Park on a day so hot that for the first time on the walk I wore shorts. It looked as though this settled weather was here for a few days. It was the first of the walk. Just past Hanlith on the River Aire the grand panorama of limestone country from Malham Cove to Gordale Scar opened out. It was marvellous. Not having seen this last time I had no idea such a view existed and for several minutes I stood and stared and thought 'this is what I'm doing the walk for'.

In Malham village it was school trip day. Children were everywhere. In the Information Centre the anti-camper policies then prevalent in the Dales National Park were in evidence both in the literature and verbally. I was informed there were no sites between Malham and Hawes and that wild camping was not allowed. Contrary to what they said I knew of several farms that took campers so I decided to go anyway. At the Cove I stood right at the bottom of this huge curved cliff and looked up, then right at the top, and looked down again. Again after the sombre gritstone moors the limestone scenery, sparkling in the sun, seemed quite light-hearted and uplifting. The ascent of Fountains Fell in the heat took an extraordinarily long time. The path crawled gradually across the slope and I counted four stone 'men' (and a half) on the summit. The view was excellent with Great Whernside's whaleback clear throughout the ascent and then from the summit plateau Ingleborough and Penyghent outlined against the sinking sun — real mountains at last! Feeling lively I ran down to the road and then walked to Dale Head Farm where ten pence allowed me a kettle of water and a pitch on rough pasture at 1,400 feet. It is surprisingly easy to run down hills with a heavy pack. I didn't try it the other way. Derek was already here. I had now walked 627 miles and although I didn't know it was halfway through the walk.

Half an hour from Dale Head and I was on the summit of Penyghent looking at a spectacular view. Between the tabletop shape of Ingleborough and the bulky sprawl of Whernside were clearly silhouetted the beautiful, magical mountains of the Lake District. The Scafells, Crinkle Crags, Bowfell and Great Gable; all were there. It was one of the best views of the whole walk. By 11 am I was in Horton-in-Ribblesdale having run most of the way down on what looked like being the hottest day yet. Best buy here was a tin of Nivea cream to ward off sunburn on the long hot haul to Hawes where I met Derek again and several other Way walkers on a crowded noisy site. People arrived all evening and unfortunately well into the night. The roar of motorbikes and the cursing of people trying to pitch tents in the dark plus the pain of sunburnt shoulders and legs made for a poor night's sleep.

Great Shunner Fell at least gave me a view this time after the five-mile slog to its summit; a hazy view with dark evil-looking clouds glowing red from the sun piled up on the horizon dramatically. Ahead and below lay the dark slash that was Swaledale. I half ran down to Thwaite, to slake my thirst on ice cream and cans of Coke.

In celebration of the Whit Bank Holiday, Keld had sprouted two gaudy campsites; the glaring orange, red and blue tents marring the otherwise quiet subtlety of the brown and green dale. On the moorland trek to Tan Hill there was a disturbance of a different kind. Crossing Ladd Hill I heard a raucous shrieking and saw a curlew jumping up and down in front of a ewe and her lamb who were standing staring at it. The cause of the bird's agitation became clear as the sheep scuttled off at my approach: right where they had been standing was the curlew's nest with two eggs and a newly hatched chick in it. I left quickly to allow the upset parent to return. At Tan Hill I joined five other backpackers camped behind the Inn on the rubbish tip that constitutes this wild pitch. Some of the litter is undoubtedly dumped by car-borne tourists but gas canisters and lightweight meal wrappers can only be left by campers who ought to know better.

Descending to Middleton-in-Teesdale I startled nesting birds constantly. Grouse with chicks spluttered into the air at every other step and in the valley I was twice mobbed by frantic lapwings who were joined by golden plovers and then redshanks. I saw several grouse chicks as they froze where they were whilst the parents tried to distract me by feigning injury.

Hungry and hot I decided to sit out the humid heavy afternoon and walk on in the cool of the evening. So I retired to a cafe, read *The Observer* and consumed three coffees, a cheese salad, a round of cheese sandwiches and a slice of lemon meringue. As an afterthought I drank two cans of shandy and ate an ice cream before setting off. My appetite seemed to be growing!

A raging red sunset developed as I walked beside the Tees past High Force and Cauldron Snout looking for a place to camp. The vivid orange of some tents glared out from across the river. I kept on as there was no bridge. When I reached the next one, spelt 'Saur' in Wainwright's guidebook, 'Sayer' on the signpost and not marked on the O.S. map, I found three tents pitched by Langdon Beck. The payment of twenty pence at Saur/Sayer Farm allowed me to join them. The following day saw me up at High Cup Nick, down to Dufton and a lunch of pickled eggs and shandy in the pub followed by a walk along a lane thick with primroses, bluebells, kingcups, stitchwort and violets, before returning to the tops and yet again good views. This trip along the Pennine Way was giving me all the panoramas I'd missed last time plus some spectacular sunsets, another of which I watched from the summit of Cross Fell before descending to Greg's Hut. The bothy had been in very recent use for a fire was still burning in the grate though whoever had been there did not return. Again I had this popular bothy to myself. Since my first visit a few carefully protected pine saplings had been planted outside.

The Pennine Way so far had coincided with my planned End to End route but beyond the valley of the South Tyne it turns eastwards before heading north through the Cheviot Hills. I wanted to take a more direct route to Scotland so at Greenhead I intended to leave the Pennine Way and head north for the Southern Uplands and as straight a line as possible through the Glasgow-Edinburgh gap to Loch Lomond and the Highlands. Firstly though I kept to the Pennine Way through Alston and along the South Tyne valley. The discovery of a post office in the unpleasantly named Slaggyford selling cans of shandy and ice cream followed closely by a pub were highlights of an otherwise unmemorable day which ended in an illegal but well-hidden pitch in a field by Hartley's Burn. This area I found depressing, especially around Langley Colliery where dark low moorland is rendered worse by closed mine buildings, ruined barns, boarded up farms, sour pasture and the detritus of a decaying landscape. An air of futility and despair pervaded everything and even the bright sunshine of the continuing heatwave did not lighten the scene.

My trespass was kept secret by a thick white mist whose dampness spread through the tent and my now weather-worn belongings but I was soon out of it as I left the river to cross dull moors for five miles before leaving the Pennine Way just as Thirlwall Castle came into view. Gilsland post office provided me with the next batch of mail, maps and guides and I sat in the shade of a bus shelter working out the next stage of the journey. In my notebook I had written a brief résumé of the planned route, actually just a list of places, before setting off but now some of the connections were not apparent. According to these plans I had intended to walk for miles over trackless and probably boggy low hills with nowhere to restock for many days. This may have seemed a good plan back home but out here it seemed ill conceived so I changed it. Instead I decided to head for Hawick as D.G. Moir's *Scottish Hill Tracks*, (a boon for backpackers planning routes through the Scottish hills rather than over them), described a good path to the town and it was an obvious resupply point.

On my new route I headed for Bewcastle and past a farm called Moscow where I stopped for a coffee. Leaving I lost the bridleway I'd been following and had to struggle across several fields trying to follow its line. The easy route-finding along the Pennine Way was over. Eventually I arrived at the diminutive hamlet of Bewcastle which appeared to consist of one farm, one pub, one house and one church all dominated by the earthworks of a Roman fort surmounted by the remnants of a castle of Edward 1st that Cromwell had pulled down. Obviously Bewcastle had taken part in the notoriously turbulent history of the Borders. A rare and fascinating relic in the churchyard is an elaborately carved eighth-century Christian cross.

For me however Bewcastle is the place where the dry, hot

43

weather of the past fortnight suddenly broke. A huge clap of thunder startled me as I lay in a dip in the earthworks having a snack and, bundling everything unceremoniously into the pack, I ran for the church porch as the rain began. The storm raged for two hours, a typical summer afternoon thunderstorm. I sat it out in the church porch then followed it north and west towards Newcastleton along country lanes and through low moorland hills to the Border Forest Park and Kershope Forest. Ranks of dark Sitka and Norway spruce enveloped me. A picnic site with wooden tables and benches just inside the forest beside a rain-gorged torrent called Cuddy's Burn seemed a good place to camp. A small ridge tent was already pitched there beside a car, owned, it turned out, by a young German couple who were touring Britain on minor roads. They kindly gave me a meal of lentil soup, a delicious change from my usual instant potato or rice meals, and complained about English steam-baked white bread which I wasn't prepared to defend.

Despite the storm the hot weather continued though the massed clouds gave it a temporary look. I entered Scotland and the un-Scottish sounding Newcastleton, a long drawn-out single-street town from where I set out for Hawick on my first D.G. Moir route. Unpromisingly this started with seven and a half miles on roads though this did allow me to visit Hermitage Castle, a grim austere hulk that Sir Walter Scott thought the finest in Scotland. Once off the tarmac, navigation problems promptly began. The Thieves Road marked on the map rapidly disappeared on the ground though its line was easy to follow at first. However to be in hill country again, especially new hill country, felt good even if, excepting the shapely Din Fell, they were as yet just big rounded grassy humps. A shock awaited me as I crossed the shoulder of Swine Knowe. The whole valley head above the Priesthaugh Burn almost to the top of 2,000-foot Cauldclough Head had been deep ploughed in preparation for conifer planting and looked like a giant's field. No track lay through it so walking was very difficult. I camped amongst the trenches at the confluence of two burns under Dod Rig, glad to be out in the hills again but worried as to how many more of Moir's routes might not exist as most of my planned way through Scotland was based on them.

There followed the most frustrating day's walking of the whole trek leaving me as depressed at the end of it as I had felt at Treyarnon and Stafford. Hawick was reached easily by forest track on a cool cloudy day. Here I stocked up with food and all three volumes of Tolkien's *Lord of the Rings*. As I was already carrying John Fowles' *The Magus* and the Scottish Mountaineering Club's *Guide to the Southern Uplands* in addition to D.G. Moir's guidebook and my maps I now had a small but heavy library with me. Outside Hawick for the only time on the walk my intended route fell apart completely and I was forced to turn back after my way was blocked completely at Muselee by a new fenced-in forestry plantation. I cast around for a way through but there was none. Reluctantly I headed back to the road and Snoot Youth Hostel which makes good use of an old chapel. I had a six-berth 'cell' to myself as there were only two other occupants. I had walked twenty-one miles but progressed only fourteen along my route.

With no choice but to stick to the roads I did so for long miles to the valley of Etrick Water where I thankfully left the tarmac behind and headed up Penistone Knowe and the 2,014-foot Herman Law, my first mountain top since Cross Fell. I had excellent views down to the Loch of Lowes and St. Mary's Loch before descending steep hillsides to the road at Birkhill Pass where there is a plaque to Charles Lathrope, a local schoolteacher and geologist, who discovered the history of the local geological structure by the study of grapholites. These are thought to be the skeletons of tiny creatures and consist of black streaks in the rock. Their importance lies in the fact that they enable certain beds of ancient rock to be identified without doubt and it was this that Lathrope discovered.

I left the road again at the famous beauty spot of the Grey Mare's Tail waterfall which crashes impressively down from a fine hanging valley. Above this a good hill path leads to Loch Skeen set in wild surroundings at 1,700 feet. I was determined to camp here but finding a dry pitch amongst the heather and peat was not easy. I eventually located a grassy patch just big enough for the tent surrounded by white cloudberry flowers.

Overnight rain cleared to give me a fine day for the walk over Broad Law, at 2,754 feet the second highest summit in the Southern Uplands though aesthetically these hills are more like big rounded moorland tops than real mountains. I saw no-one all day and realised that I had not seen another walker since leaving the Pennine Way. The end of my stay in these hills came as I descended to Tweedale and the beginning of a forty-mile road haul to the Highlands. I wandered down to Broughton village in the first rain I'd walked in since Offa's Dyke, oscillating between the road and an overgrown, derelict, and in places impassable railway track. I camped early in a small Norway spruce plantation. It had been a weary withdrawn day despite the hills and I was glad it was over.

A couple of road-slogging footsore days took me through a rural-industrial wasteland that no walker would dream of crossing except on a through walk like mine. Everywhere around the dreary town of Forth lay old abandoned mines, ragged smallholdings, spoil heaps and deserted buildings interspersed with new forestry plantations. An atmosphere of lacklustre despair pervaded the place. The day ended in a bar at Braehead where I watched a World Cup football match on the rented television. Every bar had one of these I gathered. Scotland lost 3–1. I decided to refrain from any comment on football whilst in Scotland. For the night I wandered into a plantation to camp by a burn called Kitchen Linn though this was so filthy that I was not prepared to drink from it. Above me redshank perched on telegraph wires.

Camped in a larch wood on Bar Hill, just above what a notice described as the best preserved section of the Antonine Wall (the earlier and more northerly relation of Hadrian's Wall), the next night, I could see the line of the Campsie Fells ahead, and although only 12 miles from Glasgow I knew I was leaving the lowlands behind. A roe deer inspected the tent nervously before slipping away into the trees.

On leaving Bar Hill at 7.30 am I had little idea that it would be 3 pm and thirty miles further on when I stopped. Maps and mail collected from Kilsyth Post Office and food bought, I climbed up into the Campsies, the southern outpost of the Highlands. I was heading for Drymen and the line of the as yet unofficial West Highland Way which I intended following to Fort William. Hard walking into a fierce wind across rough pathless moorland was lightened by the sight of ranges of real mountains to the north and west. Eventually I dropped down to the Crow Road, Endrith Water and Fintry. Looking back to the edge of the

Campsie Fells with the corries of Balglass standing out, the view was impressive. Under my feet a snipe shot out of the grass to reveal two chicks.

In Drymen I was told that Cashel seven miles away on Loch Lomondside was the nearest place I could camp so I set off into the dark after a supper of chips and Coca-cola. I reached the site just before daylight and pitched the tent in the drizzle. Although tired I was pleased to be in the Highlands.

I was now on the West Highland Way which in its entirety runs 92 miles from Milngavie on the edge of Glasgow to Fort William. Although running through dramatic mountain country the West Highland Way is an easier walk than either the South West Way or the Pennine Way as it follows the glens through the hills and only once, when it crosses the ridge between Glencoe and Kinloch-leven via the Devil's Staircase, is there a steep climb. This makes the WHW an ideal trek for the backpacker who wishes to travel in rugged country easily or who, as I did on this occasion, wishes to push on north as directly and quickly as possible. The roughest part of the route in 1978 was the path alongside Loch Lomond. Beyond Rowardennan the path entered the Queen Elizabeth Forest Park. Across the loch the Arrochar Alps stood out, especially prominent being the twisted ridge line of the Cobbler. Exciting country at last I thought as I followed the narrow path through the oak, birch and hazel. The weather was cold and wet with strong gusts of wind from the west. The mountain tops appeared and disappeared through the clouds. I had intended to climb Ben Lomond but my desire not to deviate from my route coupled with my sore feet and the first two blisters I'd had in weeks, made me abandon the idea. Beyond the plush Inversnaid Hotel the terrain became much more rugged. I found occasional traces of paths, probably sheep or deer tracks, but mostly it was a scramble over fallen trees and through the big boulders that had fallen right down to the water's edge. Somewhere amongst them lies a cavern known as Rob Roy's Cave but I never found it. A couple of deer leapt off into the trees and several sheep with long curving horns gazed at me as I entered a tiny clearing and decided it was big enough for the tent. As I settled in a tawny owl called out then flew off from the branches above the tent.

47

The wind veered to the north west overnight and was blowing hard by dawn giving a day of heavy rain squalls and sunny periods for the walk to Tyndrum, through thick wet bracken and ankle-clutching bogs until the road was reached. I wore my waterproofs all day. The Hotel Invernan provided lunch in the dry, a crisp fresh salad and a pot of coffee. Crianlarich was passed through then Tyndrum reached. With their mountain vistas invisible in the clouds these little hamlets seemed dreary and dull. Tyndrum in fact is distinctly seedy. I camped there on an expensive and not very attractive caravan site sandwiched between the road and railway. I had to stay as I'd arrived too late for the post office and in it were my next batch of maps and mail.

Leaving the road the walking improved (now that the West Highland Way has formal status a footpath exists between Crainlarich and Tyndrum). I followed the remains of the old road to Bridge of Orchy, crossing and recrossing the railway line mostly by bridges but once across the rails as that bridge was no more. Ahead was the strong graceful cone of Beinn Dorain. Then the old military road took me over the shoulder of the hills via Mam Carraigh (in the Scottish hills a 'mam' is a broad, easy pass whilst a 'bealach' is a higher, narrower one) to Inveroran with a magnificent view down to Loch Tulla, along Glen Orchy and across to the Blackmount with Stob Gabhar prominent. The scenery all the way from here to the Kingshouse at the head of Glencoe is breathtaking and the old track from Forest Lodge makes for easy walking. As the Kingshouse is approached Rannoch Moor appears, grey and flat, to the right, whilst to the left rear up the massive peaks of the Buachaille Etive Mor and Sron na Creise. Across Glencoe runs the jagged crest of the Aonach Eagach.

Enthralled by the view I bounced down to the Kingshouse feeling elated then padded round the carpeted corridors searching for a colleague from the YHA Shop in Manchester and his wife, Brian and Jane Cropper, who'd arranged to meet me here. Eventually they found me in the bar making enquiries about camping outside. Unnecessary enquiries as I found I had been treated to a meal and a bed in the hotel. Sitting in the dining room in stockinged feet, boots being forbidden, eating a good meal felt most strange as did the tiny bedroom and what seemed an unnaturally soft bed. The hot water was welcome (and necessary!) too. With a few malt whiskies inside me I felt quite decadent.

Dawn produced a cloudy, windy day with the tops hidden in swirling mist and Glencoe looking traditionally dour and grim. After the further luxury of a hotel breakfast I packed up all the food Brian and Jane had generously brought for me, which included a whole cooked chicken, hoisted my now very heavy pack and set off for the Devil's Staircase and the old military road to Kinlochleven.

This was a significant part of the walk for me, as the previous August on a short backpacking trip from Fort William to Glencoe, I'd met an American walker who was walking from John O'Groats to Land's End. I walked this section with him and several months later he wrote to tell me he'd successfully completed his trek. That evening, camped on the site of the Massacre of Glencoe, near the Clachaig Inn, I'd written in my journal: 'John made me consider the idea of a Land's End–John O'Groats walk seriously — not just a vague future idea. South to North. April to July. A spring trek.' And so the seeds were sown that resulted ten months later in me being back in the same place doing the long walk myself.

The one shop open in Kinlochleven provided me with *The Observer* and a can of Coke which I took to the woods above the town to read and drink during lunch. A whole chicken didn't quite fit in with my normally vegetarian diet but I had become less strict since discovering that in many bars in Scotland the only food was a pub lunch consisting of mutton broth and Scotch pie and chips. I was prepared to eat any alternative to dehydrated food! I was also on this occasion hungry enough to finish the chicken in one go.

Fort William was reached, past the massive buttresses of Ben Nevis, Britain's highest mountain, at seven o'clock and I camped three miles outside the town on a caravan site. The next day was to be a day off as I had to collect my penultimate parcel of maps from the post office and stock up for at least six days as Ullapool was the next place I could be sure of finding supplies. The next stage was the longest cross-country section of the walk and one of the toughest too. Fort William has the atmosphere of a frontier town, a defiant industrial gesture to the hills and wildness around. Like Kinlochleven it is not an attractive country town but an industrial estate. As the only really large town on the west

49

coast of Scotland it is one of the most important Highland centres. Ben Nevis and Glencoe are major tourist attractions and most tourists pass through or stay in Fort William. There were many tourists about as I did my shopping including large numbers of young people, especially Canadians, Americans and Australians, with huge rucksacks that dwarfed mine. Walkers or climbers were notable by their absence.

From Fort William my plan was to head north and west through the remote hills around Lochs Arkaig and Quoich to Glen Shiel and then through even remoter mountains north to Torridon, Kinlochewe and eventually Ullapool. I hoped to take about a week and in fact I passed through Ullapool during the seventh day out from the Fort. I could probably pick up limited food supplies in Glen Shiel, Torridon and Kinlochewe but probably not stove fuel so I stocked up on a litre of methylated spirits to obtain which I had to sign the poisons register. Fort William's shops also provided me with foodstuffs usually unobtainable in small villages and I left loaded down with dried fruit, muesli, granola, and wholemeal bread as well as the more usual oatcakes, cheese spread and chocolate bars plus half a dozen dehydrated meals from 'Nevisport'.

I returned to the tent with two full carrier bags of food wondering how I could carry it all. Ben Nevis stood out sharp and clear on the warm sunny evening, with large snow patches still visible high up amongst the crags. On the site I enjoyed the bliss of a long soak in a hot bath. It would probably be the last one for a long time.

The pack felt very heavy (and probably weighed well over 50 lb) as I followed the Caledonian Canal to Gairlochy and walked through sombre fir woods along the Mile Dorcha (Dark Mile) before heading back up into the hills past the waterfalls in Gleann Cia-aig. Throughout there were superb views back to the Grey Corries, Aonach Mor, Carn Mor Dearg and, towering above them all, Ben Nevis, whose bulky shape was to dominate southern views for days to come. I camped in a bowl in the hills near the ruin of Fedden. The site boasted sandpipers by the stream and large numbers of the insectivorous common butterwort flower. I felt very contented.

A mixture of woods and open country accompanied me along the road by Loch Garry, past Tomdoun and finally to

Allt a'Ghobhainn and a Moir route into Glen Quoich. Exciting vistas lay ahead. Tall shapely pointed peaks soared up to the clouds. I wanted to climb them all! This magnificent scenery grew more and more impressive as I tramped up the valley of the River Loyne amidst shy red deer and not so shy Highland cattle with the peaks of Spidean Mialach and Gleouriach rising temptingly to the south. I couldn't spare the time to climb them now but I vowed to return.

I pitched the tent beside a feeder stream of the River Quoich having been accompanied up Wester Glen Quoich by a large number of cattle including two bulls which inspected me and then, luckily deciding I was harmless, lost interest. Unfortunately the midges found me much more attractive and I was forced to spend most of the evening sealed in the tent. Later when it grew cooler and the tops clouded over, the midge attack abated and I looked out. All around stood the silent hills.

From Wester Glen Quoich I intended to cross the Bealach Duibh Leac and descend to Glen Shiel. I may have done this but I'm not quite sure actually where I went. I set off on a cool slightly hazy day on a good path which petered out higher up the glen. Ahead I could see an obvious nick in the skyline which I presumed to be the pass. The rough slopes leading up to the nick were very steep and in places I needed to use my hands. From the ridge there was no sign of a path or even that anyone had ever been that way as I looked down rocky slopes to a small corrie. Gingerly I scrambled down, the heavy pack not making balancing easy. Twice I was turned back by steep crags and it was some time before I left the upper corrie by easier slopes and found a path by the Allt Mhalagain which led directly and securely to the road in Glen Shiel. I was sure I'd missed the pass and come over the ridge somewhere else but if I had I couldn't work out where. After the excitement of crossing the ridge I was quite glad of the easy downhill roadside stroll to Shiel Bridge and Loch Duich.

By the lochside I saw sandpipers, oystercatchers and several herons with, further out, flocks of ducks bobbing up and down on the water. The Road to the Isles runs here and cars whizzed by at great speed, the occupants blind to the quiet beauty they were disturbing. To reach Glen Elchaig I went via the much vaunted Falls of Glomach leaving the loch at Morvich to take the well waymarked path through Dorvsduain Forest and over the moors to the falls. I was accompanied for much of the way by a couple with a dog which, whenever I got close to them, attacked me and had to be called off. It seemed that it disliked rucksacks. Eventually they gave up and decided to reach the falls from the other side where one can drive closer to them. I saw them and their dog the next morning.

The Falls of Glomach are impressive with a 370-foot drop down a wild chasm viewable only from a narrow and crumbling path on the cliff's edge. I descended this exciting track with good views directly down into the deep gorge and with the echo of the water crashing down ringing from the rocks all around. Quite awe-inspiring. Camp was down on the glen floor.

An early start saw a long, twenty-eight-mile day that ended with a pitch on the shore of Upper Loch Torridon amongst the most beautiful mountains I had ever seen. From Glen Elchaig and Glen Lingn where the river descends in tree-lined chasms I crossed low forested hills on a track that comes out into the luxurious gardens of Attadale House with its rhododendrons and Chilean pines. A door in the garden wall lets one out onto the road. From the hill brow above Attadale I'd had my first view of the Northern Highlands in the form of the Beinn Damph and Coulin forests. I couldn't wait to reach them. Past Coulags I headed into the hills beside the Fionn-abhainn with superb views of Fuar Tholl, Sgorr Ruadh and Maol Chean-dearg whose names mean The Cold Hollow, the Red Peak and the Bold Red Head respectively.

The mountains from here to Dundonnell I found provided the most overpowering surroundings of the walk. Rising up separately from sea level in a massed array of pinnacles, serrated ridges, deep corries and savage crags these hills are made up of layers of dull red Torridonian sandstone capped on the highest peaks with harsh white crests and cones of quartz. There is a timeless primaeval air here. If true wilderness still exists in Britain then this is it.

I crossed the first range of these mountains by the Bealach na Lice, appropriately named Pass of the Flat Stone for huge flat slabs of rock are passed by here. I descended to Loch an Eion hoping to find a site up here in the heart of the hills but sandstone drains badly and all was boggy. A harsh guttural cry drew my attention to some black-throated divers on one of the many small lochans. With their delicate markings and graceful bearing they must be one of the most attractive of our waterbirds as well as one of the wildest. Then I was suddenly confronted with Liathach. A vast wall topped by a jagged ridge culminating in a shining white pyramid-shaped summit rose in front of me. An astounding view with the sides looking vertical and unscaleable. I stumbled down the path unable to tear my eyes away until they were distracted by the other two Torridonian giants, Beinn Alligin and Beinn Eighe, the latter with its silver-grey screes setting off Liathach perfectly.

Eventually, tired and footsore but elated, I reached the hamlet of Annat on the shores of Upper Loch Torridon where I camped with a view through the tent door of Liathach, Beinn Alligin and a beautiful slow red sunset. I felt totally content and strangely hyper-conscious of my environment. Everything seemed unearthly and magical.

My ecstatic notes for the 17th June begin: 'What a day! What an exciting brilliant mountain day!' In every respect it was the high point of the walk. At times in the mountains a certain transfiguration comes about, the normal pleasures of hill-walking are transformed and everything becomes more real, more immediate and totally perfect. In words it is indescribable. Either one has felt and therefore understands the intense nature of the experience or one hasn't. It is, if you like, a mystery, a personal mystical event that is unattainable by conscious means. I have had several such moments in the hills, always unpredicted and lasting from a few minutes to a whole day as on this occasion. They have only occurred when I've been alone and are too personal to really share.

The day dawned with a completely clear azure sky, and not a cloud in sight. My intention was to walk to Kinlochewe round Liathach and Beinn Eighe, a route I started by walking down beside Loch Torridon to where the Coire Mhic Nobuil path rises into the hills between Beinn Alligin and Liathach. I followed this marvellous and scenic path to its junction with the Coire Mhic Fhearchair one which I took to the corrie itself, rated as one of the best in Scotland, intending to retrace my steps and go cross country north of Beinn Eighe to Kinlochewe. But the mountains drew me in.

I entered the famous Coire Mhic Fhearchair to see a beautiful ice-blue loch backed by the amazing Triple Buttress, a massive crag made up of a third Torridonian sandstone and two-thirds shining white Cambrian quartzite. After taking in the scene my eyes were drawn to an obvious scree gully leading to the col between Ruadh Stac Mor, the mountain's highest point at 3,309 feet, and the main ridge. I could, I thought, leave the pack, scramble up to the summit and back then continue my low level route. So off I went negotiating the rough ground and boulders by the lochside to the bottom of the scree gully. If I took the pack up I could of course walk the ridge and descend to Kinlochewe, so up I scrambled over the rocks beside the very loose and worn gully. With a huge and heavy pack the scramble was quite an effort and not one I would recommend but in twenty minutes I was at the col. A brief rest and I was bounding up the last easy slopes to the summit cone itself where a couple of walkers were already sitting.

Wave after wave of hills swept to the horizon in all directions, a scene broken only to the west by the island-studded sea. South and west the dark jagged edge of the Skye Cuillin stood out and I could also identify the peaks of the Beinn Damph and Coulin forests to the south, the other Torridon tops and northwards the great wilderness round Slioch and An Teallach. Most of this overwhelming array of mountains was though, at that time, for me unidentifiable. So many more to climb, so many more potential days like this one. I revelled in the thought. After half-an-hour a more mundane thought managed to intrude on the vision and realising I still had a long way to go I set off back to the col and up to the main ridge. Reluctantly I then left the twisting, narrow ridge, seven miles long in total, to descend into Coir'an Laoigh on a steep but clear path to the road along which I plodded to reach Kinlochewe at 8.40 pm. I'd only walked twelve miles but it was good to let slip the constant attempt to achieve the maximum mileage each day.

The area north of Kinlochewe that stretches unbroken by a road to the A832 at Dundonnell is often regarded as the only unspoilt wilderness area left in Britain, the Last Great Wilderness. Inside this vast land of loch, river, bog and mountain, development has been kept to a minimum. No bulldozed tracks, no reservoirs, just a few bothies and stalkers' tracks. This is how it should be kept but every few years proposals are put forward for hydro-electric schemes to be developed here. All of us need to concern ourselves with such schemes and to support bodies such as the Scottish Wild Land Group that do everything possible to protect areas such as this.

My visit to this unique area was unfortunately only a day long. Much as I would have liked to I could not spare the time to really explore these hills. That would have to wait for another visit. Skirting the shore of Loch Maree I followed the short Abhainn an Fhasaigh from its mouth in the loch to its source in Lochan Fada, a distance of only three and a half miles. The stream makes up for its short length by thundering impressively down rowan tree lined chasms in foaming cascades. Lochan Fada is one of the wildest spots I have even been to, a remote mountain lake with nothing but bleak hills around it. From the Bealach na Croise I descended to Loch an Nid, another loch in a superb setting with the massive Mullach Coire Mhic Fhearchair dominant to the west and the rugged outline of An Teallach temptingly ahead. I passed close by this classic peak with a clear view of its jagged crest rising above a deep corrie before dropping down to camp near the road on the northern edge of this magnificent country.

I was camped six miles from the ferry across Loch Broom to Ullapool and on enquiring by telephone I found that the next boat was at noon so I had a quick dash over to Altnaharrie arriving hot and tired (for there was a steep climb involved) with only a few minutes to spare. The ferry, a tiny launch, bounced across Loch Broom to come to rest in the harbour with the strong smells of fish and tar all around. After collecting my last set of maps from the post office I spent an hour in a cafe trying to understand the route I'd planned, an activity I finally abandoned and planned a new route which involved purchasing a new map. Ullapool, a pleasant fishing village, was full of tourists and seemed huge to me as it was the biggest place I'd been in since Fort William.

The view as I left Ullapool was stupendous stretching from An Teallach across Loch Broom to the Summer Isles and up the coast to Ben Mor Coigach, Stac Pollaidh and Canisp to the dark mass of Ben More Assynt. From a vast plateau of bog and loch these primaeval jagged peaks rise straight up in steep sweeps of rock. Arriving at Inverpolly Nature Reserve I began to look for a camp site. The warden informed me that if I descended to Elphin I could camp by the river. As I did so I considered climbing these peaks and decided that the best way to do it was by bicycle! That is to say, to cycle between each peak and the next, pitching camp at the bottom of each, climbing it, then cycling on. This would remove the long road walks between each peak but still make it a self-propelled journey. An idea for the future. Towards Elphin I could see the dark wet peat landscape change to a lush land of bright green grass with outcrops of white rock. I must be in limestone country again and this was confirmed by a pamphlet on local geology obtained from the Nature Reserve. A belt of limestone runs through this area resulting in potholes and caves in sections of the Ben More Assynt massif and here in a fertile valley where the small crofting community of Elphin is based, though half the houses are now sad empty shells. I camped down by the river in long thick grass with a good view of Cul Mor and Suilven to prepare for my trek north-eastwards to the north coast.

A steady downpour led to a late start as I optimistically waited for it to clear. It kept up all day. Encased in waterproofs I tramped the road to a welcome lunch in the warmth of the Alltnacealgach Inn. From here I decided to cross the south-east spur of the Assynt range to Loch Shin. In this storm with the tops in thick cloud there was no question I felt of crossing the peaks themselves although I was to do so in similar conditions in a few years' time. I took the track to Benmore Lodge ignoring the 'Private' signs and the warnings of a forestry worker sheltering in his JCB who told me that I'd never get through and that people had died trying. The rain worsened and the wind became galeforce as a steady slog took me over the south shoulder of Meall an Aonaich, the nearest I came to the main ridge. I could barely see more than a few yards and had to keep my head down to protect my face from the cold lashing rain. I was glad to reach Loch Shin and pitch the tent just short of Coille a Bhad Leith wood. I felt that I'd followed only the edge of a storm centred on Ben More Assynt as throughout the sky was black to the north-west but lighter to the south-east. The last six miles of the day were brightened by a series of rainbows above Loch Shin as the rain died to a drizzle and the midges came out.

The latter were out early in the morning resulting in a rapid abandonment of the site and a rapid walk past lochs Ghriama and Merhland to take my last Moir route across the desolate moorland north of Ben Hee, the Hill of the Fairies. The track over the Bealach na Meirleach was good, very good in fact as I was passed on it by two vans and a car! I put the Moir away for the last time. After my doubts in the Southern Uplands the booklets had guided me through the Highlands in excellent fashion.

Behind me the Ben More Assynt group stood clear of cloud for once. Ahead Ben Loyal and Ben Hope appeared and disappeared in the view. The last hills before the north coast. They vanished for the day as I topped the pass and the rain came down hard. Descending I came to Strath More, one of the many deserted glens that cut deeply into the hills from the coast. I say deserted as these valleys were once cultivated land until the notorious Clearances took place. These resulted from the breaking of the power of the clans after the failed 1745 rising following which the lairds, their power as chiefs of armed bands gone, became anglicised and southern based seeking profit from their lands in terms of money not people. Sheep were a good source of cash and for them the glens and straths were cleared of people who either moved to the coast or emigrated. It is impossible to walk through these barren lands without being aware of the Clearances and here in Sutherland some of the most notorious took place, many carried out by Patrick Sellars and described by Donald Macleod in articles entitled 'Gloomy Memories'. The stories make horrific reading with people fleeing possession-less from burning houses. By the middle of the last century the people had gone and the glens were empty, leaving us the legacy of the depopulated Highlands we have today. Only after riots and the campaign of the Highland Land League was the first Crofter's Act passed in 1886 granting security of tenure. Even today depopulation goes on and crofts are sold at higher prices than prospective crofters can afford, as second homes for rich southerners, known in many areas as 'white settlers'. For most of the year these homes are empty and the land turns sour and the communities wither away. Given this and the development of hydro-electric schemes, tourism, the oil industry and nuclear power in a country with no National Parks or Areas of Outstanding Natural Beauty a coherent policy of land ownership and management involving the wishes of the local populace and based on principles of environmental conservation is desperately needed.

I camped that night beside the Pictish broch of Dun Donnagail. This stone mass is a typical broch, a huge cone tapering upwards with walls several feet thick but open at the top, though this one is full of rubble. A strange edifice, it reminded me of Carn Gloose, a long way behind in time and distance. There I had been beginning. Here I was ending. This realisation came upon me as I worked out I had four days to go. I felt odd about it. I wanted to finish quickly and yet I didn't want to finish at all. I liked this way of life.

The weather caused a brisk, five and a quarter hours, seventeen-mile walk to Tongue. It was a repeat of the Assynt day and I was battered by strong winds and heavy rain. The Moine Path, the old moorland route from Strath More to the Kyle of Tongue, led me under the mist-shrouded northern ramparts of Ben Hope round the edge of the vast peat moss known as A'Mhoine. The crossing seemed interminable but it was in fact a two and a half hour nothing-to-see, head down, storm-charging bog slog. Decayed bridges crossed raging torrents as the storm blasted straight down from the Arctic. In Tongue, a small village strung out along the A8383, I camped on a site with half a dozen other wind-battered tents. I dried out in the tent over several cups of hot coffee lying fully clothed in the sleeping bag as it was quite cold before retreating to the hotel bar. Only sixty or so road miles remained.

Mist and rain continued as I walked along the north coast occasionally seeing a rocky headland and a few hazy islands that reminded me, as did all this last section including the weather, of the South West Coast and the dreams I'd had then. They'd been realised now but already new ones were taking their place. Dotted along the road were tiny hamlets kept alive by a mixture of crofting, fishing and tourism, the remnants of the old communities. At one of them, Strathy, I camped amongst sand dunes within sound of the sea. The calm peaceful evening was beautiful but engendered in me a melancholy feeling. With only forty or so miles to go, the big adventure was all but over.

At the information centre in Melvich the assistant told me with pride how she'd directed a man to lodgings a few days ago who'd walked all the way from Land's End. She was so full of this that I felt unable to tell her I'd done so too and merely purchased a public transport timetable to find out the times of trains to Manchester.

The walking continued in wind, rain and mist as I came down off the desolate peat moors to woods and the village of Reay followed by richer agricultural land with farms, fields and cattle. Approaching Thurso screaming terns dive-bombed me to be joined by gulls, oystercatchers, lapwings and curlews and, at one point a short-eared owl.

At 3.45 pm on June 25th the journey ended. A cold misty day with slight drizzle saw me walk the last 21 miles in $6^1/2$ hours, impatient to finish. I could just see the island of Strom and the nearer Orkneys. There was nowhere else to walk. I wandered amongst the tourists at John O'Groats. It looked like Land's End, especially the shattered cliffs out at Duncansby Head to which I walked after pitching the tent for the last time. I felt both glad and sad though I couldn't really accept it was over. Tomorrow on the train it would sink in: 1,255 miles walked in 65 days, the whole journey lasting 71 days. And a wonderful journey it had been. In the tent everything seemed normal. Travelling had become my way of life. Returning to 'normal' life would probably be much harder than the journey. That evening I sat in the hotel bar over a celebratory pint amongst Orkney seamen stormbound here watching the World Cup Final on the television. I was engrossed in a feeling of quiet satisfaction mixed with sadness. A dream of years was over.

3

Scotland

FROM CORROUR TO ULLAPOOL OVER 92 MUNROS

The most enjoyable part of the Land's End to John O'Groats walk had been in the Scottish Highlands and on my return from that trek I knew that was the area I wanted to explore next. This feeling was reinforced by the publication that summer of Hamish Brown's superb *Hamish's Mountain Walk,* an account of the first ever continuous trip on foot over all the Scottish 'Munros'. Before going on I'd better explain just what a 'Munro' is and what the rather obscure activity of 'Munro bagging' is all about.

In the 1880s Sir Hugh Munro, one of the early luminaries of the Scottish Mountaineering Club, compiled a list of all the tops in Scotland over 3,000 feet high, a list he subdivided into those he considered to be separate mountains and those he thought were only subsidiary summits. This list was first published in the annual SMC Journal in 1891 and contained 276 separate mountains. These have come to be known after Sir Hugh as 'Munros' and there have been many editions of 'Munro's Tables' as the list is known since that first one, and many mountaineers who have set out to climb them all, a feat first achieved by the Rev. A.E. Robertson in 1901. This activity, scorned by some, is known as 'Munro bagging'. My view is that we go into the hills for fun and whatever the individual enjoys, provided it does not damage the environment or interfere with the pleasure of others (as for example motor bike riding in the hills does), is valid. Munro bagging takes the mountaineer into many places in the Scottish hills that might otherwise never be seen and ensures that efforts are made to go out even when conditions are not ideal, providing thus an antidote to laziness or faintheartedness. Finally the pursuit of the Munros gives both a depth of experience in hillgoing that would otherwise be hard to obtain and an extensive knowledge of the Scottish hills.

As well as climbing all the Munros I had another aim which was was to climb as many of them as possible on long backpacking trips. Hamish's trek was of course the ultimate Munros' backpacking trek but I did not feel I was capable with my then scanty knowledge of the Scottish hills, of replicating it; nor did I have the four or so months to spare that it would take. In fact when I began planning my first long Munros walk in the autumn of 1978 I'd climbed just 20 of the 280 listed in the 1974 edition of Munro's Tables. (Height changes after resurveys by the Ordnance Survey have over the years led to some hills falling below the magical line and being expunged from the Tables and others, having 'grown' a few feet, being added. During my Munro bagging years there was to be a more controversial revision of the tables but for 1979 the 280 of the 1974 edition were the 'official' ones.)

One reason for choosing the Scottish Highlands for my next venture was that after the Land's End to John O'Groats walk I knew I did not want to do a walk that involved too much road work or travel through flat landscapes or towns. I wanted to do a wilderness mountain trek and Scotland is the best place for this in Britian. My horizons had not yet turned to overseas mountains, at least not seriously. Inspired by Hamish's book and visits to Torridon and the Cairngorms in the autumn of 1978, I made my first notes for a backpacking trip in Scotland that October. Throughout the winter I played with various ideas, studied the tables and the SMC Guides and pored over maps until I came up with a plan for a walk through the West Highlands taking in as many Munros as possible. Once the general line was decided I settled down to working out a detailed route. This would not be a walk connecting two points in a relatively straight line like the End to End one but a tortuous trek joining up dozens of seemingly randomly placed dots on the map. When drawn in, the line between them did not suddenly reveal a hidden shape but rather displayed what looked like tangled knitting. Some hills would be backpacked over, others would be done from base camps or bothies which I planned to use whenever possible as I'd developed a liking for these remote and basic shelters. My final plan was for a walk from Fort William to Ullapool via Knoydart and Torridon. At least I thought it

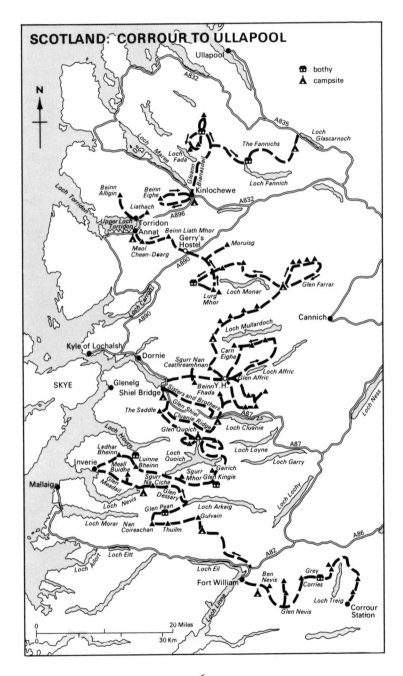

SCOTLAND: CORROUR TO ULLAPOOL

bothy

campsite

N

Ullapool

A832

A835

Loch Glascarnoch

The Fannichs

Loch Fada

Loch Fannich

Loch Maree

Gleann Bianasdail

Beinn Allighin

Beinn Eighe

Kinlochewe

Liathach

A896

A832

Upper Loch Torridon

Torridon

Annat

Beinn Liath Mhor

Gerry's Hostel

Moruisg

Maol Chean-Dearg

A890

Beinn Eighe

Loch Torridon

Loch Carron

A890

Lurg Mhor

Loch Monar

Glen Farrar

Cannich

Loch Mullardoch

Kyle of Lochalsh

Carn Eighe

Dornie

Sgurr Nan Ceathreamhnan

Loch Affric

SKYE

Glenelg

Beinn Fhada

Glen Affric

Shiel Bridge

Sisters and Brothers

Y.H.

The Saddle

Glen Shiel

A87

Loch Ness

Cluanie Ridge

Loch Cluanie

Glen Quoich

Loch Loyne

A87

Loch Hourn

Loch Quoich

Loch Garry

Ladhar Bheinn

Meall Buidhe

Luinne Bheinn

Sgurr Na Ciche

Gairich

Inverie

Glen Meadail

Sgurr Mhor

Glen Kingie

Mallaig

Glen Dessary

Glen Pean

Loch Arkaig

Loch Nevis

Gulvain

Loch Lochy

Loch Morar

Nan Coireachan

Thuilm

A86

Loch Allort

Loch Eitt

Loch Eil

Gulvain

A82

Grey Corries

Loch Eitt

Fort William

Ben Nevis

Loch Treig

Corrour Station

Loch Linnhe

Glen Nevis

A82

0   20 Miles
         30 Km

62

was final but at the very last minute I expanded it to include the Grey Corries, the Aonachs and Ben Nevis, so as to include both the highest Munro of them all and to bring my total of Munros for the walk to one hundred, though some of these I'd climbed before.

June 1979 was the month I chose for the walk as I wanted to start after the snow had gone but also before the midges became a problem and before deer stalking (which begins mid-August) made access difficult. My estimate of the mileage was 500 and I hoped to do 100 a week, less than on the Land's End to John O'Groats walk but I would be carrying supplies for many days on this one and also climbing several hills over 3,000 feet most days.

The walk began on the 30th May 1979 at 9.30 am when I stepped bleary-eyed off the night train to Fort William at Corrour station into a chill grey landscape. Despite having had virtually no sleep in the crowded carriage I set off immediately for Loch Treig and the long, long ridge up to my first Munro, Chno Dearg, which I reached three hours after leaving the train. I hoped that first day to climb the four Munros that lie either side of the reservoir of Loch Treig. The grey clouds had lifted by the time I reached the summit and the two Munros across Loch Treig looked tantalisingly close and accessible, except for the great trench that held the loch and which I had to cross to reach them. First though I trotted round to Stob Coire Sgriodan whose western side falls in steep, shattered slopes straight from the summit to the loch. A boggy, fiddly descent took me down to Fersit as tiredness set in, made worse by the now hot and humid day.

The ascent opposite looked forbiddingly steep with Meall Cian Dearg totally insurmountable. In fact the cliffs of the latter were easily ascended by an exhausting scrabble up steep grass and I arrived on a boggy plateau soaked in sweat and surrounded by a cloud of midges which at least ensured I kept moving. When I did sit down higher up and away from the midges I immediately dozed off, only to wake with a start wondering where I was. One and a half tubes of glucose tablets were gulped down to try and provide a little energy for the plod up to Stob a 'Choire Mheadain past old, rotten cornices, for the reward of a view of the vast sweep of the Highlands from Schiehallion, Ben More and Stob Binnein, Ben Lui and the Glencoe tops, to Ben Nevis in the south and west, then north to hills I couldn't name and which it was hard to realise I was going to climb in the next month. The view kept me occupied as still only half awake I walked on to Stob Coire Easain, the last and highest of the day's Munros at 3,658 feet. It was warm on the summit and the remnants of old snow were audibly melting. I was too tired to linger though and a rapid, direct and bouncy descent led to the Lairig Leathach and more specifically the small bothy that nestled magnificently under Stob Ban, the first of the next day's hills. Across the glen the tremendous rock buttresses of Sgurr Innse showed me that many hills not reaching the 3,000-foot line (Sgurr Inse is 2,600 feet high) are more interesting than many that do.

Twelve hours' sleep saw me recovered from the train journey and made for a lunchtime start for the traverse of the Grey Corries, that long ridge distinguished by its quartzite screes, containing four Munros, that takes the walker west towards Ben Nevis and the sea. Unfortunately a cloud base of about 1,500 feet rather curtailed the views and so I spent the day in that still, silent and unreal world that is cloud-walking. A compass bearing took me from the outlier Stob Ban onto the main ridge from where it was just a question of continuing, though loose quartzite rubble and greasy moss made the going slow and unpleasant and the damp cold air meant I needed to wear my balaclava (a thin nylon one to save weight rather than a thick wool one) and Goretex jacket.

Approaching Stob Coire an Laoigh I came up against a more serious difficulty: snow. Lots of it; old, rotten and treacherous where it lay on the knife-edge of the ridge itself. Without an ice axe I felt very insecure especially after I felt one slab move under me. Where possible I traversed under the snow but too often I was forced to gingerly cross narrow corniced sections of hard windslab. Sgurr Choinnich, the last Munro on the ridge, (the other one being Stob Coire Clairigh), had even more snow but once over it I thankfully abandoned the ridge to descend boggy slopes towards the ruin of Steall in Glen Nevis where I planned to camp. After five and a half hours in the dense cloud it was quite a revelation to drop out of it into a world that stretched more than a few yards in any direction. Below lay Glen Nevis, bleak, wet and grey; the only movement coming from a small herd of deer. As I pitched the tent by the Water of

Nevis a cuckoo was calling from a clump of trees and I could hear the shrill cry of a sandpiper above the rushing water.

Fears of more snow on the higher hills of the Aonachs and Ben Nevis were realised on a beautiful, clear, warm spring day. Large snowfields were crossed on the haul up to the 4,054-foot Aonach Beag and I was glad of the good weather for large disintegrating cornices overhung the cliffs that drop away to the east of the summit. My nerve went on an attempted descent to the col of Aonach Mor as, unable to see the run-out, I was afraid of a slide down the steepening snow slope. Oh, for an ice axe! Turning back I descended by my ascent route and then set off for the Carn Mor Dearg–Aonach Mor col. In recompense for my rebuff I had the pleasure of walking up a beautiful valley with the Aonachs to the east, Ben Nevis and the Carn Mor Dearg arete to the west and down the centre the clear gushing stream, rushing over slabs of granite, twisting and crashing into whirlpools of pale green while deep calm sections undercut the banks. Higher up old snow bridges spanned the water. Leaving the pack at the col I scrambled up Aonach Mor passing two descending parties, the first people I'd seen since Corrour. On the descent I realised I no longer had time that day to climb Carn Mor Dearg and Ben Nevis so I decided to bypass them. I had climbed them before. Also the snow I could see on the arete between the two and on the last 1,000-foot steep slope up to the summit of the Ben was potentially too dangerous to climb without an ice axe. From the summit of Aonach Mor the snow-streaked bulk of Ben Nevis was truly awe-inspiring. Ironically I could see that the formidable snow slopes on Aonach Beag petered out a few yards below where I'd turned back.

Returning down the glen to Steall I reflected on the unneccessary miles and feet of ascent I'd carried my full pack. I felt tired on the track through the Glen Nevis gorge and the road to a farm campsite and stopped at one point to cool off my hot feet in a stream. I needed to be near Fort William as my first food and map parcel were waiting at the post office to be collected and as the next day was a Saturday, if I didn't pick it up in the morning I'd have to wait until Monday.

The energy sapping heat of the previous two days continued making even shopping a wearisome activity but the chores were over by lunchtime leaving me time to nip up and down Ben Nevis (there and back taking five hours) in the afternoon. The long hot stony haul finished over extensive snow fields which gave me cold wet feet and the wind on the summit was cool enough to effect a quick change from shorts and T-shirt to breeches and Goretex. But the view was good, a rarity up here on the roof of Britain. I had now done eleven Munros in four days, a good start to the trek.

A hazy, humid, ennervating day accompanied the only road slog of the walk as I travelled eleven miles along the A830 from Fort William to Fassfern with a very heavy pack; supplies enough for five days in it. Footsore and weary I was relieved to leave the tarmac and head up Glen Suileag. These were the days before lightweight boots and before I realised that running shoes are excellent for road walking and even hill use in summer, so I was wearing a hefty pair of 5-lb traditional leather boots of a type I would now regard with horror. Then I simply accepted that backpacking meant sore feet, especially if roads had to be walked. After a walk beside the birch-banked Leth Allt a last stumble led down to Glen Fionnlighe and a pitch at the base of Gulvain ready for the climb up this Munro the next morning. Wood anemones, primroses, violets and lesser celandine gave an air of colour and spring to the walk but the heat brought out the midges and evening was again spent in the tent inhaling the acrid fumes of a burning mosquito coil. The sun had seriously affected my food supplies and I was faced with dealing with liquid margarine, sweaty cheese and squelchy chocolate.

Distant thunder and a light spattering of rain on the tent accompanied a sticky restless night. Too hot in the tent I didn't dare open the doors for fear of admitting the midges. As I ascended the steep grassy slopes of Gulvain more thunder rumbled away to the east. From the long curving summit ridge the view was insubstantial due to the increasing haze. A laborious descent and traverse led round to Lochan a 'Chomlainn in boggy Glen Camgharaidh where I surprised several hundred deer. Cutting across the Streaps ridge after lunch at the loch to Gleann a 'Chaorainn I admired these magnificent hills; all rock and water and steepness. A jagged ridge led up to the tiny summit that sadly only reaches 2,988 feet.

Mentally revitalised by the growing splendour of the scenery I cut up to the Sgurr Thuilm ridge and soon reached my second Munro of the day from where I was staggered by my first real view of Knoydart, dark under the growing cloud. A twisted, gnarled landscape unfolded itself. Along the switchback ridge to Sgurr nan Coireachan I began to hurry, trying to beat the white sea mist I could see rolling in up the valleys and over the lower hills. But the mist beat me and, as I became enveloped in the cold dampness, I just touched the cairn and started down. At first the descent, a direct one as I wanted to cross the river in Glen Pean above Lochan Leum an t-Sagairt (where it should be shallower than further downstream), was straightforward, but lower down I had a time-consuming scramble around innumerable tree-girt crags. Hazy, atmospheric Glen Pean, narrow and hemmed in by arching curves of rock, was a gloomy but impressive vista. The river ford went so easily my feet remained dry but rounding the lochan, crammed as it was into the narrow glen, posed a problem. The map showed a path on the right bank but here steep crags rose straight out of the water and I could find no way through them. Forced back I had to recross the river to where a path ran just above the water and then cross the river for the third time which I did with one leap before the final boggy trudge to Pean Bothy. It had been an excellent day and I settled contentedly into the spacious hut. Late in the evening the door latch rattled and on opening the door I found myself face to face with a deer which despite the light I was shining in its face backed off only a few yards and began to graze.

During the night the weather broke and I was woken a couple of times by the pounding of wind and rain on the bothy roof. Dawn produced rain and a cloud base of about 1,000 feet. A damp plod through the new forestry plantations took me round into Glen Dessary from where I made a direct ascent of another Sgurr nan Coireachean. Compass bearings led me to the col with Garbh Chioch Mhor, then just a top, but since promoted to full Munro status. The negotiation of the convoluted and rugged ridge of this peak would have been very difficult in the mist but for the existence of the stone wall that runs along it, for the ridge twists and turns constantly to present the walker with a complex tangle of crags, cols and minor summits edged to the north by several large cliffs down which I occasionally found myself staring. Once the top was reached the next Munro, Sgurr na Ciche, seemed to arrive very quickly and easily. The tiny summit of this latter peak is strewn with bits of old trig points. Nothing else being visible and everything being sodden — ground, grass, air and me — I descended rapidly south and west to the Allt Coire na Ciche and the path down to Mam na Cloche Airde, the pass between Glen Dessary and Loch Nevis. I only left the mist behind when I reached sea level. As I came out on the lochside I passed the red splash of a tent by the ruin of Finiskaig and then two others by Sourlies Bothy which was overfull with soldiers who made it obvious they resented anyone else coming in so I pitched my tent outside to be joined soon by yet two more. This remote spot was becoming quite crowded. In the stillness I could hear waders calling out on the mudflats and as it grew dark the squeaking of bats. Huge kingcups grew by the stream.

Loch Nevis is one of the most beautiful of the west coast sea lochs and I made the most of my visit as I ambled round its rocky seaweed-strewn shores to ford the River Carnoch, an easy task at low tide. Then, the bridge shown on the maps did not exist. Now that the Ordnance Survey have finally got round to removing it from their maps (it was pulled down in the 1930s) the estate has rebuilt it! Up at the wide pass of Mam Meadaill I left the pack for a quick ascent of Meall Bhuidhe, my Munro for the day. Clearing skies gave a good view down to Inverie Bay and a spectacular one back to Sgurr na Ciche and the hills of the last two days.

Down at Inverie, the only village on mainland Britain with no road connections and therefore reachable only by boat or on foot, I found I'd missed the post office by fifteen minutes but the postmistress seeing me standing outside her small wooden shed came and opened it up for me and I reclaimed my food parcel. Already tired of my diet of dried food I purchased a tin of baked beans, another of mandarin oranges and a fresh orange for supper from the small shop. The three-course meal tasted wonderful! Near camp a sandpiper did its broken wing act and noting where it had begun I located a shallow depression in the grass containing four pale, finely speckled eggs.

Out of Inverie by way of Gleann na Guisarain I struck up seemingly endless slopes through wet, thick cloud to Ladhar

Bheinn's ridge and, eventually, the summit. The descent to the Bealach Coire Dhorcail was complicated by a series of small crags and I was quite surprised when I came out on the pass itself. Further down I left the still, silent, white cloud to see Loch Hourn below and further down again I enjoyed the cunningly made zig-zag path that leads through new bracken and bluebells then banks of primroses to the valley floor. I stayed at Barrisdale in the stalkers' bothy for a fee of fifty pence which as well as a bed provided the luxuries of a gas cooker, electric lights, easy chairs and, most wonderful of all, a flush toilet. The money went to the only inhabitants, the prawn fisherman and his son who lived next door and who, for a fee, will ferry you across the loch to the road at Arnisdale. Also in the bothy were two other Munro baggers though they were travelling through Scotland by car and had walked into here to climb Ladhar Bheinn and Luinne Bheinn. Coming from the north they were able to give me useful information about what lay ahead of me and we talked for hours.

With rain steadily falling and the cloud base only a few feet up the hillside I had a leisurely breakfast. By 10.15 am the rain had become drizzle but the paths were running with water as I headed up Gleann Unndalain into the cloud to carry out the now usual scamper up a Munro, in this case Luinne Bheinn, after leaving the pack at a pass. The good stalker's path continued down past secretive Lochan nam Breac to vanish into the waters of the reservoir of Loch Quoich whose artificial shoreline gave an unpleasant scramble to the Allt a 'Choire Reidh and another ascent to another pass and another discarding of the pack before another Munro, this time Sgurr Mor. I was heading east and leaving Knoydart now. Glen Kingie, to which I descended, is wide, open and lonely; very different from the narrow, cluttered Knoydart glens. I was entering the country of the big east-west ridges that I was to follow over forty-nine Munros for the next thirteen days to Achnashellach and Torridon country. A splash across the Kingie took me to Kinbreak bothy, which at first glance looked ruined as the door was hanging off its hinges and torn plastic flapped at the windows. However the habitable part of the building is upstairs where a long low attic with a few benches and loose floorboards provides weathertight accommodation. With only one tiny window (there is a skylight now) I found

I needed candles lit even in daylight. Feeling chilly as all my clothes and my down sleeping bag were damp after the days of rain I lit a fire and suddenly the dark room felt like home.

I was due to meet a friend the next day in Glen Quoich, an arrangement made by phone in Inverie. Alain Kahan, who I'd known since college, was travelling up on the bus from Fort William leaving it at Cluanie to walk into the glen and, hopefully, meet me. I had three Munros to climb before arriving there so I needed to hurry as I didn't leave Kinbreak until 11.30 am due to sleeping in late. Gairich was soon reached then left to drop down to Loch Quoich from where an unpleasant fly-ridden slog took me to the dam and the road. Arriving there at 5 pm with the weather hot, humid and muggy I realised I had to choose between the Munros and Alain and as the Munros couldn't object if I failed to turn up I headed up the road for the track to Glen Quoich. The calm conditions produced perfect reflections in the water as I hurried along. On approaching Alltbeithe, a boarded up building in Glen Quoich, I could see a figure moving down Easter Glen Quoich towards me. It had to be Alain. We met at Alltbeithe as we'd planned though we'd hardly expected to reach it at the same time. Camp was on a dry grassy islet in the River Quoich rather than on the boggy land either side of the river. I wanted a good site as I intended staying two nights so that I could pick up the two Munros I'd skipped that day. Alain unloaded his pack of goodies he'd brought for me: a new Goretex jacket (my current one was the same I'd used on the End to End walk and was becoming a little worn), a plastic mug (mine had broken leaving me to drink from the paraffin-tainted cover of the stove), Nikwax for my boots, a wholemeal loaf and letters from friends. As his pack had weighed 43 lb he was quite happy to get rid of that lot.

Climbing up Gleouriach felt strange without a heavy load as I'd just completed a 7-day, 105-mile, 10-Munro section of moving on every day. Although I didn't know it at the time that was the longest, hardest stretch of the walk. Three consecutive days was the most I was to do with a full pack from then on and I was to cover much less mileage for each Munro. In fact during the following seven days I only carried a full pack on three of them and 25 Munros were covered in 114 miles of walking. A pleasant narrow rocky ridge led from Sron na Breun Leitr to the Gleouriach summit which gave good views into the shattered corries to the east and over to the cliffs of the far spur. A nice ridge walk continued down to a col before I walked up Spidean Mialach to enjoy the views down into the wild recesses of the northern corries of this pair of Munros; a great contrast to the uniform green slopes on the south side I'd walked below the day before. The weather was improving rapidly and by the time we reached our islet it was hot and sunny. Looking for flowers around the site Alain came up with wintergreen, orchids, pansies, violets and wood sorrell. Dippers bobbed in the stony stream and we saw a heron ponderously flapping up Wester Glen Quoich whilst martins helped remove the swarms of insects. Keen to bag another Munro I left Alain sunbathing and set off into Coire a Chaorainn intent on Sgurr a Mhaoraich to make up the trio for the day. I found the corrie a superbly wild tumble of huge rockfalls topped by shattered, jagged, crumbling spires. Luckily an easy way can be found by the stream to the low point on the ridge. Then a scrabble up loose moss and rock leads to the summit cairn. The evening light enhanced the grand views: back to the Knoydart hills, along a sparkling Loch Hourn to Ben Sgriol, north to The Saddle then round to the hills to come, the long Shiel and Affric ridges. The ridge over Sgurr Coire nan Einicheallach led straight down to the tent and supper at our delectable site.

Clearing weather accompanied us up to Sgurr a 'Bhac Chalais, a very minor peak, but one which gave us a good look at the shattered south-east face of Sgurr na Sgine, the first Munro of the day. A difficult scramble down steep rocky slopes led down to the col from this peak though on looking back an easy grassy rake just west of where we'd descended could be seen. A few days later I was to wish I'd studied that rake a bit better. A wall took us round the western edge of Sgurr na Sgine from where we climbed rough slopes to reach the top sooner than expected for once. Down again at the Bealach Coire Mhalagain I left the packs with Alain and ascended The Saddle by a grassy spur, crossing some surprisingly extensive snow patches on the way. From the tiny summit, aretes of broken rock spread out in every direction, and my ascent route looked to be the only easy one. The distant views were lost in a heat haze but this didn't matter as it was the immediate rock scenery that caught the eye. Back at the bealach I rejoined Alain and we

descended to Glen Shiel where Alain hitched a lift to the
Five Sisters camp site whilst I, being a purist, slogged along
the four miles of tarmac. The site was waterlogged but did
have hot showers, a shop and a cafe.

By dawn the site was partially flooded due to heavy
overnight rain and I woke to find the tent groundsheet
sodden and my sleeping bag damp despite being on a
Karrimat. I'd placed a plastic bivvy bag under the
groundsheet for extra protection but this had proved worse
than useless as a small lake had formed between the two
impermeable layers. I moved camp immediately to a stonier
but drier pitch across the way then, to compensate for such
an abrupt start to the day, I breakfasted on an omelette and
coffee in the cafe. During breakfast I suddenly realised that
I felt like a day off, an idea which was welcomed by Alain,
and which, given what was to happen, turned out to be a
wise decision.

I'd hoped to cash some money at the post office but the
tiny counter in a filling station office only sold stamps and
didn't have savings bank facilities. The nearest place that
had them was Dornie, eight miles away. I would need that
day off. I checked the times of the post bus to Dornie and sat
down to wait. As it came hurtling round a corner I stuck my
hand out but to no avail. I doubt the driver even saw me as
the red blur flashed past. I set off to walk and hopefully
hitch a lift. Two hours and a long road bash later, I arrived
hot and sweaty, in Dornie after an annoyingly sunny and
clear day.

Dornie had some compensations in the form of several
shops, which, as I needed twelve days' food, were very
useful, the choice in Shiel Bridge being limited to say the
least. On the way back I hitched a lift in a few minutes from
a French youth hosteller seeing the Highlands and Islands
by hired car.

Planning the next few days in the hotel bar that evening
we decided to take just Alain's tent, which although slightly
heavier was roomier than mine, plus his Trangia meths
stove and two-pint billy plus food for two days. The
traverse of the big ridges on the north and south sides of
Glen Shiel would, all being well, see us back at Shiel Bridge
in two days and, with many miles and feet of ascent involved
we wanted our packs to be as light as possible. The rest of
the gear we'd leave in my tent on the site.

The rucksacks did feel lighter as we pounded up the road to turn off by the Allt Mhalagain for the Bealach Duibh Leac. This was where I'd gone wrong the previous year on the Land's End–John O'Groats walk and I did it again this year. The tops were in mist but I still didn't feel happy about the bumpy, broken ridge we walked along from the bealach. Although the compass bearing seemed right and there was a wall to follow as there should have been, it somehow felt wrong. Luckily as this feeling grew and I began to cast around for some evidence of its correctness the cloud lifted briefly and I could see Wester Glen Quoich. To the north though and not the south where it should have been! I quickly realised what had happened. The bealach lies up a branch of the main valley but, carelessly, we had continued up Coire Toitell to come out on the ridge between Sgurr na Sgine and Sgurr a 'Bhac Chaolais. We had then climbed the latter by the grassy rake I'd noticed when we'd had difficulty descending from the peak two days previously! The wall we should have been following could be picked up on the summit of Sgurr a 'Bhac Chaolais so we climbed it for the second time that day, and the third altogether,and set off down to the bealach having spent a couple of hours and much energy on this diversion.

The ridge itself with its seven Munros proved quite straightforward. The highlight of this high level traverse is the ridge and summit of Aonach air Cirith, an interesting broken arete. Just before tackling this we were awestruck by the sight of a golden eagle soaring quite close to us above Easter Glen Quoich. A magnificent sight. After the long stretch of the ridge leading to Druim Shionnach Alain opted to head north down to Loch Cluanie to set up camp whilst I continued up the last Munro of the day, Creag A'Mhaim. After reaching the summit I dropped down to the old road and in increasingly heavy rain walked briskly to where Alain had pitched the tent. He had chosen a good sheltered dry spot near a bridge and overlooking the loch. We had just enough time for a sandwich and a pint in the Cluanie Inn before it closed and we had to turn out in the rain and wind to get back to our tent.

The storm continued all the next day. Alain decided, sensibly, on a long lie-in and a hitch-hike back to Shiel Bridge. Still hoping to complete the round of Glen Shiel I left him with most of the gear and headed up the An

Caorann Beag to the Bealach a 'Choinnich. The wind was tremendous and hail began to fall, whitening the tops above me. Even with all my clothing on including full waterproofs, hat and gloves I was barely keeping warm. On the ridge to Ciste Dubh I took a real battering and on the return to the bealach I realised that to try and fight this storm all the way back to Shiel Bridge along an exposed ridge and without the means for an overnight stop if I failed to complete the ridge would be foolish. Even going downhill into the gale was causing difficulties. So, reluctantly, I descended to the road and hitch-hiked to Shiel Bridge, breaking for the first time the continuity of the walk. Safely back the afternoon was spent drying out in the cafe replanning the next few days and hoping that the rapidly spreading puddles on the site wouldn't reach the tents. Whilst the storm kept up I would have to stay put but once it abated I intended to complete the North Glen Shiel Ridge as a day walk before continuing my northwards walk.

This ridge includes the well known Five Sisters of Kintail, two of which are Munros, and then continues with four more Munros, sometimes known as the Brothers, one of which, the outlier Ciste Dubh, I'd climbed in the storm. The others I picked up the following day which was calm and dry though with thick mist on the tops. Apart from a minor route-finding error when I mistook Sgurr na Carnach for Sgurr na Ciste Duibhe the day was uneventful, not to say dull. After completing the ridge I descended to the glen and hitch-hiked back to camp. Although physically fine I felt mentally tired, mostly due to the bad weather. I was beginning to wonder about the value of traversing long ridges of Munros when I didn't see anything — and temporarily losing my whereabouts was the most interesting thing that happened. Perhaps Alain had the right idea. He'd spent the day visiting some Pictish brochs.

Leaving Alain waiting for a lift back to Fort William and the bus to Manchester I had an indulgent morning as it would be eight days before I reached the next place that sold food. I began in the camp site cafe with an egg roll and three cups of coffee. Moving on to the hotel snack bar I had another coffee and a toasted cheese sandwich then, finding a restaurant a hundred or so yards further along, I went the whole hog and had a full meal of egg, tomatoes, chips and peas plus, of course, a coffee!

Feeling, unsurprisingly, full and lethargic I left the road and headed up Glen Choinneachain for the narrow, dramatic-looking cleft of the Bealach an Sgairne, the Gates of Affric. Dumping the pack, heavy with nine days' supplies, at the bealach I slogged up into the cloud to the summit of A'Ghlasbheinn, all bumps and little tops. Beinn Fhada on the other side of the pass proved easier despite being higher; its long, slow, stony slope with large cornices broken and disintegrating to the north and east offered a more gentle gradient. For once I felt uneasy in the silent white mist and I kept looking round to check I was alone. I cannot explain this feeling as I saw and heard nothing and it had never occurred in similar conditions on other hills.

From the pass I followed another walker down into open, desolate, upper Glen Affric at the far end of which could be seen clear, egg-shell blue sky and sunlight though around me the hills were still cloud-capped. I was heading for Glen Affric Youth Hostel which is more like a sophisticated bothy than a modern-style hostel. The main building is an old iron estate lodge, pleasantly primitive inside with creaking, sprung bunk beds and Calor Gas cooking rings. Water comes from the stream outside and an open, peat-fed, fire provides the only heating. It lies seven miles from the nearest road. I arrived to find four walkers and the warden seated round the fire. The person I'd followed down the glen was part of an attempt by Edinburgh University Mountaineering Club to climb all the Munros in twenty-four hours. The other three were all also Munroists, perhaps not surprising here, and two of them were using the hostel as a base for nine days of peak bagging. One of them had actually been the warden here when Hamish Brown stopped over on his 1974 trek over all the Munros. I was staying for three nights whilst I 'collected' the Munros on either side of Glen Affric; three nights during which I would sleep in a bed for the first time in sixteen days.

In time-honoured hostel fashion the old metal bunks creaked loudly and the floors vibrated whenever someone moved so we were all up early each day. Over breakfast that first morning I had a long talk with the warden about his life here at such a remote hostel where all food and fuel had to be carried in and where one a week he had to travel the twenty-one miles to Cannich to bank the hostel fees and

75

stock up on supplies. For this job Will had bought a motorbike which he managed to ride to within four miles of the hostel. Glen Affric is only open for three months of the year and although isolated it is regularly used so the warden doesn't have a chance to be lonely.

Five Munros lie to the south and south-east of the hostel and these were my first goal as they form a convenient horseshoe with just one, Carn Ghluasaid, out on a limb. Crossing the River Affric by the bridge below the hostel I went straight up the steep slopes of the Mullach Fraoch-choire into the dense mist. Not lingering on the summit I continued along an unexpected and interesting pinnacled ridge which lent character to the hill before climbing A'Chralaig. Near the huge well-built beehive-like summit cairn on the latter a ptarmigan began its broken-wing decoy trick and careful investigation disclosed a tiny motionless chick almost invisible against the mottled ground, which I photographed before moving away to grant relief to the now frantic parent. As I moved on I could feel the sun through the clouds and a breeze began to stir the mists. During the descent to the Bealach Choire a Chait the cloud began to break up to reveal Loch Cluanie far below. The feeling of freedom caused by being out of the mist after so many days in it made for a burst of energy and I raced up Sgurr nan Conbhairean and then on to the undistinguished Carn Ghluasaid. On looking back to the Mullach I was most impressed to see a fine pyramid topped peak with the pinnacles I'd crossed standing out clearly. In this group the Mullach, A'Chralaig and Sgurr nan Conbhairean are the real peaks, the other two Munros being merely raised points on the outlying spurs of Conbhairean. All have wild, rocky corries on the Glen Affric side. I descended quickly to my fifth Munro, Tigh Mor Na Seilge, then dropped directly down grassy slopes to Gleann na Ciche and a forestry track back to Glen Affric. The round had taken nine hours and for the first time in several days I hadn't worn my Goretex jacket.

Next day proved to be an epic: I spent $12^{1}/_{2}$ hours walking 30 miles over 5 Munros. Firstly came a long walk down beautiful Glen Affric from the wild open terrain of the upper glen, to the woods and lochs below Athnamulloch with many impressive huge old Scots pines. Looking back up the glen my eyes were led along the wooded shores of

Loch Affric bounded either side by hills, to the dominant shape of the snow-splashed Beinn Fhada. Where the road began I left the glen and went up Gleann nam Fiadh by a bulldozed track to join a good stalker's path by the Allt Toll Easa which led to the col below Toll Creagach up which I was surprised to see about a dozen walkers toiling. I followed them up featureless stony slopes to the nondescript summit. Forty-five minutes later I was on top of Tom a'Choinich and picked up a pair of woollen gloves probably dropped by one of the large party I could now see descending to Glen Affric. Not finding the owner I left them later in the hostel.

From Tom a'Choinich the walk improved. The way to Carn Eige was over pinnacles and along narrow ridges that are not even hinted at on the map. Not a rock is marked either though Loch a 'Choire Dhomhain is set dramatically in a rock girt corrie. At one point a fascinating spiral rock staircase takes one up a steep rocky slope that I found out later from the SMC *Guidebook to the Western Highlands* was man-made though at the time I wasn't sure. Carn Eige at 3,880 feet is the highest peak north of the Great Glen topping its near neighbour and my fifth Munro of the day, Mam Sodhail, by all of eighteen feet. First though came the real killer of the day's walk: the trek out from Carn Eige to the outlying 3,294-foot Beinn Fhionnlaidh, the fiftieth Munro of the whole walk. Or rather not so much the trek out as the trek back since the col between the two is just below 3,000 feet leaving a 900-foot climb back to Carn Eige. Back on Carn Eige (2 hours 15 minutes after leaving Toll Creagach), I ate my last chocolate biscuit and drank my last mouthful of water. Luckily it was a quick down and up to the huge hollow rectangular cairn on Mam Sodhail near which stands the remnants of a small building. From the SMC Guidebook I learnt that in the 1840s, Mam Sodhail, along with Sgurr na Lapaich to the north, was an important station of the primary triangulation of Scotland. Apparently the cairn was then twenty-three feet high.

Long stony slopes led to the Bealach Coire Ghaidheil and a stalker's path down into Glen Affric. A heavily laden walker passed me heading for a bivvy on Mam Sodhail. I was just glad to stumble into the hostel, eat a hasty meal and collapse into bed. It had been a long, long day.

Glorious views and the best weather of the whole walk

accompanied me on the trek over An Socach and up the unpronounceable Sgurr nan Ceathreamhnan (Kerranan comes close I'm told), a fine pointed peak. As I ascended it a magnificent panorama began to unfold. A jumble of Shiel, Cluanie and Quoich hills reached out to Knoydart where the familar shape of Sgurr na Ciche was clearly visible. Further south lay a large lump which I realised with a shock was Ben Nevis as Carn Mor Dearg, Aonach Beag, the Grey Corries and the Munros of the first day of the trek came into view. From the actual summit of Ceathreamhnan the Black Cuillin of Skye and the Torridon peaks, particularly Liathach, held the eye. I stayed half an hour, eating, photographing, trying to identify but mostly just looking. It was very hot and, clad in shorts and a T-shirt, I felt for once that it was summer. I could have sat there all day.

But a third Munro beckoned so off down the long lumpy ridge to Creag a'Choire Aird I went to views of Loch Mullardoch and Gleann Sithidh. I descended to the latter and, removing my boots and socks, had a delightfully cool paddle across the stream to camp near where the Allt na Cniche joins the Abhainn Sithidh. It was only 4 pm but this was a pleasant enough spot to spend an afternoon and I used the time to rinse out some socks and air my sleeping bag and sheet liner. As I was washing my pans out after dinner a walker paddled across the river wearing the most amazing, hot-looking, loud tartan woollen breeches. A chat revealed he was camped at Iron Lodge with two walkers I'd seen earlier and had spent the day on the Carn Eige hills. I was to meet one of this party five days later on Beinn Liath Mhor leading a school party. In the meantime I was glad to be backpacking again. The last time I'd pitched the tent had been eight days previously at Shiel Bridge.

Two hours of toiling and very amateur botany (for the otherwise dull slopes were covered with flowers including many orchids), took me up An Socach, the first of the four Munros lying north of Loch Mullardoch. Clouds streaming in from the west signalled the end of the brief spell of clear weather and on the summit I changed shorts for breeches and donned my shirt. Clouds boiled up in the corries below as another haul took me up An Riabhachan to see the surrounding tops disappear in the growing haze. Two more Munros, Sgurr na Lapaich and Carn Nan Gobhar, followed with views down into the grim corrie of Loch Tuill

Bhearnach before a descent into Garbh-coire. The name means rough corrie and it is: all tussocks, bog and boulders but not steep so I bounced down in a dream, fantasising about a bothying trip to Knoydart with some friends. The empty, featureless loneliness of these hills was beginning to affect me. Too much time spent ascending and descending dull slopes was causing a loss of inspiration. Mats of pink moss campion lent splashes of colour to the descent and the Scots pine woodlands in the glen restored my spirits only to have them sink again at the sight of the hydro-electric scars which have sadly marred Glen Strathfarrar. Camp was by the River Farrar on excellent firm turf speckled with yellow flowers, mostly vetches and trefoils. By the river a sandpiper called and I saw a dipper through the alders that fringed the bank.

A day walk over the four Strathfarrar Munros followed during a violently stormy day. The ridge became a long stagger of compass bearings, brief glimpses through torn cloud at the cols and hard walking into the blasting wind interspersed with moments of shelter spent cowering behind little stone walls and summit cairns. Sgurr Fhuar-thuill, Sgurr a Choire Ghlais, Carn nan Gobhar and finally the long relentless gentle slopes of Sgurr na Ruaidhe came and went until I thankfully dropped down into Coire Mhuillidh. Snow-spattered Carn nan Gobhar and Sgurr na Lapaich rising above Inchvuilt wood, light and dark with Scots pine and silver birch, looked almost alpine as I headed back to camp in the clearing evening light. A walker heading towards me turned out to be one of the Munroists from Glen Affric hostel who'd just completed the same walk as me in the other direction. We must have passed each other in the storm. Back in the tent I realised that I would have to run my planned next three days into two as I was almost out of food and would soon be eating my emergency rations.

A stormy night in which the tent flapped hard led to little sleep and an early start. All the pegs stayed in despite what seemed to be the imminent launching of the tent into space on several occasions during the night. The local stalker, met by the lochside, gave me advice on an ascent route up the first of the day's four Munros, Maoile Lunndaidh, on whose top the wind was ferocious. Beyond the next peak, Sgurr a 'Chaorachain, inaccurate information and lack of research led me astray. I was looking for a Munro listed in the Tables as Creag Toll A'Choin. No peak of this name exists on the O.S., map but I was used by now to inconsistencies between the Tables and the O.S. Deciding that perhaps Bidean an Eoin Deirg was the Munro as it was the only other hill around I left my pack and went off and climbed it to discover later that it is only a top. Creag a Toll a'Choin is in fact an alternative name for Maoile Lunndaidh but in the Tables both were marked on the maps as Munros and it was from the maps I'd compiled my list for the walk, neglecting to check them off against the text. I was in fact looking for a non-existent hill!

Again the cloud and cold, cold rain came in and with it the wind which meant a rapid, blowy ascent of Sgurr Choinnich, the third and final Munro for the day. I couldn't face another night out in this wind and rain with a wet tent and a damp down sleeping bag. I was becoming increasingly tired as the days went by, the food ran out and disturbed night followed disturbed night, so I headed down from the Bealach Bhearnais along the boggy trackless glen to the bothy I knew lay there, and which would offer a dry and secure haven from the storm. I reached it in heavy rain to find, in the small single room, two other walkers established for the night. Once I stopped I began to shiver for I was only wearing a thermal vest under my Goretex jacket. Even after donning my wool shirt and pile jacket it took two pints of hot, sweet coffee and an hour or more before I began to feel warm. And this was the 22nd June, the second day of summer! One of my campanions for the night managed to light a fire which took a little of the chill from the damp air.

With barely enough food to last the day I had to reach Gerry's Hostel in Glen Carron the next day, as there was a small store there, easy enough by a direct route but I also wanted to climb four Munros, two of which lay in the opposite direction to Gerry's! So, in thick cloud, I splashed off through the bog and up to the col and Bidein a'Choire Sheasgaich where I dumped the pack before scrambling up through steep, broken crags to the summit and then to Lurg Mhor. In three hours I was back at the pack to eat my compressed emergency rations, dusty blocks called, hope-fully, 'cake with chocolate' and 'bread with cheese' plus two oatcakes with margarine. From the Bealach Bhearnais, reached over Beinn Tarsuinn, I paddled down the path before wading the swollen Allt a Chorais. Leaving the pack again I quickly walked up the good zig-zag path to Sgurr nan Ceannichean and Moruisg and back. Again it took me three hours from pack to pack. I finally reached Gerry's at 9 pm after an 11½ hour day.

The hostel, a private one, was nicely disorganised. Six other people were in residence but my interest was in the basic store. The purchase of a box of Alpen, 3 eggs, a tin of baked beans, a jar of honey, a tin of condensed milk, several Mars Bars and a packet of chocolate wholemeal biscuits had me beside myself with excitement. The only thing lacking was coffee. Having only three bags left I was carefully stewing every last drop out of each one. Supper was baked beans with two eggs stirred in, followed by biscuits. It was delicous! Replete I spent the evening warming myself in front of a big fire listening to Beethoven's First Symphony on the record player and watching my stockings steam on the hot water tank. I felt relieved to be there and a little pleased too. Despite underestimating my food needs, in eight days I'd climbed 30 Munros and walked 140 miles. The total for the trek was now 70 Munros and 390 miles.

Breakfast of a boiled egg, two large bowls of Alpen laced with honey and condensed milk meant I didn't feel hungry for another four or five hours, a most unusual situation! Crossing the Kyle of Lochalsh railway near Achnashellach I set off up the Coire Lair track admiring the dominant bulk of Fuar Tholl ahead. As I climbed the long slopes of Beinn Liath Mhor, the first of the day's three Munros, the clouds gradually dispersed and I arrived on the ridge in sunshine. The mile-long walk to the highest point gave grand views over Coire Lair to Fuar Tholl and Sgorr Ruadh. Near the top I passed a long trail of schoolboys, and counting them as I went by I found there were forty in all! I had met the teacher on Sgurr nan Ceathreamhnan five days previously and he pointed out to me the orange dots of their tents in the woods by the Easan Dorcha.

Ptarmigan were everywhere, both on the descent and the pull up the easy, broken sides of Sgorr Ruadh from where I could see the graceful line of the ridge I'd just left. The logical continuation of this round of Coire Lair would be via Fuar Tholl to Achnashellach but as I wanted my third Munro, I dropped down to the Bealach Ban and the path to the Bealach na Lice and Loch an Eion, crossing again my Land's End–John O'Groats route. The pack abandoned by the lochside, I toiled up the steep northern face of Maol Chean-dearg as the cloud rolled in off the sea. The ascent route is an intricate one through loose rock, along grassy rakes and round small crags but the easier ways are cairned. I arrived on the top in thick cloud so I descended immediately to collect the pack and drop down to Torridon and a camp on the beach after another long day — 11 hours 15 minutes this time.

Vast amounts of money went on vast amounts of food which I lugged back to the tent before setting off for Beinn Alligin at 2 pm. A strong wind and the usual dense cloud ensured a quick up and down to reach the tent in a downpour. The multiplicity of paths made me realise that I was in the most frequented area of hills since Ben Nevis, not that I saw many others in the storm. Enjoying a more relaxed period after the rigours of the past week the next day I again didn't set off until after lunch, this time to ascend Liathach. I didn't even need these peaks for my round of the Munros for I'd done them all before. In the wind, rain and cloud the Liathach ridge was exhilarating but I was to make two more ascents before I had a view from this fine mountain. The weather forecast, picked up in the hotel bar that night, was for a gradual improvement spreading northwards.

Not fancying a road walk to Kinlochewe, nor carrying my now very heavy pack over Beinn Eighe in a storm, I continued my decline into decadence by catching the post bus the ten miles up the glen, the only break in the continuity of my walk from Corrour. Still, I rationalised, this was a Munro bagging trip not a point to point backpacking trek. I was just in need of a day off and I spent the afternoon relaxing in Kinlochewe, and enjoying the sunshine. By evening it was raining again as it was the next day, the beginning of my last week of the trek. The drizzly morning with scudding clouds didn't look too promising but by 10.30 am, Beinn Eighe was clear. I went straight up Coire Domhain into a strong wind to finish with a scrabble up unpleasant scree to Sgurr an Fhir Duibhe where I was confronted with the vast desert of loose stone that is Beinn Eighe. The wind roared up out of the corries as I followed the always interesting and often exciting ridge over Sgurr Ban and Spidean Coire nan Clach with excellent views of Beinn Alligin, Liathach, the Beinn Damph and Coulin

Forest hills and the lochs Clair and Coulin glittering blue in the sunlight. Around them lay cool greenery. North were the huge, stony corries with just the bright flashes of water to break the sterility except on A'Choinneach, the sward of green grass and moss here are startlingly different from the quartzite scree and boulder of the rest of the hill. As on my visit on the End to End walk the view from the summit, Ruadh-stac Mor, held me, despite the terrific wind. The wild primaeval view of endless mountains stretched to the jagged skyline of An Teallach before softening into the rounded Fannichs and country I was heading into, hills as yet unknown that I was to climb.

In Coire Mhic Fhearchair waves were rolling white-topped across the loch, driven by the wind, and the waterfall at the corrie's lip was being blown back up into the air. Above the turmoil stood the aloof, unaffected Triple Buttress. Eschewing the road back to Kinlochewe I kept north then east into the stony wastes of Maol Cheannan; it was rough going amongst heather and boulders but with good views of the north side of Beinn Eighe and down to Loch Maree as well as of the odd quartzite cliffs of Meall a'Ghiubhais. The swollen, boulder strewn and rapid Allt Coire Ruadh-staca was difficult to ford, forcing me upstream some way but providing views into the vast maw of its eponymous corrie. Once across the torrent I entered Toll a'Ghiubhais, a strangely flat upland valley with a slow meandering stream and the impressive cliffs of Ruadh-stac Beag rising above. Looking up the unnamed corrie between Ruadh-stac Beag and Creag Dubh it seemed as though there were four separate mountains at the head of it. Myself I'd give Beinn Eighe three Munros if not four! Kinlochewe was finally reached in the now usual afternoon rain. I didn't mind for once. I'd had clear conditions for one of the Torridon three.

Another wild night of wind and rain hammering against the tent had me awake in the small hours. Others were awake too as I could hear voices and occasionally a light would sweep the tent. By dawn many of the other tents had gone. I slept again, waking finally at 10.30 am, a late rising for the walk to the bothy at Shenavall, where I intended staying for a couple of days whilst I climbed the Munros around this remote shelter. Despite not leaving until 12.30 with my pack again heavy with a week's food I had an excellent day with plenty to see, more than would have been possible on the cloud-covered tops. Whinchats seemed to adorn every fence post and furze bush as I walked beside the Kinlochewe River to Glen Bianasdail and its raging stream. A magnificent sight but worrying as I knew I would have to cross the stream at its source three miles away in Lochan Fada. The glen is a pleasure to walk up. Steep, narrow and rugged it gives good views back to Beinn Eighe which today popped out of the clouds every so often looking larger than possible, whilst near its head loomed Mullach Coire Mhic Fhearchair and pinnacled Sgurr Dubh. Twice in the lower glen I saw herds of wild goats. Long haired and primitive looking they moved away from me but did not seem afraid.

The river at Lochan Fada confirmed my fears. The stepping stones I'd crossed on the End to End walk were invisible under the torrent. A little downstream I found a place where the current was not quite so strong and, using a branch as a third leg, I waded across with my rucksack hipbelt undone for quick jettisoning if I slipped. The water was thigh deep, very cold and the current strong. When I reached the far bank my feet ached from the cold and I was glad I had dry socks to don.

The drizzle did not detract from the superb desolation of remote Lochan Fada. Myriads of sundew and butterwort covered the ground as I plodded wetly up to the Bealach na Croise. Sundew is a slightly sinister plant but I hoped they all grew fat on a diet of midges. More goats, golden plover and greenshank enlivened the long descent. At one point six goats were wandering along narrow ledges on some low crags. The two largest had frequent butting matches, one starting when a kid butted one of them in the rear and then hid, leaving the other adult to take the blame. They were very entertaining and watching them occupied fifteen minutes or so of the afternoon. Farther down the glen came the shrill cry of sandpipers and the demented flutterings of large, hairy egger moths in the heather.

Shenavall bothy, reached after $8^1/2$ hours walking from Kinlochewe, lies in a magnificent setting looking out across Loch na Sheallag to the jagged ridge of Beinn Dearg, another fine non-Munro. I've been up it since. It's worth the effort. The bothy itself is a fine one with several rooms. In one three others sat round a roaring fire. I set up my bedding in another room before accepting their invitation to join them. We told tales of our adventures far into the night. That day they'd set out to climb the six Munros south of Shenavall but had found the rivers impassable. The rain and wind beating against the bothy made it unlikely the situation would improve the next day. My companions and I had nearly met on several occasions during the previous month we discovered. When I was on Ben Nevis they were across the glen on the Mamores and on Beinn Fhada the day I climbed Sgurr nan Ceathreanhan. They'd stayed at Barrisdale Bothy and at Gerry's too though they were using a car to move between areas rather than walking.

Another squally night was followed by a morning of wind, rain and low cloud; depressingly familiar conditions. The others set off for the 'six' again whilst I opted for An Teallach. From the shoulder of Sail Liath I struck up the ridge of this sandstone mountain in dense cloud to Sgurr Fiona and then the Munro, Bidein a'Glas Thuill. (In the revised Brown-Donaldson Tables of 1981 Sgurr Fiona is given Munro status too.) Descent was by a gully off the col with Glas Mheall Mor and into Coire A'Glas Thuill. Once below the cloud and on my way back to the bothy I could see impressive, mist-wreathed pinnacles and gullies below the hidden summit. Working my way round Glas Mheall Liath I entered Toll an Lochain as I wanted to see this rival to Beinn Eighe's Coire Mhic Fhearchair. The weather made the corrie dark and gloomy with no skyline, just an absorption of the grey rocks into the dense grey cloud. It's certainly a magnificent corrie on a magnificent mountain. One day I hope to visit it in clear conditions though my two subsequent visits have taken place in similar weather to this first one.

Cold rain drove me out of the corrie and back to Shenavall. I'd been away only six and a half hours, so after a late lunch I went down to the river to collect kindling and sticks from amongst the gorse bushes for a fire at the bothy; I also sawed up some of the large larch logs stacked up outside. I lit a fire and was joined by two Scandinavian walkers en route from Ullapool to Poolewe. I was surprised that they should know of such an area when the majority of British, and certainly English, walkers probably don't know where it is. The others soon returned after a long but successful twelve and a half hour day on the 'six'. The rivers were dropping they reported.

July 1st was wet and windy and cloudy. I was off by 9 am to ford the knee-deep rivers and head for the 'six'. I was going for a long walk-in, preferable in my view to a long walk-out. Good tracks up Gleann na Muice and Gleann na Muice Beag to Lochan Mich-illean led to another ford of the Allt Brutbach an Easain. I went up into the dense cloud and drizzle to find the trig point on the first Munro, Ruadh Stac Mhor, before using the compass to take me down and round to A'Mhaighdean, a claimant for the title of the most remote Munro. Beinn Tarsuinn followed, my 100th Munro in all and the 80th on this trek, so I had a Mars Bar on top by way of celebration. The hill warrants some attention having an interesting, rocky and in places quite narrow ridge. In retrospect I decided it was the best of the six though I didn't see any of them. I was just below the cloud at the next col but not long enough to see anything other than a close up of a golden plover. Toiling up Mullach Coire Mhic Fhearchair I thought it a stony hill but it's nothing compared with the next one, Sgurr Ban. I ascended slowly over loose boulders and descended over similar. To add to my 'pleasure' it began to rain heavily and the visibility deteriorated even more.

At least on Beinn A'Chlaideimph there were fewer rocks and the going was easier though by now I just wanted to finish. A long descent to the west of Creag Ghlas and an easy river crossing left me with about a mile of path to the now empty bothy. Wood had been left and a note saying there was more a mile or so up the river but I was too tired and hungry to go out and collect it. I'd walked 19 miles and been out eleven and three quarters of an hour. The hunger was abated by mushroom soup, macaroni cheese and lemon curd sandwiches. As I went to sleep I could hear the wind hammering against the roof.

A feeling that the end of the trek was near grew as I left Shenavall to retrace my steps to Loch an Nid. I was en route for the Fannichs, a group of eight Munros lying to the north of Loch Fannich. Shortly past Achnegie I met three backpackers heading west for Carnmore. These were the only backpackers I met during the whole walk. All the other walkers encountered were Munro baggers rather than cross-country trekkers (I was both) and I had met no-one else carrying a tent.

I had a definite feeling of sadness on leaving the Torridon

area when I turned east towards Loch a'Bhraoin. The hills now rose green and level sided cut by regular water runnels. Gone was the chaos of rock, stone and water that makes up the great mountains of north-west Scotland. This area felt more desolate and empty and I was aware of less sensory stimulation as I began the long pull up grassy, heathery slopes onto A'Chailleach. Once on the tops the south-west wind was strong and cold and the cloud so wet it was hat-and-coat time again. Compass bearings were necessary to take me to Sgurr Breac and onto O.S. Sheet 20, the last one of the walk. Due to a lack of distinctiveness the route finding is more difficult here than in the somewhat similar hills between Glen Affric and Glen Carron. From Sgurr Breac a south-east bearing took me to the Allt Leac a'Bhealaich and the track down to Loch Fannich, a reservoir like Monar and Mullardoch. The bothy at the Nest of Fannich was shelter for the night. Part of the building is locked up for use by the owner but there is plenty of room left for overnight visitors and I installed myself in a large downstairs room and lit a fire with wood from the ample supply stacked in the porch. Trees surround the bothy and much dead wood had been collected outside to be brought in to dry when there was room.

I had only a couple of days' food left and realised I would have to restock if, as I had originally planned, I went on to climb the Beinn Dearg hills after the Fannichs. I was, anyway, coming round to the feeling I might end the walk after the Fannichs. I was three days over my original schedule and tired of slogging over hills in thick cloud on compass bearings. A few days of clear weather would have made all the difference but since leaving Affric I'd only had three of those (and with rain at the end of two of them) out of twelve days. Out of the thirty-three Munros climbed in that period it had only been clear on six. There were seven remaining Fannichs. Would it be fine for what was probably the last day of the walk?

It was. Both fine and the last day, that is. And a long day too, over seven Munros in seventeen miles. At 5 am two white horses outside the bothy door woke me but I didn't arise until 9. The first Munro, Sgurr nan Each, was in mist though the wind had dropped and the cloud was drier so I wore no coat or hat. The walking was easy over turf and occasional boulders with peaty ground at the cols. Compass bearings took me over Sgurr nan Clach Geala and Meall a'Chrasgaidh and up to Sgurr Mor, at 3,637 feet the highest of this group. I had an increasing feeling that the cloud was about to lift, a feeling reinforced by glimpses of blue sky. On the col with Beinn Liath Mhor Fannaich I had a view down to Loch Broom and over to cloud-capped An Teallach. I returned into the cloud on the contour round the final slopes of Sgurr Mor to the ridge to Meall Gorm and then An Coileachan. Along this stretch I kept popping in and out of the cloud to finally leave it on the last Munro which gave good views back to Beinn Eighe whilst further south the Affric and Farrar hills appeared intermittently through the drifting clouds.

On the descent via Loch Gorm I turned to see all the Fannichs clear of cloud; a fine group of hills. When I pitched camp on a dry patch of turf by the Abhainn a 'Ghiubhais about two miles from a road, my last wild pitch of the trek, I decided to leave the decision about whether to continue or not until I saw what the weather was like the next day. An added argument for stopping was the state of my MSR stove which was burning slowly and badly and obviously needed a complete overhaul.

I woke to a hot muggy day with the cloud low and thick. I felt tired. One does this for fun so there is no point pushing oneself too far. In five weeks I'd walked 525 miles and climbed 92 Munros, of which 42 had given views, the other 50 being shrouded in cloud. I felt quite satisfied with this. I walked to the main road, an obvious place to stop, and there, on the A835 near Loch Glascarnoch, the trek ended. Ullapool was just a short hitch-hike away.

This trek left me with one desire: to do more long backpacking trips in the Scottish Highlands. The next year saw me on the first 'Ultimate Challenge' (an event based on an idea of Hamish Brown) that is now held every May. Running from west to east across Scotland the U.C. has no set route but all entrants have to submit their own detailed plans for either a high-level (12 peaks to be included) or low-level trek. That first year the event was three weeks long and I submitted and walked a 300-mile route from Locheilort to Montrose over 56 Munros.

With plans for my first long walk abroad simmering in my head I put great efforts into finishing my round of the

Munros in 1981 with another U.C. crossing from Oban to Montrose of 250 miles (the event now reduced to a fortnight in length) over 36 Munros, followed in July by a 525-mile walk in 35 days over my final 55 mainland Munros. This last walk I turned into a trek from the southernmost Munro, Ben Lomond, to the northernmost, Ben Hope, for greater interest. The Munros not climbed on these four long walks (which 'collected' a total of 239 in 1,625 miles and 102 days of walking) had been ascended during shorter visits to the Highlands, including winter ones, and whilst working as an instructor for Outward Bound Loch Eil. The final few, on Skye, were completed in August 1981 with the end coming on Sgurr nan Gillean on a perfect summer's day, a fitting finale to a marvellous mountain adventure.

Not that my involvement with the Munros ended with that first round. The Scottish hills are the finest in Britain and a superb area for long distance backpacking trips. Now I'd climbed the main ones I could take my time revisiting them and trying to ascend them in fine weather (a much harder task than simply climbing them all!) as well as having a look at some of the Corbetts and 'tops', many of them fine hills in their own right. The U.C. pulled me back again too and I made another crossing in 1983, this time with a companion, from Mallaig to Montrose over 20 Munros in 225 miles, and again in 1984 from Strathcarron to Montrose over 29 Munros and 7 Corbetts. I'll be undertaking more long backpacking treks in the Highlands before long I'm sure.

4

France & Spain

THE PYRENEES:
A BACKPACKER'S PARADISE

Free from the call of the Munros I could now turn my thoughts further afield and seek adventure abroad for the first time. The big push to complete the Munros in 1981 had been undertaken so that I would be free to attempt the Pacific Crest Trail in the USA in 1982. That walk would take me up to 14,494 feet above sea level with hundreds of miles of it over 10,000 feet. How would I react to walking at this altitude when the highest I'd been before was 4,500 feet on Ben Nevis? To try and find out in advance I decided a trip to the higher mountains on the European mainland would be a good idea. The Alps were the obvious choice but I was deterred by stories of overcrowding, overdevelopment, overregulation and a lack of wilderness suitable for backpacking. Manicured trails, huts every few miles and strict regulations on camping did not appeal to me though of course I didn't know if the Alps were really like this or not. (A later cross-country ski tour of the Vanoise Alps showed me that this region at least is.)

So, if not the Alps where? The Pyrenees appeared from the knowledge I'd gleaned from books and articles in the outdoor press, mostly by Kev Reynolds and Showell Styles to be more suitable for the wilderness backpacking I wanted to undertake. September looked a good month to go and hasty planning showed that the Central Pyrenees could be reached by rail and a round trip made from Luchon-des-Bagneres in France, as good a reason as any for choosing that area. I was not making my first venture abroad alone for two regular backpacking companions were with me: Graham Huntington who'd been on the Offa's Dyke part of the End to End walk and Alain Kahan who'd been on the Glen Shiel part of the Corrour to Ullapool trek.

Although nowhere near as well known, the Pyrenees are second only to the Alps in scale amongst Europe's mountain ranges. Stretching almost four hundred kilometres from the Atlantic to the Mediterranean the Pyrenees consist of two overlapping mountain chains along the watershed of which runs the border between France and Spain. Most of the main peaks are along this political boundary but some, including the highest, lie south of it in Spain and on my first trip it would be these I would visit.

Our sketchy plan, concocted mainly from guidebooks, was to visit the two highest areas of the Pyrenees, the Posets and the Maladetta, spending about a week in each and, hopefully, climbing the highest peaks in each one. From Luchon we would cross the Port D'Oo, descend into the Valle de Estos in Spain and set up a base camp there. After a week supplies would be picked up in Benasque before we headed up into the Maladetta and another base camp to be used for peak bagging before finally returning to Luchon and France via the Port de Venasque. As our climbs would involve crossing glaciers and some rock scrambling we took ice axes, crampons, a rope, and a few slings and karabiners as well as our camping gear, so we had heavy packs to hump by train and boat to Luchon.

After wet summers in Scotland, North Wales and Manchester respectively we were all looking forward to two weeks of hot sun and clear skies as we set off on the 5.30 am train from Manchester Piccadilly on September 4th. At 9.30 the next morning we were in Luchon breakfasting at an outdoor cafe in the morning sunshine before looking for a taxi to the trail head in the Valle de Estos. A taxi found, we embarked on the first climb of the walk, and 2,600 feet and 3 miles later (quite enough after a 28-hour journey), we made our first camp, a superb one on the south side of Lac Sausatt. Immediately on this first short walk I was impressed by the grandeur of the Pyrenees and the abundance of flowers and wildlife.

The second day we crossed into Spain via the spectacular 9,540 foot pass of the Port d'Oo passing on the way the deep blue ice-floe-covered Lac Glace which is ringed by jagged peaks, snow fields and glaciers, some of which we had to cross. The path took us along the northern and eastern edge of the Pic des Spijoles with its multi-coloured rust and grey crags, then over small snow fields and along ledges to the Col des Gourgs Blancs before the final haul up boulders and loose scree to the Port d'Oo. A cold wind here soon had us changing shorts for breeches and then, as we began the descent, adding waterproofs as rain swept in. The arid stony slopes leading into Spain seemed pathless, although a trail was marked on the map, but finding a way down into the valley below was quite easy. We just kept going downhill!

Some time was spent finding a sheltered and, as we thought, well drained pitch in the valley as we intended to stay for a few nights and eat our way through some of our supplies before moving on. The Valle de Estos is a lovely valley of steep bluffs, twisting ravines, and pine forests with

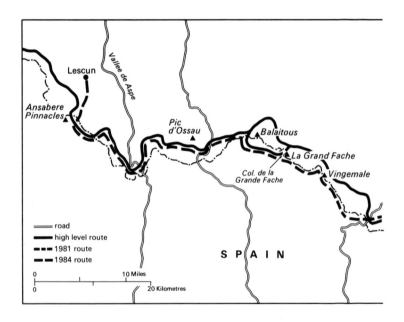

many flowers decorating the meadows and slopes even as late in the season as this so the day spent exploring it was a delight. We saw many birds including kestrels, vultures, Alpine choughs, redstarts and dippers. The short ravine where the Clarabide joins the Estos ended in a delightful hidden waterfall whilst at the head of the valley the Puerto de Gistain gave good views though even better were those from Point 2790, reached by a narrow rocky ridge. Beyond the long green cleft of the Estos could be seen the distant Maladetta whilst much nearer stood the towering Pico de

Posets, the frontier peaks and Pico de Machimala. Satisfied with our exploration of this intricate and interesting valley we returned to camp via a series of moraine tops and tiny side valleys to the north of the river with just one glimpse of a herd of isards, the chamois of the Pyrenees. Back at the site we collected wood to light a fire and burn all the rubbish that despoiled the area round the site. We also threw back into the stream all the rocks used by previous campers to hold down their tent pegs.

All day clouds had poured across the sky from the south

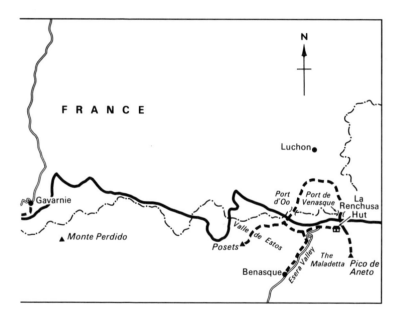

west and there had been a chill breeze and the occasional rumble of distant thunder. Light rain fell at 11 pm but the threatened storm really began in earnest between one and two o'clock in the morning with an hour of pyrotechnics and torrential rain. This settled down to a heavy downpour that went on into the morning until the skies darkened again and another violent storm arrived. Rain hammered down from towering, black, swirling skies while high above thunder cracked and boomed and lightning flashes split the darkness. The ground, parched bone dry the day before, could absorb no more and pools of water started to develop rapidly, spreading slowly across the earth towards the tent Graham and I were sharing. Now we knew why the scars of old drainage ditches covered the apparently well-drained site. Theoretically I disapprove of digging drainage channels but when faced with being flooded out or moat building I was soon running round in bare feet and Goretex jacket frantically heading the water off. For two hours Graham and I carried out our crude civil engineering operation, discovering in the process a new use for our much abused ice axes as trenching tools. The guidebooks had told of summer thunderstorms but had assured us that they only occurred during the late afternoon and at night and never lasted long. Twenty-four-hour storms like this one had not been expected. The rain eased off mid-afternoon and we watched a shepherd bring a herd of a hundred or more sheep plus several dozen goats all with bells round their necks up the valley to leave them just down from our camp. We were glad we had brought a large dome tent as it meant we weren't cramped during our day in camp. Alain, camped on higher ground than us in his little solo wedge tent, hardly stirred all day, spending his time reading, eating and brewing endless cups of tea. Spending enforced days of leisure lazing in the tent in beautiful remote locations is one of the hidden pleasures of backpacking though they are better when you don't have to spend time digging ditches!

The morning after the storm dawned bright and clear so Graham and I set off to climb the Pico de Posets, at 10,968 feet the second highest peak in the Pyrenees. Graded *facile,* the easiest Alpine grade, the ascent via the Coma de la Paul is reckoned to be quite simple though the guidebook recommends taking rope, ice axe, crampons and helmet. We had everything but the latter. However we never made the summit due to my reliance on our Spanish maps which I mistakenly treated as though they were up to Ordnance Survey standard. After the confusion this caused we used the guidebooks for detailed information. A feature on the ground but not on the map led to my attempting the final section of the ascent by the wrong route and I almost became cragfast up a particularly loose and dirty gully. Graham had wisely remained at the col below. I reached the top of the gully to find myself facing a steep series of rock terraces. Possibly it was climbable but I didn't know what lay above and I knew I must have gone wrong so I climbed gingerly back down the nasty little chute, at one point lowering the pack on the rope down a short vertical section before being able to climb down myself. By the time I had extricated myself from the gully and we had realised where we had gone wrong and where the correct route lay, clouds had begun to form around the summit so, not wishing to be caught up high in a storm like the previous day's, we made a hasty descent. Despite our failure to climb the mountain the day was made memorable by the sight of ten isards grazing on a hillside only a hundred yards away from us as we made our way down. We beat the rain to the tent by about a minute but after an hour's downpour it cleared again allowing us to emerge to light a fire with the wood Alain had gathered and tell him of our adventure. Not being a mountain climber he'd preferred to spend the day wandering amongst the woods and seeing how many species of flowers he could find.

Our supplies running low, we descended the valley to a road and the old medieval town of Benasque. The walk down through conifer forests in sunshine and above the roaring river was idyllic. It being a Saturday we met many other walkers, especially near the road. After pitching the tents by the confluence of the Estos and the Esera we walked down the road into Benasque to stock up with a rather bizarre collection of food as the only breakfast cereals we could find were Sugar Smacks and the only practical dried food, packet soups and pasta of which we were to become very tired over the next week. I was to leave my Sugar Smacks behind in a refuge after a few soggy tasteless breakfasts. As well as the cereal, soups and pasta I stocked up on chocolate, cocoa, sugar, toasted biscuits, a pound of Emmental cheese and what I described in my journal as 'some sort of instant pudding'. Benasque itself is an unspoilt little town with many steep-sided narrow cobbled streets and some interesting buildings though new development is taking place. By now its character may have gone. A bar called The Rhododendron provided an excellent lunch.

Our camp was only at 3,940 feet and the night there was very warm. Our return to the heights was delayed the next morning when Alain discovered we'd left all his papers, including passport and train tickets, in the bar where we'd had lunch. Luckily he quickly arranged a lift with some rather baffled campers, who were packing up nearby, back to Benasque and equally luckily his documents had been picked up and kept by bar staff so he hadn't lost anything. To reach the Maladetta we walked up the Esera valley to camp just above the Renclusa Hut, a large wardened mountain refuge. The initial part of the walk was marred by the scars of a new road which stops suddenly half way up the valley. Where it is intended to go finally I was unable to find out but as part of it has already collapsed perhaps it will never be finished leaving the upper Esera relatively unspoilt. I say relatively as the lack of a proper road did not stop the traffic and we were astonished to see family saloons bumping along a dirt track to a large camp site in the valley immediately below the Renclusa (the road has since been extended to the campsite which now boasts a cafe). We camped away from the hut as the immediate surroundings were squalid in the extreme. Literally decades of rubbish, mostly empty tin cans and butane cartridges, were dumped down the slopes nearest to the hut, a practice we found common to all the huts we saw in both France and Spain and one that has spread to the over-used camp sites in the huts' vicinity too.

We were camped here because the Renclusa is the starting point for the Normale Route (Grade: *peu difficile,* recommended equipment: crampons, ice axe, rope) up the highest peak in the Pyrenees, the 11,063-foot Pico de Aneto, which Graham and I wanted to climb. The weather the first day here being cloudy and damp no-one else stirred so I set out alone. The ascent, although easy, involves over a mile across the Aneto Glacier and I needed the ice axe and crampons here. I kept a close lookout for crevasses and was very glad when the weather improved and the mist cleared. After all, I'd never been on a glacier before! At this time of year the snow cover has gone and the crevasses are exposed and easy to avoid or, when necessary, cross. I went round the upper edge of the glacier, a longer route than going straight across but far less crevassed. Although alone I felt fairly safe as there were several other parties on the glacier. After five hours the summit of Aneto was reached via the airy rock scramble known, curiously, as the Puente de Mahoma (Mahomet's Bridge), an impressive ridge consisting of great blocks of granite and giving views straight down to the glacier below. The view from the summit was vast but less

96

grand than from lower down as Aneto is so much higher than the surrounding mountains. The top, unfortunately, rivals Ben Nevis or Snowdon for litter and unnecessary junk, in this case a motley collection of religious icons. I had the summit to myself for half an hour before an English party arrived followed by a French one and a lone Argentinian. Return was via the main glacier track along with a roped party of two and an unroped party of six Spaniards. There were many crevasses to be stepped across, some wide, some narrow, deep and evil looking slits. However I was soon adopted by the Spanish party whose leader stood astride the bigger crevasses helping people across and including me in those he helped. Once across the other side they plied me with food and drink from the bottles of wine, cans of beer and sumptuous fresh salads, meat and cheeses they were carrying. Although we could not speak each other's language our shared sense of triumph at having climbed Aneto linked us closely. I was, though, a bit shocked when, on seeing me stowing my rubbish in my pack, a Spanish woman came over to me smiling and shaking her head, took my rubbish, added it to the carrier bag of bottles, cans and paper she had collected and then hurled the whole lot down a crevasse!

I'd enjoyed the ascent so much that when the next day dawned sunny and clear and Graham fancied the climb I went and did it again! This time we roped up and crossed the glacier by the direct and heavily crevassed route, the way I'd returned the previous day. Despite the improved weather there were very few people about and none on the summit. We were back at camp in eight hours. I spent that night sleeping out in my new Goretex bivvy bag as there was a clear sky with a full moon. It was a dry but cold night and the bivvy bag definitely extended the range of my lightweight down sleeping bag. Each time I woke up I could see the moon above the ring of pine trees and snow-clad, pale gold glowing rock peaks. It was my birthday and there was nowhere else in the world I'd rather have been.

At dawn I lay on my back watching the sun light up the peaks. We had to return to France as Alain was going home in a couple of days, his holiday cut short by a job interview. The impressive, narrow notch of the Port de Venasque in the rock wall of the frontier gave views of the Posets, Maladetta and the Mulleres hills. Leaving the packs and my companions I climbed the Pic de Sauvegarde for one of the best views of the walk; as well as the peaks seen from the pass I could see the long line of the frontier peaks and the wooded hills and valleys that led down to distant Luchon. It was with great reluctance that I descended back to the pass and we switchbacked down the tight turns of the steep path to the unattended Refuge de Venasque where we slept the night. Down in France a haze was creeping up the valleys.

For the past few days the weather had grown hotter and hotter and now we were at lower altitudes it was very hot indeed. Alain left us above the Hospice de France to walk back to Luchon whilst Graham and I took a contouring trail through the cool and airy beech, pine and spruce forests of the Bois de Sajust and Bois de Bedourade before crossing the Cirque de Glere and ascending a steep and seemingly endless unshaded path to the Col de Sacroux and then the Col de Pinata below which we pitched camp. We were crossing the grain of the land now, up and down over the steep-sided spurs jutting out from the frontier peaks into France. The well maintained and spectacularly situated trail contouring high above the valleys was the best path we came across yet we saw hardly anyone on it though on the worn-out grinds to the mountain huts we met dozens of people.

This was, sadly, our last camp site and we stayed there for two nights. The last full day I spent climbing the Pic de Maupas, an enjoyable 10,200-foot peak with an interesting final scramble up to the summit ridge and good views south along the frontier and, for the final time, into Spain. I also had a good view of an approaching storm from the huge iron tubing pyramid that decorates the summit so made a rapid descent, reaching camp just before the rain. A final night of thunderstorms and heavy rain left drizzle and low cloud for the walk down into Luchon. My first Pyrenees backpacking trip was over but I'd been captivated by this beautiful wilderness country and knew I'd return.

* * *

Three years passed and it was the summer of 1984 before I found the time to go back to the Pyrenees. Again Graham Huntington was my companion and again we hauled heavy sacks though this time without the climbing gear as we were intent on a pure, linear backpacking trip along a section of the Haute Route Pyrenee, a high-level route that stretches the full length of the chain from the Atlantic to the Mediterranean. Although there are many Alpine-style huts along the HRP, to really appreciate this route I think you have to camp or bivouac. Only by doing so can you obtain a true feeling of wilderness and the beautiful solitude to be found in these mountains as you pitch your tiny tent or, even better, lay out your sleeping bag under the stars surrounded by a serrated skyline of peaks.

However, after a 32-hour journey began on September 8th involving six trains, one boat and three buses and ending with a three and three-quarter-mile steep uphill road walk the aesthetic nature of our first camp site was far from our minds as we stumbled off the road into a field and climbed into our sleeping bags. We were just outside the hamlet of Lescun, high above the Aspe Valley. Above Lescun rise the first of the High Pyrenees as you travel from the Atlantic so with only two weeks available we'd decided to start here and walk eastwards to Gavarnie. This, we reckoned, would take eight days leaving us two or three over to explore the area around the Cirque de Gavarnie. Accordingly our packs bulged as we had eight days' worth of food and fuel. The HRP makes no concessions to resupplying needs so unless you use the huts, which we could neither afford nor wished to do, or are prepared to drop down into the valleys to find a shop, you have to carry all your supplies for long sections.

Our first night's bivvy was interrupted by heavy rain half way through the night. Graham had sensibly slept in his Goretex bivvy bag from the start but, as the night had begun dry and warm, I hadn't so I had to find mine quickly and wriggle into it. I then slept soundly for another four hours whilst the downpour continued. A few drips crept in through the bivvy bag zip but I learnt that the way to counter that is to roll over and lie with the zip underneath you. What the experience did show was that it is possible to sleep out in the open in heavy rain in a down sleeping bag and a Goretex bivvy bag and remain completely dry. Come morning and all we had to do was bundle everything into the packs, race into Lescun and indulge in a protracted breakfast in the cafe to watch the deluge.

When we finally set off up towards the invisible

mountains the rain was easing off though low clouds and a cold wind remained. Our destination was the head of the valley of the Gave d'Ansabere below the limestone pinnacles of the Cirque d'Ansabere. We reached it in $3^{1}/2$ hours and set up camp just below some crude but inhabited shepherds' huts, the Cabanes d'Ansabere. We were to see many of these shelters, some very primitive, some well-built, on our trek for shepherds still spend their summers high in the mountain pastures with their flocks. Our site was just above timberline, and the mature beech forest we'd climbed through had given way to small clusters of wizened, weather-smashed dwarf beech which formed dense thickets only a few feet high. Glimpses of the Ansabere pinnacles were granted us in the swirling cloud but not enough to prepare us for the glory that greeted us with the dawn. There, shining white in the new sun's rays, rose the towers of limestone. 'Absolutely magnificent' I wrote in my journal. I was able to appreciate the view too, having slept for $11^{1}/2$ hours! A frost lay on the tent flysheet and the sky was completely clear.

Now on the HRP itself, our first full day's journey took us away from the pinnacles, over the border into Spain for a brief section, and then back into France. The HRP lies mainly in France, being a creation of the French Alpine Club, but the topography, as here, occasionally necessitates the route straying into Spain. The international frontier itself runs along the main crest of the Pyrenees which the HRP follows as closely as possible. As we climbed up to the Lac d'Ansabere en route for the border we saw large numbers of birds of prey circling above us. As we neared them we could see that they were taking off from the hillside round the lake, some of them in fact from the lip of the cirque itself. We identified these big, unwieldy, ponderous birds as vultures and came within a few feet of some of them as we entered the cirque.

A steep climb up a trackless grassy hillside led to the frontier and a totally different landscape. Instead of the green, wooded valleys of the French side we looked across ridge after ridge of typically Spanish mesa terrain cut by dusty, arid-looking valleys. Behind us clouds drifted over the peaks and the lower valleys were hidden in dense white mist. In Spain not a cloud sullied the sky and the sun blazed down. This is quite normal and one of the delights of the

Pyrenees is the sharp contrast between the cool, damp, misty, green, forested French valleys and the hot, arid, Mediterranean Spanish side. If the weather is wet in France then go to Spain! A lake in Spain, the Ibon de Acherito, beckoned us down before we began a traverse through green-turfed but waterless shallow valleys with potholes and sinkholes and little limestone outcrops. This pasture-land uncannily resembles that of the Yorkshire Dales.

Back on the frontier at the Col de Pau we immediately plunged into thick French mist, happily on an excellent waymarked path which took us either just below or actually on the crest itself round the Pic de Burcq to the Col de Saoubathou. Here the cloud cleared abruptly (or we walked out of it, I'm not sure which) and we had a superb view across the Aspe Valley to the Pic du Midi D'Ossau. This rock peak, known as the Pic du Midi for short, is only 9,460 feet high, nothing exceptional in Pyrenean terms (there are many peaks over 9,000 feet) but its distinctive steep shape stands out for miles because there are no other summits that are so high nearby. It is without doubt a very impressive mountain.

The crossing of the Vallee de Aspe, through which a road runs over to Spain, was the next stage of the trek and a major one too as it meant a long descent across one side of this major valley followed by a long climb back up the other. The Col d'Arrouy gave a breathtaking and unexpected view of the frontier peaks of the Cirque d'Aspe before the trail dropped down into the pleasantly shady forest of beech, silver fir and black pine. Just above the woods was another shepherd's hut, the Cabane Grosse, aptly named as it turned out. A sign near the hut offered cheese for sale so whilst I sat on the packs and petted the dozens of dogs that were around, as there were at every cabane, Graham went and bought some cheese. He came back with a vast hunk that had cost 88 francs! He'd only asked for a kilo but clearly had at least twice that amount. We knew what we'd be having for lunch from now on! After taking a few photographs of a particularly large and magnificent Pyrenean mountain dog we continued, our packs heavy with cheese. Dropping rapidly into the forest the trail took us to the Gave d'Aspe and the road before starting to climb again up the treeless south-facing hillside covered with colourful Mediterranean plants and alive with bright-winged grasshoppers and darting lizards. The hot, hot climb ended with more woods then finally the tiny Refuge Lary where we spent the night with three other backpackers, two of them French and one English.

All the following day the Pic du Midi drew nearer and we had many wonderful views of its soaring cliffs. A well-used path led past a necklace of attractive lakes above the Gave de Bious and under the strangely twisted rock summit of the Pic Casterau. A tour of these lakes is a popular day's outing and we met many other walkers for the first time on the trek. Still in limestone country we saw many disappearing streams and one large marble 'sink' which we climbed down into for a quick inspection. Once on the slopes of the Pic du Midi itself we left behind the easy pastureland walking and had to traverse a huge field of boulders jettisoned from the mountain's crumbling sides. This led to the Col de Peyreget and views ahead to the higher peaks to come, the Balaitous and Vingemale. A few hundred feet below the pass we decided to bivvy on some grassy shelves by two small pools. Situated just below the south face of the Pic du Midi this was one of the most spectacular camp sites I've ever had. During the evening we heard voices and eventually located two climbers descending the face. For some time we watched their downward progress on what seemed from where we were, to be very loose rock as they downclimbed some bits and abseiled others. Finally just as it was growing dark they reached the bottom and clattered off down the scree.

We weren't having much luck with bivouacs this trip. This was our second one and for the second time it rained, though not until dawn. I woke at 7 am to a black sky and a storm rushing in. Thunder, rain, hail and strong winds had arrived by eight o'clock and we were hurriedly packing. A rapid descent followed to the rich beech woods of the Brousset valley where the rain stopped and we could remove our waterproofs. The ramshackle bar/restaurant by the roadside at Soques served lukewarm coffee which was hardly worth stopping for and soon we were heading up the Arrius valley.

A slight confusion over the route during our telephone and letter planning between North Wales and North Yorkshire had resulted in us being short of one map, a fact we'd only discovered a few days into the trek. Now we had reached the point where our maps ran out and we were dependent on the guidebooks. We were also embarking on a section of the HRP described as crossing 'high, remote passes. . .and several stretches of rough and awkward terrain'. With the weather still unsettled it did not seem to be the place to be without a map so we decided to take an alternative route on the Spanish side of the Balaitous, the next mountain on the route, which both guidebooks said was easier than the 'official' route and which, more importantly, was on our maps. This left us with only a short 'mapless' section to do.

The way to the Arremoulit Refuge was on a clear path though on steep zig-zags through a desolate, rock landscape dotted with cold pools and lakes. No green sheep pastures here. The valley below the Lac d'Artouste was white with cloud but we remained in the cold, grey open. From the hut we instantly went wrong and climbed to the Col d'Arremoulit instead of the Col de Palas. Fortunately both lead to the Lacs d'Arriel where we were heading and the descent from the wrong col was, although very steep, on a narrow but good path. It was only when we tried to get our bearings from the lakes, which were on our maps, that we realised our error. From the col we'd had an awesome view of the grim rock, ice and snow ramparts of the Balaitous and were glad we weren't going to attempt to cross those complex and steep slopes without a map. The Balaitous is so inaccessible that one early pioneer, Charles Packe, took two attempts in 1862 and 1864 before managing to climb it, wandering 'for seven days on and almost all round the mountain before setting his foot at last on its real summit'. The nature of our surroundings combined with the weather, grey clouds swirling round the summits with a cold, thin wind carrying hints of rain, had a great effect on me and I noted in my journal that 'I actually shook and felt quite nervous on the descent to the Lacs d'Arriel'. Somehow the scenery was on too grand a scale, too inhospitable for human beings to fit in. The shelter of the tent was most welcome and gave a human scale to the terrain. For once I did not even think of bivouacing.

In keeping with the surroundings, the night was rough and stormy. Dawn broke cold and grey with rain spattering against the flysheet and a bone-chilling wind whistling off the lake. A series of small, dammed lakes fills the narrow valley of the Arriel, hemmed in on either side by steep rocky slopes and crags. Wrapped up in our warm clothing and waterproofs we followed the narrow path that twists and turns along the very edge of these tarns often crossing via broken stone causeways when there was no space for it to continue. This supposedly easier route than the one north of the Balaitous massif could be a trap in heavy rain or during snowmelt. The waters of the lakes and the connecting streams would only have to rise a little to prevent any exit from these hemmed-in, claustrophobic little cirques. It was a relief to leave this dark valley and traverse the slopes above the more open valley of the Rio Aguas-Limpias on a good path. To the north the frontier peaks were still draped with clouds but to the south the Spanish peaks basked in sunshine. We were out of the rain now but the cold wind still blew. Eventually we came to the large Ibon de Respumaso reservoir and a deserted construction village. We looked in the chapel. It was full of bivvy gear and obviously in regular use as a shelter. The route was very simple, just keep on up the valley. This was helpful as the detail on our French maps of this Spanish terrain was minimal and the guidebooks gave far less of a description than for other sections of the HRP, presumably because this was only an 'alternative'.

More complex ground led from the unfinished dam of the Campo Plano towards the Col de la Fache, a high frontier pass at 8,740 feet. Above the col rises the great pyramid of the Grande Fache (9,860 feet) which kept appearing before us as the clouds lifted, then dropped again. On a steep scree slope just above two small lakes directly below the col, our way was barred by an unstable looking bank of old snow whose bottom section had broken off and lay glistening in the blue waters below, leaving a nasty hole between it and the main slope to catch anyone who slipped. I tested the snow gingerly. It was very slippery. With only Brasher Boots and no ice axes we decided not to risk it and managed to find a way round the other shores of the lakes which only involved a short paddle. Earlier in the season I imagine an ice axe would be essential here. As it was we were glad to reach the col and leave this desolate landscape behind. A long day ended with a rapid descent on an excellent path into the softer surrounds of the Marcadau valley where we pitched the tent. We both felt that if this was the easier alternative route then the 'official' one must be very serious for this was by far and away the hardest and most dangerous day we'd had yet.

Clouds still lay on the tops but it was calm when we set off the next morning past the huge Refuge Wallon, a cross between a hotel and an Alpine hut, outside of which there were many people and several tents. So far the only other tents we'd seen had been in the vicinity of huts as had most of the people we'd met. We had several high passes to cross and another visit to Spain, although only a short one, and we were approaching the third major peak of our walk, the Vingemale, the others being the Pic du Midi D'Ossau and the Balaitous. Firstly, we had to regain lost height by climbing slowly up the peaceful and pleasant valley of the Gave d'Arratille, wooded in its lower reaches then rocky and lake dotted higher up. As we ascended the valley we fell in with two other British backpackers. They too had taken the alternative route south of the Balaitous and found it tougher than expected. They'd also taken the right route from the Arremoulit Refuge over the Col du Palas and told us that the descent from the col on pathless, loose scree above cliffs was very difficult with heavy packs. Obviously our route with its path is in fact easier than that given in the guidebooks. At the frontier pass of the Col d'Arratille we parted company as they were heading down into Spain to resupply and visit Ordessa whilst we were just cutting across the scree under the Pic Alph. Meillon to the Col des Mulets before returning to France. As always the Spanish side was hot and sunny. During the straightforward descent to the flat glacial plain of the Oulettes du Vingemale we could see our path winding back up the opposite hillside. On the plain two tents were pitched, a fantastic site facing the hanging glaciers of the mighty 10,820-foot Vingemale. Although the summit remained wreathed in cloud for all but a few sunlit minutes this huge north face was still over-powering and impressive and we had it in view for most of our ascent to our third high col of the day, the Hourquette d'Ossue (8,970 feet) from where we could look down onto the glacier. Eight hundred feet below us on the other side of the col lay the Refuge Baysellance, closed for the season (it was September 17th) but still occupied. From there a really enjoyable, tightly built path above a steep-sided, narrow valley with many waterfalls and sections of glacial debris led to another morainic plain, the Oulettes d'Ossue, where we camped. We were at a roadhead here and although we didn't know it our journey was almost over. Short of food (yes, we'd eaten all that cheese!) we walked down the road into the tourist village of Gavarnie. This tiny mountain hamlet is totally dominated by the tourist trade to the extent that although there are twenty or more trinket and bauble shops there is only one small and limited grocery store. Donkeys and horses are everywhere for from here tourists are taken on the animals' backs to view the spectacular Cirque de Gavarnie. Once we'd sorted out food, money, films, bus times and obtained a weather forecast (rain!) we headed back up into the sanctuary of the hills. We were aiming to camp high up near the Refuge des Sarradets ready for an ascent of the highest peak in the Gavarnie Cirque, the 9,900-foot Pic du Marbore. However darkening skies and heavier packs caused us to stop and camp in the narrow Vallee de Pouey Aspe just below a very steep section of the trail. We were to be glad of our caution for during the night a savage storm began with high winds, lashing rain and, by dawn, heavy snow. Coming from the north-east it was very cold and we were quite content to spend the day the gale raged curled up in our sleeping bags reading and having endless brew-ups. We were also thankful that we'd brought a reasonable-sized tent and not gone for saving every ounce of weight. We seemed to be on the snowline for it was melting as it fell round the tent but plastering the slopes above. A short walk up the valley to stretch our legs in the afternoon confirmed our decision to stay put. The ground was treacherously smooth with wet snow and hail and the path up the steep hillside above our camp had vanished under the snow.

A brilliant day followed, sunny but sharp with cold. The white mountains sparkled in the sun. The snow was not thawing and it felt like winter had begun. With only our summer gear, to climb would have been folly, so with good grace we retreated, admiring on our descent the newly white-mantled peaks. Back in the valley we wandered up to the Cirque de Gavarnie to admire this vast wonder of nature along with dozens of tourists. Then it was back to Gavarnie and the village camp site before the bus the next day. My second trip to the Pyrenees was over and I came away even more convinced that here is a paradise for backpackers.

Camp in the Valle de Estos: Spanish Pyrenees, 1981.

above: Glastonbury Tor: Land's End to John O'Groats walk.
below: The summit of Ben Nevis: Corrour to Ullapool walk.

The Vallée de Pouey Aspé: French Pyrenees, 1984.

Above: Deep snow in the San Bernardino mountains of Southern California: Pacific Crest Trail.
Opposite: Tunnel Falls on the Eagle Creek Trail, Oregon: Pacific Crest Trail.
Below: Larry Lake fording Tilden Creek, Yosemite National Park: Pacific Crest Trail.

Above: Scott Steiner surveying the Bob Marshall Wilderness: Continental Divide.
Opposite: Climbing towards the Divide in the Bob Marshall Wilderness: Continental Divide.
Overleaf: Looking down to the Markarfljot River Gorge: Iceland.
Below: The author cooking over a camp fire at Roaring Fork Basin, Teton National Forest: Continental Divide.

5

USA

THE PACIFIC CREST TRAIL

Mile after mile of pristine mountain scenery spread out under a blue sky. The sun sparkling on lakes and creeks in timberline cirques above which rise great golden granite cliffs. A pair of backpackers striding up a narrow switch-backing trail to a camp under the stars. Image after image like these flashed up on the screen. I was in Leicester watching a slide show given by a ranger from the USA's National Park Service who'd swapped posts for a year with a ranger from the Peak National Park. The slides were of Yosemite National Park in the Sierra Nevada mountains of the USA which back then in 1975 I'd barely heard about. I left that slide show impressed by the sheer scale of that vast wilderness and struggling to digest the numerous facts I'd learnt. I began thinking about the prospect of backpacking in an area where for even a short trip a week's supplies would be needed; where bears and coyotes and other wild animals still roam; where the peaks reach up to 14,000 feet and the sun shines all summer. How or when I could go I had no idea, but I knew that one day I would go and see this wilderness for myself.

Sometime during the next two years I discovered, I cannot recollect exactly how, the existence of the Pacific Crest Trail. Now I had a specific walk I wanted to do. It seemed a distant goal when I set off on the End to End Walk in 1978 but by 1981 I was planning on walking it the very next year. The Pacific Crest Trail, or PCT as it is popularly known, stretches from Mexico to Canada for 2,600 miles along the chain of mountains that lies furthest to the west in the USA, the last mountains before the Pacific Ocean is reached. In the south there is no continuous chain, just a series of east-west trending ranges split by narrow tongues of desert creeping in from the great interior to the east, the huge region of deserts that holds the Pacific Crest

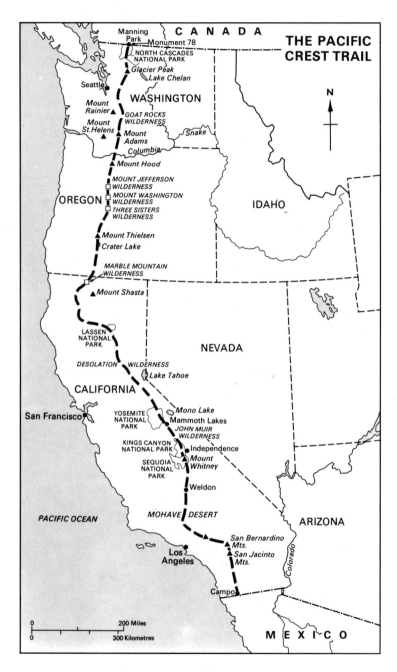

mountains and the Rocky Mountains apart. Then four or so hundred miles north of the Mexican border the land rises up and the Sierra Nevada and the Cascades stretch unbroken for 2,000 miles all the way to Canada.

The Pacific Crest Trail twists in and out of these mountains; alternating between the desert and the transverse ranges, the San Jacintos, San Bernardinos and San Gabriels, in Southern California; crossing the hot, arid flatlands of the Mohave Desert; rising to over 13,000 feet as it passes through the magnificent Sierra Nevada in Sequoia, King's Canyon and Yosemite National Parks; winding through dense lake-dotted conifer forests past the solitary glacier-covered volcanoes of Northern California and Oregon; descending to its low point of 150 feet at the Columbia River and then finishing in a glorious 500-mile flourish amongst the tremendous North Cascades. En route the PCT passes through 7 National Parks, 24 National Forests and 6 State Parks.

My PCT walk was planned on and off for four years during which I read all I could about the trail and the areas it passes through, poring over lists of gear and compiling lists of food and post offices to send it to. This was to be my first major backpacking trip abroad and over twice as long as any walk I'd done before so careful preparation was needed. Much of the planning was done in conjunction with Warren Rogers of the Pacific Crest Club who provides information and help for all PCT walkers. Warren led the teams of YMCA boys who over four summers from 1935 to 1938 explored a Mexico–Canada route that is the basis for the PCT. Establishing the trail then became Warren's goal and its existence is a tribute to the decades of work he has put in and the help and inspiration he has given to those keen to walk in his footsteps. Since being designated an official National Scenic Trail in 1968 much work has been done on the PCT and most of the route is complete, leaving only short sections where diversions have to be made round private land. Guidebooks are available and I had both the Wilderness Press two-volume set and the Pacific Crest Club's strip maps. I ripped up the first to save weight and had sections sent on to me, whilst Warren sent me batches of the latter every few hundred miles.

Eventually the planning stage was over and on March 31st, 1982, I flew out to Los Angeles to be met by Warren

Rogers who'd invited me to stay with him and his wife Mary whilst I made my final preparations. My main task was to drive out to see Charlie Yacoobin in North Hollywood whose company Trail Foods was to send me 26 food parcels over the next six months. That done and various bits and bobs added to the packages Warren drove me to the start of the PCT at the tiny border hamlet of Campo. The long and scenic car journey over, Warren wished me luck and left me standing by the rucksack I was to live out of for half a year. Alone in the dusk on the campsite in Campo I realised that the adventure really was beginning.

On April 3rd I took my first steps towards Canada, having first turned south and walked the few miles to the broken-down barbed wire fence by a dirt road in nondescript semi-desert scrub that marks the border with Mexico. That first day is now etched in my memory but at the time I remember a sense of unreality and feeling distanced from everything. I left the border with a strange mixture of suppressed elation and anti-climax. The excitement I was experiencing hardly seemed to accord with what I was actually doing, which was trudging down a hot, dusty road. Campo is only a temporary start to the PCT as the land to the west is privately owned and as yet access for the trail has not been negotiated. I didn't mind the uninspiring start. It was enough just to be on my way. One day there will no doubt be signs and noticeboards designating the spot where the PCT reaches Mexico. However I felt happier starting alone with no sign of what I was attempting to do, no finger post pointing towards Canada with 2,600 miles written on it. I didn't want to think of the PCT as 'official'. For this year at least it was to be my private and personal trail no matter how many others I met along the way. This understated start was appropriate to that.

The clearest memory I have of those first long, hot days in the Southern California chapparal is of the sun; white and relentless in the sharp, blue, cloudless sky. In this featureless terrain with its wide, flat horizons, the slowly moving sun was the only sign of the progression of time and, used to the rapidly changing scenery and climate of Britain's closed-in hills, I felt as though I was walking on the spot. I travelled on wide, sandy trails through the mass of tangled shrubbery, dry, thorny, often shoulder-height and impenetrable, that is the chapparal. With the heat went a dearth of water. The first few days taught me that I must carry full containers and drink deeply at every water source. Of course heat and thirst are the classic symptoms of desert travel together with burning feet and mine were so hot, sore and swollen after just fourteen miles that off came my 5-lb mountain boots and on went my light, cool running shoes. I was to carry those boots many miles. They proved more comfortable on my back than on my feet!

This initial stretch of semi-desert was crossed in two days and a more rugged landscape developed as I approached the Laguna Mountains. Monolothic red rock boulders lined the trail as it switchbacked upwards. Sitting in the shade of one of these sandstone pillars I met my first other PCT hikers, Scott and Jim. We exchanged greetings and I gazed nervously and with awe at the high packframes that lay beside them. Did they really need all that gear and if so was I badly under equipped? I was relieved to discover that this was their third day out and that they were finding their packs a problem. I never met or heard of them again so never learnt if they made it to Canada.

The Lagunas gave me my first taste of the glorious conifer forests that I was to revel in from here to Canada as well as a view east to the lifeless void of the Anza-Borrego Desert sliding away into the heat haze. The cool Jeffrey pine forest was welcome after the searing heat of the chapparal. Jeffrey pines are the commonest conifers in Southern California as they are extremely drought resistant. They can grow to a height of 170 feet and will grow at altitudes of 5,000 to 9,000 feet. I became very familiar with this specifically Pacific Coast tree in the mountainous sections of Southern California. As I entered the shade of these spreading, rich reddish-barked trees for the first time the change was dramatic. In just a few hundred yards I moved from the exposed burning openness of the semi-desert to walking on snow patches under the tall pines. Someone had been skiing here recently and I followed the parallel tracks across the forest floor. Over a week later I would meet the skier but for now I was alone.

A meal of tortillas and enchiladas in a Mexican restaurant (much more appetising than my instant noodles and packet soups), eaten in the little mountain town of Mount Laguna, was typical fare in this Spanish influenced part of the USA. Laguna was spacious, a timbered little town with a new, almost pioneer atmosphere about it. The dark brown, low wood houses and wide dusty avenues blended into the surrounding forest, a forest that the town had not quite escaped from, so that the buildings seemed to be hiding cautiously amongst the trees. On picking up the first of my twenty-six food parcels at the post office and crossing off the town from the list in my journal I began to understand that my journey had actually begun but the enormity of it, of setting out to walk 2,600 miles, I was unable to think about it.

Through the Lagunas the PCT follows the Desert Divide Trail with striking views down to the ridged badlands of the Anza-Borrego Desert 4,000 feet below. The Laguna Mountains, at around 6,000 feet high (small in US terms), are an uplifted granite block with a scarp slope to the east and it was along the top of this that I walked. Westwards the mountains dipped slowly away into rolling pine and oak forests to finally merge with the undulating chapparal country. A sterile brown in colour, the desert hills came to life at dawn and dusk when they caught the rays of the setting and rising sun. Then Oriflamme Mountain was aptly named.

Pulling me on was the distant, tiny snow peak of the 10,804-foot Mount San Jacinto. Four days saw me across seventy miles of chapparal on dusty tracks past deserted gold mines in 'cowboy movie' canyons, through tiny hamlets like Banner and San Felipe, over the verdant mini-prairies of cattle ranches and then up beside the havens of wooded canyons with creeks that trickled into the San Jacintos. During those four days I encountered the start of the annual gathering of the 'trailers', as each year's crop of hopeful PCT backpackers are known. In the tiny hamlet of Warner Springs I met, sprawled in front of the post office, Joel and Jeannie, two footsore trailers and their equally footsore dog, Riley. Soon two more turned up, from Finland of all places! The gathering had begun. From now on I regularly met and heard of other trailers straggling slowly northwards from Mexico until it felt as though a small community was on the move. Key contact points were post offices and cheap restaurants, both essential to the wellbeing and survival of trailers. Trail registers were to be found in most post offices and in these you could check to see who had been through, look for messages and hints of what lay ahead as well as leave messages and hints for those behind. At this early stage, the two most frequent topics were the state of one's feet and the state of the snow up ahead. Rumours were spreading of deep, late snow in the Sierras, of avalanches and deaths. At Warner Springs a phone call to the San Jacinto State Park Ranger Station elicited the information that there was still ten feet of snow above 6,000 feet but that it was compact.

Unfortunately for me it didn't remain that way. Seven miles out of the desert town of Anza I camped in the foothills of the San Jacintos. It began to rain, the first rain of the walk. Rain on snow has a softening effect and sure enough when I climbed up to the first drifts near Cedar Springs I found them deep and soft. I was finally in real wilderness and soon in real wilderness weather too as a furious and unpredicted storm broke out. Within minutes I was being lashed with wind driven rain and the visibility had dropped to around ten yards. The slog through the two-foot-deep snow was arduous and on the steeper slopes I needed the ice axe for balance. I'd felt foolish carrying it through the chapparal but I was glad of it now. The trail was invisible under the snow and I was walking on compass bearings when I reached the narrow ridge between Spitler and Apache Peaks. The rain stopped but the strong winds and mist continued with gusts lifting the cloud edge occasionally to give an unreal brief glimpse 7,000 feet down to the desert floor where Palm Springs basked in bright sunlight. Suddenly out of the gloom a large red tent appeared and the four occupants told me they'd tried to reach Apache Springs, where I was hoping to camp, but had had to turn back because of the snow. They were just out for the weekend but had met three other trailers a few hours previously. This was my first knowledge of the three backpackers I was to travel through the snows of the High Sierra with and who were to become close friends.

That night I melted snow for water for the first time and hoped for an overnight frost to harden the snow in the morning but it failed to materialise. In fact the lowest overnight temperature was 47°F. Despite this I attempted to push on but the snow was even softer than the day before and I couldn't find the buried trail or navigate properly in the thick mist and featureless forest. I felt increasingly insecure as the terrain steepened and balls of snow slid off down the slope and my footsteps collapsed under me. After an hour of great effort and little progress I turned back defeated and returned to the Spitler-Apache ridge where I was rewarded for my prudence with a second breakfast of blueberry cobbler from the still safely ensconsed campers. Several hours later I arrived in the pleasant mountain resort of Idyllwild in the pouring rain.

At the ranger's station I discovered that the PCT down from San Jacinto was not complete and that the Forest Service recommended route was by the road through Idyllwild anyway. The trailer gathering continued and we soon had a little encampment of our own on the campground. The other five trailers had walked the road from Anza to avoid the snow. As well as Joel and Jeannie, Ken (the skier whose tracks I'd seen in the Lagunas) was there plus another couple, Ron and Cheryl. Inevitably the discussion centred round the snow in the Sierras. Despite my San Jacinto experience I was determined to go through them, snow or no snow, but I was coming to the conclusion that it would be unwise to go alone. Only Ken of my present company was even considering going through if the snow remained. The others intended avoiding all snow, and would road walk instead.

Back on the trail again I descended in the dying remnants of the storm through the wooded foothills of the San Jacintos to the town of Cabazon. The town sits in the San Gorgonio Pass, a tongue of desert protruding into the mountains dwarfed by the massive walls of Mounts San Jacinto and San Gorgonio that rise 10,000 feet either side of the pass in the space of a few miles. Wandering round Cabazon I came upon three battered, weatherworn, not to say haggard looking figures. These were Scott Steiner, Dave Rhebhen and Larry Lake and while I'd been in Idyllwild they'd been battling against the storm in the San Jacintos at times totally lost and once only progressing three miles in a whole day. The final bushwhack into Cabazon had been through steep, trailless chapparal which had left them scratched and scarred.

The Trailer Assembly Point in Cabazon was the fire station behind which we all camped on a small patch of grass surrounded by water sprinklers. Into this space were crammed nine backpackers and all their gear. That evening we repaired to a rather sleazy pizza and beer parlour where, over several pitchers of Coors beer, we discussed future plans and a deal was struck. Dave, Scott and Larry were intending to go through the Sierras in the snow and I was pleased when they invited me to join them. The others evidently thought we were both reckless and crazy. They intended either to hitch-hike round the Sierras or, in Ken's case, walk up the road below the Sierras in Owens valley.

I had now completed 150 miles of the PCT and felt that the first stage of the journey was over. I no longer felt like a novice on the trail and I no longer looked like one either! Ahead lay the wooded slopes of the San Bernardino and San Gabriel Mountains and beyond them the arid wastes of the Mohave Desert. Leaving the unbelievably noisy and hot San Gorgonio Pass, threaded as it is by both a freeway and the Southern Pacific Railroad, I climbed thankfully into the hills beside the dirt filled, grey rushing waters of Whitewater Creek to camp with my three prospective Sierra companions under the shade of a canyon live oak tree. I didn't bother with the tent and lay in my sleeping bag watching the last light of the day fading on the red and orange strata of the canyon walls.

For the next three days I travelled with Scott, Dave and Larry and we began to get to know each other. Initially Larry had set out on his own but had met the others within a few days of leaving the Mexican border and had travelled with them ever since. Like Scott he was a veteran of the 4,000-mile Appalachian Trail in the eastern USA whereas Dave was on his first long backpacking trip. Although this was their country they were still 4,000 miles from home as they were all from the eastern states and on their first visit to the west. This distance from home gave us something in common as other trailers we met could go home for a rest or to wait until the snow melted, whereas none of us had that option.

A difficult and frustrating ascent of the flood-swept boulder-strewn canyon of Mission Creek took us into the San Bernardinos and the finest scenery of the trail so far. For fifty miles the PCT wound through these forested, still snow-covered, gentle hills. At Big Bear City I left my companions. This was a supply point for them but not for me, my next one being at Wrightwood, another six days' walk further on. I was quite happy to be on my own again. Conversation and companionship, although pleasant, distracted from the subtle beauty of the surroundings and intruded into the silence. Before Wrightwood I had a long, gradual and enjoyable descent to the next desert gash, the Cajun Pass. I began this slow farewell to the San Bernardinos by leaving the forest zone and descending to Holcomb Creek, walking high above the tumbling waters as the scenery became more and more arid. The weather was hot but the snow-fed creek was cold as I found during the three knee-deep fords needed to reach Holcomb Crossing Trail Camp, a well used but clean backcountry camp site. The place was deserted on this occasion however. Having set up camp under the Jeffrey pines, for the first time I lit a camp fire just for myself and sat watching the flickering flames and the dark starry sky beyond whilst the temperature dropped. Suddenly I felt very self-contained and very remote, huddled by my pathetically tiny orange spot of warmth with all around the vast dark wilderness. At the same time I felt a sense of euphoria at being alone in, but part of, the natural world that I had come to seek.

Deep Creek followed Holcomb Creek and the desert rivers, golden brown in the sunlight and black with pools and white with rapids, led enticingly on to the snowy San Gabriel Mountains, edged to the north by the endless flatness of the Mohave Desert. As I neared Cajun Pass I entered more accessible country and walked many miles of tarmac as I encountered paved roads, cars and people. The convoluted sedimentary rocks around the gash of the pass formed deep tortuous canyons graced with names like Little Horsethief and hot, barren desert hills such as Cleghorn Mountain. Unstable, narrow, alluvial aretes with soft sand slopes set at impossible angles, and showing signs of many landslips, dominated the sides of the pass which lies on the notorious San Andreas Fault, one of the world's major earthquake zones. The pass is a major route through the mountains with both a freeway and a railroad. The PCT is ignominiously funnelled through a culvert under the latter which must be a low point for a wilderness trail. Above this slogan-sprayed square concrete tunnel screamed the high speed traffic.

After waiting to cross the railroad whilst a mile-long goods train negotiated a steep bend I ascended above the pale desert sentinels of the Mormon Rocks named by the Mormon Pioneers who were some of the first white settlers to come through the pass. Latter day manifestations of the pioneer spirit showed themselves as I wandered up the seemingly endless Lyttle Creek Ridge for I appeared to be in the middle of a gunfight. From each little side canyon echoed the cracks and richochets of small arms fire as weekend gunmen practised their skills. I was glad on reaching the cool of the pines and the first snow to escape from the heat and the gunsmoke. During the long traverse of Blue Ridge the dominant feature was the white, hazy mass of Mount San Antonio, at 10,064 feet the highest peak in the San Gabriels. The haze, spreading insidiously up and out from the ever closer Los Angeles basin, was to be an unpleasant presence over the next few weeks. This poisonous brew of automobile fumes is causing extensive needle damage to the conifers of the Angeles and San Bernardino National Forests. Limber pines over 2,000 years old are finally dying under the onslaught of the noxious wastes.

The descent back to the San Andreas Fault was the most frightening episode of the Southern California section of the walk. Walking gingerly on hard packed icy snow I soon lost the line of the trail and ended up going down the wrong canyon via steep loose snow, steep loose scree and steep loose mud. At every step the ground slipped from under me. Very scared I slithered and skidded down 3,000 feet of this, hanging off my ice axe until the slope eased off and I entered the small mountain town of Wrightwood. Unfortunately I then had to climb right back up to the ridge again with a rucksack that now weighed 56lb due to its load of new supplies. I bivouaced in Vincent Gap under an interior live oak tree with blackened fire rings, rusty cans and broken glass all around. Earlier I'd seen three sets of boot prints in the snow and felt sure Scott, Dave and Larry were nearby.

Voices from the road trickled down to me as I packed up and I was delighted though not too surprised to see my companions. Above us lay the 9,339-foot Mount Baden-Powell over which the PCT lay. Larry, with no ice axe or crampons, opted for the snowbound road so only three of us began the climb. The snow was just right for step kicking and we were soon on the summit which lay just above timberline with a few gnarled, ancient stunted limber pines struggling up the slopes towards us. White mountain tops spread out to the south, all the way back to the still snowy

San Jacinto, whilst to the west we could see a snowy ridge leading down to the desert foothills and the Mohave plain we'd been walking above for weeks.

The two-week spell of good weather continued as we dropped slowly down towards the desert. I was sleeping outside every night now and revelling in it. One of the most delightful experiences of the whole walk was to lie under the trees listening to the quiet subtle sounds of the night and looking out to the distant lights of the universe.

On the last day of April we straggled into the desert hamlet of Acton. The Transverse Ranges were behind us and only the Mohave Desert now lay between us and the Sierra Nevada. First though we accepted the generous offer of a local resident, Delree Todd, to take us into Los Angeles forty miles away to buy the extra gear we'd need for the Sierras. So I spent May Day traipsing round four mammoth backpacking stores, a shopping spree that left me bereft of $250 but the proud possessor of 12-point crampons, Sherpa Sno-Claw featherweight snow-shoes, Goretex gaiters, fibre-fill bootees, 10 topographic maps of the Sierras plus the Sierra Club *Naturalist's Guide to the Sierra Nevada*. Now I had to hump this lot across the desert! This was my first day off since the one in Idyllwild sixteen days ago though the overwhelming noise and bustle of LA meant it was not very relaxing.

Back in Acton, trailers were gathering on the edge of the Mohave Desert, eleven in all, contemplating the problems ahead of excessive heat and lack of water. From the hills on the desert's edge the trail could be seen stretching for miles tortuously winding round dusty slopes. It was a depressing sight as it meant hours of unchanging, unchallenging walking. The only relief during these hot, shadeless days was the discovery of a few barely flowing creeklets to assuage our permanent thirsts. Dulled by the heat as we descended in a mindless daze into San Francisquito Canyon we were not prepared for our first close encounter with a rattlesnake.

A sudden, abrupt and very loud rattle from the long grass at Larry's feet caused chaos. Larry leapt backwards colliding heavily with Scott whilst Dave and I piled into the rear. Then we saw the snake, a dark four-foot-long thickset coil that straightened out and slid off into the undergrowth. Eventually our hearts stopped hammering and cautiously we continued. I was surprised at the loudness of the rattle and alarmed at how easy it was to almost step on a snake. Almost subconsciously I began avoiding long grass and the vicinity of bushes.

Ironically as we reached the Mohave proper the weather changed and the clear sunny skies faded away into grey clouds and rain. But instead of the lifeless sand and gravel I'd expected, the ground was a brilliant mat of orange and yellow flowers, mostly poppies. The desert was in bloom. Across the Mohave are spread a series of isolated homes whose residents have over the years built up a network of overnight stops and water supply points for PCT walkers; an essential service. For 35 miles the PCT followed the line of the Los Angeles aquaduct and every mile there was an inspection hole just wide enough to permit the entry of an arm bearing a water bottle. Below rushed the cold snowmelt water essential to LA and, out here, to PCT hikers. On the hottest day of our desert crossing we stopped by one of these water holes, set up our groundsheets as sun awnings and sat out the midday heat. Under the awnings it was 80°F. At 5 pm we set off again to walk in the cool of the evening by the light of the moon. However snakes proved a problem as they were hard to spot in the dark. We were used now to meeting them in daylight but after Larry nearly stepped on a small sidewinder we did no more night walking.

Hot nights made for restless sleep but the spectacular orange and red desert gold sunrises made up for this as did endless canned drinks at Cantil, a tiny collection of houses with a store near the northern edge of the Mohave. Here I met Wayne Fuiten, a PCT hiker who'd left Campo on April 12th and reached here before us having averaged 19 miles a day with no rest days. An ex-military man he was highly organised and hiked to a precise schedule clicking off every step on a counter and stopping for five minutes every hour. He stayed with us to Weldon, then hitched north to avoid the Sierra snow, returning there later in the summer. I met up with him again in northern Oregon but we never actually hiked together as my random stops and widely varying mileages leapfrogged his organised progress.

At Kelso Creek we passed the 500-mile mark. A fifth of the PCT was gone. I slept badly the night before the final 17 miles to Weldon, excited by the thought of reaching this goal. Since Campo, Weldon had meant the end of the beginning, the end of the initiation period and the start of the real adeventure, the start of the Range of Light, the magical Sierra Nevada. The knowledge that these mountains were still snowbound and as far as I knew yet untravelled this year only added spice to my anticipation. Weldon, a small village strung out along a highway, became our base for a few days whilst we organised our expedition through the Sierras.

Our trek through the Sierra Nevada began on the 12th May with a four-day walk through woods and waterlogged meadows up to the 9,350-foot Siretta Pass, where there was still a little snow, and down to the tiny roadhead resort of Kennedy Meadows with some good views of the massive granite cliffs of the Yosemite-Valley-like Dome Wilderness. At Kennedy Meadows the store had a food parcel for me, the biggest and heaviest of the trip with eighteen days' food in it. I added a little more which was lucky as the next section took 22 days. My pack was almost too heavy to lift. A few days of gradual climbing up through the woods took us to the snowline and the beginning of a tough, exhausting, glorious high-level trek, mostly about 10,000 feet, mostly in sunshine, and always in the most wonderful mountain country. Finally I was in the wilderness, the pictures of which, seen back in Leicester, had inspired the whole journey.

We camped on snow most nights with the temperatures usually falling well below freezing, the lowest being one morning when it was just 14°F inside my tent. These cold nights meant that early in the morning the snow was like concrete and we would set off using crampons. By late afternoon even the skis Scott and Dave were using and the snowshoes Larry and I had were sinking into the deep, soft snow. Due to this we tried to set off at dawn and stop by mid afternoon. A daily routine was soon established, unlike further south where the constant changes from chapparal to desert to forest to mountains had made for very different days. We would rise before dawn and cook and eat breakfast shivering over our tiny stoves and waiting for the first warming rays of the sun. The PCT in the High Sierra follows the same route as the John Muir Trail climbing over a series of high passes in between which it drops down into forested canyons. We tried to place each camp as close to the next pass as possible so that we could cross it whilst the snow was still firm then try and descend quickly in order to climb as high as possible up towards the next pass before the snow became too soft.

Black bears are common in the High Sierra and due to the popularity in the summer of the John Muir Trail many of them have become used to raiding camp sites for food. Due to this it is essential to protect your food from them by hanging it high up in a tree. Once upon a time you could simply throw a line over a branch, haul up your food then tie off the line round a tree trunk. But the bears, not being stupid, soon found that if they found a cord and broke it, a bag of food would usually appear. So now you have to protect both the food and the supporting line by a tedious and complicated procedure called counterbalancing. This involves finding a suitable branch fifteen to twenty feet up, throwing a rock over it tied to the cord, hauling the bag of food up to the branch, tying on another bag of food to the other end of the cord as high up as you can reach then hurling that bag up into the air in the hope that the two bags will end up side by side at least ten feet off the ground and five feet away from the trunk of the tree (bears can climb) and below the branch. I always set this up as soon as we reached camp, actually hauling up my food when I'd eaten. I must say I hated doing it but losing my precious food to a bear appealed even less. Mornings were worst as I had to leave my warm sleeping bag and rescue my food from its tree (usually by jumping up and down with the ice axe until I could snag the bags) before I could have breakfast. Of course when we camped well above timberline we could not do this but we always did when camped in the forest — and fresh bear tracks and droppings, found every few days here, made sure we never forgot.

The scenery was stupendous with range after range of golden granite peaks soaring above the snowfields and the deep, wooded canyons down which crashed tumbling creeks from the still-frozen mountain lakes. Although the spring thaw was underway we were still able to cross most of the creeks on snow bridges and walk across the higher tarns. A huge tilted block, the High Sierra has the scarp slope on its east side and when we touched on this we could see 9,000 feet down to the arid, desert floor of Owens Valley and the pink alkaline flats that once were the bed of Owens Lake. In the forests we were often on steep, insecure slopes where we dodged from tree to tree and where our snowshoes and skis were useless. Quickly we learnt to stay in the canyon bottoms, descending and ascending them, rather than trying to follow the line of the hidden trail which usually traversed high up on the canyon sides.

I'd never used either snowshoes or skis and had chosen the former as I didn't think the High Sierra was the place to learn to ski. It soon became apparent that on terrain where they could be used the skis were both faster and more fun, though in the forests when strapped to rucksacks they were a nuisance, as they frequently got caught in branches. In contrast the snowshoes were slow but sure and no problem when carried on the pack. Mine had built-in crampons and a flexible foot so they could be used for kicking up steep slopes, though they proved a little insecure on steep descents. Where we had to wade (the only word) through deep, soft snow, progress was slow and tiring and this was where the few injuries we received came about as we often caught our legs on hidden rocks and tree stumps when falling through the snow. Post-holding was an apt description for this most inefficient of all modes of mountain travel. However whether post-holding, cramponing or snowshoeing progress was slow, an average of ten miles a day for the 200 miles through the High Sierra from Kennedy Meadows to Mammoth Lakes, our next supply point. The 23 days this took included three not actually walking the PCT. One of these was spent climbing 14,494-foot Mount Whitney, the highest peak in the USA outside of Alaska, and two waiting whilst the others went to collect a food cache they had hidden before they started the trail.

The first week saw us into the snow and above 10,000 feet for the first time though we were to become used to this altitude, staying above it for virtually the whole 200 miles with many camps at over 11,000 feet. When below 10,000 feet we dipped down into the alpine forest of foxtail, whitebark and lodgepole pines but mostly we were above timberline in a monochrome world of black and white where the blue of the sky and the changing colours of the sun from dark red to orange to gold to yellow to white and back again were the only relief from the black and white mountain scenery. Yellow-bellied marmots basked on rocks, standing up on their hind legs and whistling loudly on seeing us. These large bulky rodents became a common sight around rock piles and on scree slopes. The creeks in the forests, whose snowbridges had now collapsed, were still fairly easily crossed as the snowmelt was not fully underway but we did have a problem at Rock Creek when a boot fell off Dave's pack when he crossed a ford and was washed rapidly downstream. Luckily I saw it wedged under a log jam a few hundred yards away, and managed to recover it after a slimy and slippery crawl out on a thin branch.

May 21st saw us at Crabtree Meadow, the starting point for the climb up Mount Whitney. Although not on the PCT none of us wanted to miss this, the highest peak in the 48 states, so we agreed to spend a day attempting the ascent. From our campsite at 10,300 feet on a small snow free patch of ground we could see the soaring spires of Mounts Young and Hitchcock and the jagged silhouette of the Whitney Pinnacles. A white snowshoe hare darted in front of our tents. Above us the lodgepole pines stood silent in the calm air. 'A superb site, perhaps best yet' I wrote in my journal, an opinion that was to be aired many times in the Sierra. Scott, Dave and I had all done a little snow and ice mountaineering and were familiar with the use of ice axe and crampons. Larry however had picked up his first ever tools at Weldon, having realised he'd need them after the San Jacinto crossing so I spent a few hours teaching him the rudiments of ice axe breaking. Hardly an adequate preparation for the Whitney climb but the best we could do. The two skiers revelled in a few hours' cross-country skiing downhill without the burden of packs. Watching them I vowed to learn cross-country skiing the following winter. A three-hour evening thunderstorm convinced us of the need for a very early start. We didn't want to be caught in such a storm high on the mountain.

Awake at the ghastly hour of half past four we were off by six on the 18-mile round trip. A wander up a narrow canyon under glaciated rock walls led to a traverse of steep snow slopes where we needed crampons to the start of a series of only partially snow-covered switchbacks to the main ridge at Trail Crest. In summer this is a popular mountain walk, easy but spectacular. So many people want to do it in fact that there is a permit system and a few weeks after our ascent we heard that the mountain was fully booked up throughout the summer. Today though, before the snow melt had opened up the area to summer hikers, we had it to ourselves. Along the crest we wound between sharp pinnacles above granite-lined corries with, far below, the tiny circles of frozen lakes and the black spread of the forest. The narrow trail was often snow covered and precarious, especially where it rounded the bulging sides of the buttresses for here it was often steeply banked and we would teeter round on our crampons facing inwards and clinging perilously to the rock. There were a few places where I would have felt easier with a rope and a belay. Gaps between the pinnacles gave stupendous views straight down to the desert floor of Owens Valley. A vast snowfield made up the final slopes to the summit which was reached just after midday. The land fell away to the desert to the east but on the other three sides spread the sharp ridges and peaks of endless snow-spattered mountains rising above vast snow-filled basins. Away to the west an angry thunderstorm was raging.

After an hour on the summit taking photographs, recovering from the climb (though the altitude had affected me less than expected and I felt only slightly breathless), and trying to ignore the signs of the summer crowds (a toilet shed and a concrete ice-filled shelter), we began the descent. To speed this up and to avoid the traverse below the pinnacles we decided to go straight down from the top and try and descend one of the gullies we'd passed below early in the day. The initial snowfield and steep talus went easily until we arrived at the top of the steep, narrow, twisting gullies. We selected a safe looking one we estimated to be between 1,000 and 1,500 feet long and began to glissade down it on our sides, ice axes at the ready. Dave then Scott slid off down the hard snow to reach the security of the wide run-out at the bottom. Then Larry set off. I watched as he rapidly picked up speed until he came to the first kink in the gully. Here he shot out of view in a cloud of snow and rock. There was a loud yell and then silence. I waited, shocked, convinced Larry was either dead or seriously injured. Finally I heard a faint cry: 'I've lost my ice axe!' Unable to see where Larry was I scrambled carefully down the loose rock beside the gully. Where he had lost control some stones stuck up out of the snow and to the side I found his axe, wedged between two small rocks. Below lay Larry himself, spreadeagled on his back in the middle of the slope. I asked him if he could move to the side of the gully as I was frightened of colliding with him if I glissaded down. He tried but immediately started to slide so I climbed slowly down to him, facing inwards and kicking steps in the hard snow whilst using the axes as daggers to support myself. My crampons were strapped on the pack Larry was carrying as we'd only taken one pack between us. It was probable though that it was the two pairs of crampons on the pack that had halted his dangerous slide. I reached him and then talked him down until his confidence returned and he was able to glissade the last, safe few hundred feet. Finally and with relief we reached Scott and Dave who had watched all this from below. We were very lucky. A serious accident miles from our camp and any help could have had unthinkable consequences. The final snow plod back to the tents brought us there at seven o'clock, thirteen hours after setting off.

In camp we found we'd had visitors. Two PCT hikers we'd last seen in Weldon, Phil and Andy, had passed through on skis. They left a note in one of the tents for us saying they weren't stopping to climb Whitney. Beyond Crabtree Meadows we reached the highest section of the PCT in the High Sierra. Our timberline camp sites were all superb and every day we climbed high above the forest to high snowbound passes before descending to ford swirling creeks. I used crampons and snowshoes all the time, often wading creeks in the latter! Forester Pass, at 13,100 feet the highest point on the PCT ('it's all downhill from here to Canada!', remarked Scott), gave another minor epic due this time to my stupidity. The ascent to the pass was very steep and at one point involved crossing a snow-filled gully high up on the rock face. Dave and Scott both crossed safely and climbed up to the tiny pass itself. Half the gully was in shadow and half in the sun. I'd noticed how when they crossed the sunny half Scott and Dave had set off little snow slides and I began to worry about avalanches. When I reached the edge of the sunny section I decided to climb straight up the gully rather than continue across. Now front-pointing up steep, hard snow for 40 feet with one ice axe and an 85 + lb pack at 13,000 feet is not a sensible idea. About 15 feet from the top I was faced with a final vertical section of soft snow. As soon as I tried to climb it it collapsed and I slid back to where I'd started. I eventually reached the pass after Dave had belayed me on his 5-mm rope and passed down his axe to me. Between Dave and Scott heaving on the rope and me pulling up on two axes I managed to flounder on to the pass. Larry, waiting patiently below, decided sensibly to follow the easier route.

Since Crabtree Meadows we'd been in Sequoia National Park but at Forester Pass we left this to immediately enter King's Canyon National Park, the heartland of the High Sierra.

Two days later the others left me beside Bullfrog Lake at 10,600 feet whilst they descended via Kearsage Pass to Onion Valley to try and locate a food cache Scott and Dave had left there over two months previously. In return for them bringing me some extra supplies I'd agreed to look after the tents and all their spare gear so they could travel really light. As we arrived at Bullfrog Lake we caught up with Phil and Andy packing up to also descend to Onion Valley. The camp was on snow by the lakeshore at timberline with a few half buried whitebark and lodgepole pines nearby. I stayed here for three nights and days, the others returning on the afternoon of the third day. This stationary sojourn in the mountains gave a different perspective to the journey. I was able to see just how fast the snow was melting. Every few hours I had to re-peg the sagging tents and by the time the others came back each one was perched on a little platform of hard snow several inches above the surrounding ground. Because of the collapsing tents I couldn't go far so I spent my time wandering round the lake watching it grow in size as the snow and ice thawed, staring up at the surrounding peaks, crossing the creeks on the diminishing snow bridges and sitting outside the tent reading, writing and watching the black and white Clarke's nutcrackers, rosy finches and mountain chickadees in the nearby trees. At night mountain coyotes howled in the forest. Late afternoon on my second day at Bullfrog Lake rain fell, the first for six weeks.

With the return of Phil and Andy bearing gifts of food and fuel and even a newspaper, my solitude was over and the journey recommenced. The 11,978-foot Glen Pass was crossed after a steep, avalanche-prone climb followed by a glissade down the other side during which procedure I lost control and regained it by letting my pack descend on its own only to see it bounce on a rock, burst open and spread the contents all over the mountainside. Miraculously only a pen was broken. Even my cameras, placed in the pack for protection, remained undamaged in their padded cases. Ironically Larry's pack frame broke at a weld even though he hadn't dropped it and we had to tie it up with cord. The scenery remained magnificent throughout this section though as we neared Mammoth Lakes our thoughts turned increasingly to food. Twenty-three days of dehydrated rations was a little too long!

At Woods Creek our route dipped below 9,000 feet and we walked on the trail, for the first time in over a week. The creeks down here were roaring snowmelt torrents but luckily there was a log bridge over Woods Creek itself. With birds singing, green shoots sprouting from the black sodden soil left by the melting snow and butterflies on the wing, it felt like spring. The forest was richer too with great incense cedars, red firs and ponderosa pines plus aspens and willows by the creek. However our descent to 8,400 feet meant a long haul all the way back up to the 12,100-foot Pinchot Pass from where we had a marvellous high-level traverse above the glaciated canyon of the South Fork Kings River with the coloured bands of metamorphic rock making up Striped Peak and Cardinal Peak which were always in view. 'Superlative Alpine scenery — as usual' I wrote.

Our highest camp was above the frozen Helen Lake at 11,600 feet, below 11,955-foot Muir Pass, named in honour of the nineteenth-century conservationist pioneer John Muir whose campaigns led to the creation of the National Park Service and whose favourite area was the High Sierra. It was Muir who called it the Range of Light. Our view from this camp of the 14,000-foot high Palisade range was spectacular, even managing to distract me at dawn from the 20°F temperature. Forest, snow-filled canyon, mountain pass; the simple daily sequence continued to repeat itself until finally on June 6th we reached the road outside the ski resort of Mammoth Lakes and hitch-hiked, thankfully obtaining lifts quickly, into town. The longest section of our crossing of the High Sierra was over. Our first act was to find a restaurant and eat a huge meal. We then pitched the tents on the campground, returned to the restaurant and ate another!

A day and a half was spent recovering, eating, washing, shopping and generally relaxing. We needed the rest as we still had 200 miles of the Sierra Nevada to travel through for which we would need to carry all our supplies. With the increasing rapidity of the snowmelt we knew that the creek crossings could be very hazardous especially as the trail was generally at lower elevations and often below timberline in the next section. With the latter in mind I bought 60 feet of 7-mm rope as from this point we were to split into two pairs, Dave and Scott and Larry and myself. In a gear shop we weighed our bulging packs. I was horrified when mine came to 92lb but Larry's new one (his pack frame having finally collapsed despite many running repairs), took the scale to its maximum of 100lb! And this even though we'd dispensed with our crampons and snowshoes, reckoning that the snow would now be too soft and patchy to make them worth carrying.

Much of our route now lay in the sombre confines of red fir forest. Known also as the Snow Forest, this forest of giant conifers creates such a shade that the snow remains here longer than anywhere else, a fact which gave us difficult navigation problems at times and also made for slow, arduous progress. We climbed above 11,000 feet for the last time at Donohue Pass from where we descended into Yosemite National Park. Down Lyall Canyon we went to the tiny cluster of houses at Tuolumne Meadows where a road crosses the Sierra Nevada, the first since that at Weldon so long ago. The store here opened the day we arrived, the road having just been cleared of snow. Either side of the road for just a few miles we met some other hikers. Apart from Andy and Phil, who had split up in Mammoth Lakes (Andy to hitch-hike north tired of the snow and Phil, whose home town Mammoth was, to wait for the snow to melt), we had met just two people between Kennedy Meadows and Mammoth Lakes and our feeling that we were part of a north-bound backpacking community had vanished.

The next six days in the Yosemite backcountry were the toughest of the whole walk. The route here is reputed to have the most steep, long ascents and descents on the PCT and the hardest creek crossings so when you do it, as we did, at the height of the spring thaw with deep snow still lying in the woods and on the passes and the creeks full of snowmelt water you are guaranteed a difficult time. Even the meadows were hard to cross as the snow here had melted and frozen to form dish-shaped suncups, some of them several feet deep and several feet across. And to finish it off there were heavy summer thunderstorms nearly every afternoon.

But it is the creeks that I remember most vividly: crawling across slippery, insecure logs inches above the deafening torrent of McCabe Creek; the waist-deep roped fords of Return Creek and Spiller Creek; more logs over unfordable Kerrick Creek; a desperate chest-deep crossing of Stubblefield Canyon Creek and finally a $1\frac{1}{2}$-hour-long crossing of Tilden Creek. It took a long time because the creek was so savage that we needed a fixed rope to ford it with our packs. Larry crossed first, without his pack, and fell in but managed to scramble onto the far bank. With the rope tied between two trees and attached to it by a karabiner linked to a waist belt (made from his bear-bagging cord) Larry returned, collected his pack and took it to the other side. Then it was my turn. Larry weighed over 12 stone and was over six foot high and found it difficult. At 5 feet 8 inches and 10 stone I just swung from the karabiner edging along on my heels, the force of the waist-deep water bending me double. To retrieve the rope Larry went back again to tie it by a knot he said came undone when you pulled the cord attached to it but which he hadn't wanted to risk when we crossed with the packs. Unfortunately, just as he reached the bank he let go of the cord! And so he had to cross yet again and repeat the procedure. This meant he'd forded Tilden Creek seven times. That day finished with a dash across an open meadow as a storm broke above us and lightening cracked all around. We had progressed just seven miles.

On and off we met Scott and Dave who'd had similar epics to us. Gentler walking beyond Yosemite National Park took us finally to Echo Lake and the end of our marathon High Sierra crossing. It had been the toughest backpacking trek I'd ever undertaken yet also the most satisfying and the most spectacular in terms of the country passed through. The 400 miles had taken 44 days. In total I'd now walked 942 miles in 83 days and was going to have to increase my daily mileage considerably if I was to reach Canada by early autumn. In Little Norway, a hamlet above Echo Lake, Larry and I were interviewed for the North Lake Tahoe Bonanza paper as the first backpackers of the year to make it through the Sierras. Scott and Dave had arrived with us but had already left when the reporter turned up for a few days relaxation by Lake Tahoe. Although we were now in the easier terrain of the lower northern Sierras Larry and I decided to stay together until we were out of the snow as we expected to encounter more over the next few hundred miles.

The people at Little Norway were very friendly and allowed us to sleep in their woodshed and use the bar as an office-cum-packing room. We both sent off all the gear we thought we could do without, about 10lb worth in my case, to lighten our packs. As food pick-up points were now only a week or so apart we also had far less weight of food to carry and I felt that, at around 55-60lb, my pack was down to manageable proportions again. During our day of rest and chores at Little Norway two other PCT hikers turned up. One was the first south-bound hiker we'd met. He'd started at Burney in Oregon and was heading for Mount Whitney and had already had problems with snow and creek crossings. We were unable to be reassuring about what lay ahead and when we left he was still considering whether to continue or not. The other walker arrived by bus! He'd made it through the Sierras as far as Tuolumne Meadows with three others who'd abandoned the trail there. He'd continued but had been swept away in Spiller Creek in Yosemite and had twisted and gashed his ankle climbing out. After limping all the way back to Tuolumne he'd decided to give Yosemite a miss and wait for his foot to heal.

From Little Norway we followed the shore of Upper Echo Lake to enter the lake-dotted paradise of Desolation Wilderness. Wildernesss Areas, of which I was to pass through many between here and Canada, are areas in National Forests designated officially as wilderness and protected from all forms of development. Desolation still had much snow but it was soft and thawing and the timberline lakes, Aloha, Heather and Susie shone a brilliant blue under the sun whilst above them towered the steep rocks of Pyramid Peak and the Crystal Range. Dicks Pass at 9,300 feet was the last one on the PCT at this elevation and we descended from it past more lakes, Dicks, Fontanillis, Upper Velma and Middle Velma, into the deep snow of the red fir forest. Many other hikers were out and about now as the 'hiking season' had begun and Desolation Wilderness is a popular area.

Easy travel on mostly snow-free trails in the forest, soon

put the daily mileage above twenty for the first time on the walk. The hitherto fine weather deteriorated and the third night out from Echo Lake it began to rain, a rain that kept up for the next four days. When it wasn't actually raining a low, thick mist dampened everything in and out of the tents. The North Fork American River proved a difficult ford, especially as we no longer had the rope, but once across, an easy walk down the Old Soda Springs Trail led to the little hamlet of Soda Springs which had two luxuries, a 'deli' called the Cheese Store where we lunched on omelettes and coffee, and a laundrette, the first since Mammoth Lakes. Here I collected my smallest food parcel with supplies for just three days in it. Heading back into the woods we spent a night in a hut called Peter Grubb's where we had a huge fire and dried out our gear. Not that it stayed very dry for the wet, misty weather stayed with us for the two days to the next little town, Sierra City, an old gold mining settlement. The hills through this northern section of the Sierras which soon were to merge imperceptibly with the southernmost slopes of the Cascade Range were gentle rounded ones only occasionally rising above the timberline. The going was easy on good trails, forestry tracks and dirt roads despite the large areas of snow that still remained. Yet somehow the sense of excitement and adventure we'd felt in the High Sierra had gone. The rain of course didn't help our morale.

A night in the cabin of forest firefighter Bob Frost in Sierra City where we had showers and again dried out our wet gear, set us up for the five-day trek to Belden, the next tiny cluster of habitation on a trans-mountain highway. Each road cut through a deep pass so we had to descend thousands of feet to these places and then unfortunately climb back out again. In contrast to the High Sierra, the passes had become low points on the route again rather than the highest ones. The climb up from Sierra City was particularly brutal, partly because of the heat and partly because the switchbacks really are steep. Beyond the massive outcrops of the Sierra Buttes we became lost in the snow for the last time in an area of confusing logging roads along one of which the trail had been relocated. Over the next few weeks camping in logged areas and walking on logging roads was to become normal but the weather finally cleared and ahead were views of the snow pyramids of volcanic Mount Shasta and Lassen Peak to draw us on. Also flowers were bursting into bloom all around us and we were surrounded by lupins, paintbrush and mountain mule's ears. It was summer and we had returned to trail backpacking. As the PCT followed the waterless crest here we even had to start carrying water again. Sore feet became a problem too. The heavy boots which had been perfect for the snow of the Sierras were proving too hot for summer forest trails.

On July 6th we reached Belden, descending the overgrown 36 switchbacks down the last six miles to the town in an hour, noting the large quantities of poison oak growing all around, a nasty but innocuous looking plant to be avoided if at all possible. The Belden Post Office PCT Register showed that there were at least twenty PCT backpackers ahead of us who'd skipped the Sierras. At 2,300 feet we were lower than we'd been for two months. From Belden we climbed up through black oak and Douglas fir forest, then the middle layers of ponderosa pines, incense cedars, white fir, sugar pine and finally the dense red fir woods. This range of magnificent trees was for me the best part of the PCT in the northern Sierras.

But we were leaving the Sierras for the volcanic terrain of the Cascades now and two days out of Belden we entered Lassen Volcanic National park. There were many tranquil and subtly beautiful tree-shrouded pools here but also mosquitos by the thousand. Of most interest though were the thermal features, usually smelt before being seen as a strong stench of sulphur permeated the forest. The fumarole of Terminal Geyser spouted water and clouds of steam through a series of yellow sulphur crusted vents whilst Boiling Springs Lake gently steamed in the sunshine, its waters at a constant 125°F. The lake is blue-green in colour due to warm-water algae and is surrounded by small vents puffing out steam and bubbling mud pots slurping away noisily.

Beyond the vulcanism of Lassen we reached another settlement, Old Station, where we pitched camp on Hat Creek Campground then spent a day hitch-hiking into the larger town of Burney in search of supplies. We were looking for shoes and a backpacking store in particular. My heavy boots needed resoling but I planned instead to send them home and buy a lighter pair. Larry needed a new fuel tank cap for his petrol stove as the current one was leaking and caught fire when he tried to use it. This meant we were both cooking on my stove and therefore had to stay together. After two months of travelling with others I wanted to go back to solo backpacking but I couldn't do this until Larry had a working stove. Unfortunately Burney had neither boots nor stove parts, just food, books and socks so our day off was in vain.

An awful, hot, dusty and exhausting trek along the highway for thirty miles took us from Old Station to Burney Falls State Park. En route we visited the curious lava tube called Subway Cave and stopped at every cafe plus a laundromat where I sat in my Goretex salopettes whilst every other bit of clothing was washed. Burney Falls itself is a superb, spring-fed 129-foot waterfall. In the height of the summer the river above the falls dries up and the water spouting though holes in the rocks is all that feeds the falls but on our visit both river and springs were flowing in force. Here we met a solo backpacker called Susie who was hiking the PCT from her home near Lassen to Canada and had only been on the trail a few days.

More days of forest hiking broken by creeks and lakes followed as we began the long 150-mile loop the PCT makes around isolated Mount Shasta. The highlight of the five-day walk from Burney to Castella on the edge of Castle Crags State Park was my first encounter with a bear. Rounding a corner in the trail we heard a sound in the undergrowth above us. Looking up we saw, about fifty feet away, a bear with two cubs feasting on some berries. As one of the cubs came down the hillside toward us the mother stood up for a better view. Having heard many stories of how dangerous she-bears are if they think their cubs are under threat we didn't linger but hurried off down the trail. I was pleased though at finally seeing a bear. Not that they are a problem here. I hadn't bear-bagged my food since leaving Yosemite.

Castella lies in a crowded valley with the Southern Pacific Railway, Interstate 5 and the Sacramento River crammed side by side. Scott and Dave had already passed through as they had hitch-hiked from Burney, but they were hiking to Seiad Valley from here then hitching again to Crater Lake in Oregon to cut out the least interesting sections of the PCT as they didn't have enough time to complete the whole trail. A note said that their stove had actually exploded! Larry was not the only one with problems. A local man who likes to help out trailers offered us a lift into the nearby town of Mount Shasta which we gladly accepted, hoping there to find the equipment we'd failed to find in Burney. This time our day off was worth it as Mount Shasta had an excellent backpacking store called The Fifth Season. Here after much deliberation and against the advice of the staff who thought I was crazy to consider walking 1,300 miles in such light footwear, I bought a pair of $2^{1}/_{2}$-lb Asolo Approach nylon/suede walking shoes with the then new studded KLETS sole. Throwing caution to the winds I committed myself to them by sending home not only my boots but also my running shoes. Larry obtained his stove fuel tank cap so, back in Castella, we finally agreed to split up. I'd travelled 1,000 miles of the 1,300 I'd walked so far with other backpackers and it was nearly three months since I'd been alone, now I had the last 1,200 miles to myself.

Larry left before me on the 160-mile trek to Seiad Valley, a walk mainly through forest that took me eight days. I enjoyed going at my own pace again, stopping when I wanted to and camping when and where I liked. I also started to see far more wildlife, quickly realising just how much more disturbance two people make compared with one. Mule deer were especially common and I saw many birds and another bear. The massive turreted cliffs of Castle Crags were partially encircled then I headed along the crest of the hills, the white cone of Mount Shasta dominating the view. The scenery, pleasant but subdued most of the time since Lassen, sprang into life again briefly as I passed through the Salmon-Trinity and Marble Mountain Wildernesses with their timberline trails, soaring, delicate tarns, marble pavements and other scenery typical of limestone country, much of it reminding me of the Yorkshire Dales back home in Britain. Black Marble Mountain with its long ridge of white marble capped at one end by dark sandstone reminded me of a giant version of Penyghent on the Pennine Way.

However a serious problem arose two days out of Castella when the internal frame of my pack snapped near the base on one side. This made it very uncomfortable to carry as the damaged side kept collapsing. The frame was bolted in and also of a unique British type not available in the USA so it looked as though I would need a new pack. For a while though I had to struggle on with my original one.

Beautiful lakes like the timberline cliff-hemmed Paynes Lake where I camped, abounded, as did the forests of the graceful western and mountain hemlocks. Other backpackers were about especially in the Marble Mountains and I heard about other PCT walkers who'd already passed through including my erstwhile companions. Larry seemed to be several days ahead of me already so I was surprised on dropping down into Seiad Valley to find him on the campground there. He'd been here two days, held up because of the non-arrival of a parcel containing some new boots. These turned up the next day and we travelled together for the first few miles of the PCT in the Siskiyou Mountains where it turns back east to complete the loop round Mount Shasta.

Our camp on the end of the narrow ridge of Lower Devil's Peak had superb views down to Seiad Valley but attracted many mosquitos, necessitating pitching the tents during the night. Larry left early the next morning and I was never to see him again. Two days saw my first view of the Oregon Cascades with a glimpse of the distant rock spire of Mount McGloughlin and shortly afterwards I left California after four months and two thousand miles to enter the state of Oregon somewhere on an undistinguished logged slope. Susie, the backpacker Larry and I had met in Burney Falls had obviously been here as I found notes left for her from a certain Jay J. Johnson who had already been mentioned to me. He had set off nearly nine months previously to walk south along the 2,000-mile Appalachian Trail, row through the Everglades, cycle through Texas and start back north up the PCT. I wondered if I'd have a chance of meeting him and hearing about his mammoth trip. Apart from his untouched yet old-looking notes some noisy, clumsy blue grouse and a few circling red-tailed hawks were all that added interest to the forest walking until I reached Wrangle Gap Camp, described in the Wilderness Press guidebook as 'the answer to an exhausted hiker's prayer. This little-used recreation site . . . has a large stone shelter complete with fireplace, 2 stoves, tables and even a sink with running water!' Given this description I was a little startled to discover on arrival ranks of white tents and the shelter full of trestle tables and cooking gear. Even more startling though were the lines of people sitting at desks writing away furiously! A bizarre sight in the forest setting, looking as it did like a displaced examination room. Which, in fact, was what it was for the writers were students on a geology course finishing their final reports. Being outnumbered, I camped some distance away in the woods and managed to do without the sink and running water.

The students were friendly once their reports were complete, and the next day as I trudged up the dirt road towards Interstate 5 and the town of Ashland (to look for a new pack), a car full of them stopped and offered me a lift which I readily accepted. The date was August 1st and the day a Sunday, so the stores were closed. Ashland has an annual summer Shakespeare festival which was on at that time and the little town was full of references to the plays and sonnets. The main play on at that time was *Henry V*. However instead of imbibing some English culture I'm afraid I have to say I accepted the students' invitation to their end of course party and spent the evening drinking beer, talking and listening to records exactly as I had done at countless student parties back home. The night was spent sleeping on someone's floor.

My second day in Ashland was spent deliberating what pack to buy at the Sun Cycle outdoor shop. They had no internal frames big enough for all my gear, a fact I ascertained by taking in my old pack, dumping the contents on the floor and then trying to repack them in the biggest one they had, much to the amusement of the tolerant and helpful staff. So swallowing my prejudices against pack frames, I chose a North Face Back Magic I model, partly because I knew the company had a reputation for fine products and partly because Dave had picked one up in Mammoth Lakes after his internal frame pack broke and had been very pleased with it. I hoped the 87-litre capacity, front loading, two compartment pack (totally different from my single compartment, top loading old one) would prove adequate as it cost me $177.50 I didn't have. The one that had accompanied me this far, an old friend now, I sadly sent off to its British makers for repair.

Another night on a floor and then Rene who had fed and accommodated me for two days and her friend Ruth drove me back up to the point where I'd been picked up by the students and I continued the trek with my strange-feeling new pack. The PCT in southern Oregon follows the crest of the Cascades which here are low, forested hills with occasional rock outcrops, and large fisherman-dotted lakes; pleasant terrain that made for fast but not spectacular progress. The first night out from Ashland I shared Grouse Gap Shelter with two families who spend a night here every year, and joined in their hot dog and toasted marshmallow supper as a high moon rose through the clouds above the still visible Mount Shasta. The mountain now lay to the south as I had completed my circuit round it.

Seven days through this terrain took me past the huge volcanic rock tower of Pilot Knob, the lakeside fishing resorts at Hyatt Lake and Fourmile Lake and into the valley of Honeymoon Creek. Mount Shasta receded to the south as I turned north again. Ahead lay more mountainous country with Mount McGloughlin and Lucifer Peak and especially the jagged, torn rim of Crater Lake. Grand and noble firs were trees I had not seen before but which occurred several times in this section, their massive trunks soaring above the twisting trail. A little booklet I had purchased, Tom Watts *Pacific Coast Tree Finder,* had proved most useful and I'd now identified nine pines, six firs, four cedars, two spruces and two hemlocks plus the Douglas fir which isn't a true fir at all. The sky high above was cloudy and rain fell occasionally. From Watershed Divide after miles of viewlesss walking in dense mountain hemlock forest I could see, not far ahead, the rock fang of Union Peak and the peaks ringing the southern edge of Crater Lake.

Entering the Crater Lake national Park I filled in my self-issuing permit then spent my first night at the official roadside Mazama Campground for a fee of $5. That evening I went to an outdoor slide lecture on the Cascade volcanoes which was useful and informative. A little knowledge of geology and vulcanism adds much to one's appreciation of the scenery in this area. So much so that the next day in the National Park Headquarters where my mail awaited me at the tiny post office I bought a copy of Stephen Harris' *Fire and Ice: The Story of the Cascade Volcanoes.* I learnt that the 7,000-foot high Crater Lake (which is not actually on the PCT but a few miles away though I cannot imagine any backpacker stays in the forest and fails to visit it) is not really in a crater but rather in a caldera, the hole left when a volcano blew its top then collapsed in on itself. Crater Lake is 1,932 feet deep (the deepest in the USA and the seventh deepest in the world) and five to six miles across whilst the basin it lies in is nearly 4,000 feet deep. Until about 6,500 years ago the original volcano, named Mazama, was the highest in Oregon rising to 12,000 feet, five thousand feet higher than the caldera it left behind. When the mountain erupted an estimated 15 cubic miles of ash and other material was ejected and traces of this have been found as far away as British Columbia and Alberta in Canada. The caldera then began to fill with water to give us the Crater Lake of today. The water is very pure as there are few sediments and very little surface water running into it. This accounts for the brilliant ultramarine colour that greets you as you reach the rim and look 900 feet down to this fairy tale jewel. Rarely have I been so moved on seeing a view as on first seeing Crater Lake. Despite the foreknowledge and the pictures I'd seen it was still breathtaking and I spent hours staring across it, fascinated by the deep blue colour, the circular shape and the coloured rock strata of the unbroken rim of cliffs stretching in a great curve around it.

The National Park is popular of course and a road runs right round the lake on the rim so I was not alone here. Amongst the gift shops I bought some much needed groceries before heading down from the rim to find water and to camp on the backcountry site of Lightning Springs. That night it rained heavily and I woke to thick clouds and a cold, wet wind. Back at Crater Lake grey threads of cloud raced over the rough dull waters and round the tops of the secondary volcanic cones that form islands. The mist wreaths gave an other-worldly air to the scene but I couldn't stay long as the next water lay 25 miles away on the other side of the strange 'Oregon Desert'. This is a flat area of pumice sand through which all the water drains, and which is dotted with widely spaced, stunted lodgepole pines whose roots stretch down far enough to reach the water table below. Thicker woods of mountain hemlock and western white pine hemmed the trail as I passed under 9,182-foot Mount Thielson, a splendid jagged spire made up of twisted bands of yellow and red rock. Thielson is the remaining hard plug of a volcano and so the geological opposite of Crater Lake. I camped by Mount Thielson Creek on a well-used but attractive site that boasted a toilet and a garbage pit. From the tent at dawn I had a magnificent view of the fang of Mount Thielsen soaring up above me with the rising sun shining on the rocks. A frost had occurred and the snow patches on the trail were rock hard as I passed the volcanic ridges of Sawtooth Rocks and Tipsoo Peak. Twelve boy scouts all heavily laden toiled past me heading for the Thielsen camp. Mosquito infested but interestingly named Nip and Tuck Lakes provided a camp after I'd encountered a southbound PCT backpacker just doing the Oregon section. He warned of the 'terrible' mosquitos ahead.

Tiny Cascade Summit's store had my parcel and also a reasonable selection of trail foods plus free overnight camping and showers for PCT hikers, a welcome touch! The PCT Register showed that Larry was already five days ahead of me and Scott and Dave nine. Another backpacker called Mark who was just doing the Oregon and Washington PCT (I say 'just', it's a 1,000-mile walk!) turned up so I had company for the first time in a couple of weeks. This was obviously boy scout season (it was mid August) for during the next few days I encountered literally hundreds of them including a mass camp at middle Rosary Lake that filled the woods for hundreds of yards. I passed this by as I did Wait Here Lake, after hesitating a little, to camp by Bobby Lake, a day's walk from the Three Sisters Wilderness. I had my full set of Oregon guides now and was beginning to build up a picture of the PCT in the state. Relatively flat and easy to walk it spent most of its time in the forest but every so often would burst out of the confines of the trees to cross an area of volcanic scenery that was spectacular (as at Crater Lake) and, to come were the Three Sisters Wilderness, Mount Washington Wilderness, Mount Jefferson Wilderness and Mount Hood Wilderness, each one an area where the forces of vulcanism had thrust mountains high above the surrounding hills and left behind lava flows and cinder cones to fascinate and intrigue.

Hurrying on towards the distant peaks of the Three Sisters, which appeared tantalisingly through the trees every so often, I was halted by a movement in a small, shallow lily-dotted pond. I sat down slowly and quietly on my pack and had the privilege of watching a she otter and three cubs swimming and diving in the clear water before drying themselves on a rock in the sun only a few feet away from me. As I approached the Wilderness I began to meet other backpackers, a total of fourteen on the day I entered the area. Three of these had seen Larry who was now six days ahead of me and also Scott and Dave who were only one day ahead of Larry. For the first time the remote possibility that I might catch them up flickered through my mind — a possibility soon forgotten as I crossed Koosah Mountain to see Bachelor Butte, the ragged edge of appropriately named Broken Top and red rocked South Sister standing in line with the more distant cones of Middle and North Sisters — glorious mountains all!

The shores of Camelot Lake were replete with tents so I went on to camp by the slightly less crowded Sisters Mirror Lake. Here I had a shock when I heard steps, looked up and saw Wayne Fuiten (last seen in Welden over three months before) approaching. He was not surprised however, having been following my entries in the trail registers since Crater Lake. He'd had a complicated time, taking off two weeks whilst some of the snow melted then walking south from northern California to Weldon before hitching north again and continuing towards Canada. I was now to see him most days during the rest of my walk along the Oregon PCT though his regulated walking style and my haphazard one didn't gell of course, but camp sites being few and far between we tended to use the same ones. The next day I shot nearly a whole roll of film as I went past the Three Sisters from Sisters Mirror Lake to South Mathieu Lake. In my journal that evening I wrote: 'A superb day! One of the best! Glorious mountain country and fantastic volcanic features. Hiked through meadows, forests and parkland past the Three Sisters; 10,358-foot South Sister large, rounded and complex, 10,047-foot Middle Sister a pure cone and 10,085-foot North Sister a jagged rock remnant. Plus glaciers on all of them. And then lava flows, curling rivers of frozen basalt and huge mounds of pyroclastic cinders (you can tell I was carrying a geology book!), and a switch-backing path up the flow into the breached wall of Collier Cone'. Ahead further volcanic spires soared above the dark forest, in a line fading away to the north lay Mount Washington, Three-Fingered Jack, Mount Jefferson and, barely visible, Mount Hood.

Soon I was in the Mount Washington Wilderness and undertaking the long haul up the almost barren Bellknap Crater, which was like walking on a slag heap. Underfoot lay black coke-like lava, rough and unstable, a severe test of my lightweight shoes and the balance of my new pack. Beyond

Mount Washington and a burned out ghostly lodgepole pine forest I reached Santiam Lodge; the only youth hostel on the PCT where I stayed, along with Joe, a southbound PCT backpacker who hoped to at least reach the Sierras before the autumn snow barred his way. Waynes' family had whisked him off home to Seattle but returned the next morning to give me a lift into the town of Sisters to do some shopping and cash a money order. Highlight of the day though was the traverse under the rocky spires of Three Fingered Jack with their convoluted heat-twisted strata in the southern part of the Mount Jefferson Wilderness. But the next day was even better with a walk through alpine meadows past timberline lakes under the graceful cone of the 10,497-foot Jefferson itself, one of the finest peaks I saw on the whole walk. I camped near Russell Lake looking across the unbelievably perfect, grove dotted parkland to the great, glacier-smeared north-west face of the mountain. A subtly shaded pink sunset rounded off a memorable day.

As with all the mountain sections of the trail in wooded Oregon, Mount Jefferson was soon left behind and I dropped back into the forest again. Green would be the colour for the PCT in Oregon. Two long but easy days saw me past Olallie Lake, where I lunched on Coca-cola and doughnuts ('donuts' in the USA) from the tiny store. From here I looked back across the tranquil waters to graceful Mount Jefferson, and across the 45th Meridian, half way between the equator and the North Pole. Although I had now walked hundreds of miles in dense forest in both northern California and Oregon I was still able to admire the woods around the Salmon River where majestic stands of Douglas fir, western hemlock, western red cedar and Alaska cedar rose above the trail. Camps at Trooper Springs and Timothy Lake were both spent with Wayne and I arrived at Timberline Lodge, a grandiose downhill ski complex on the slopes of Mount Hood (at 11,235 feet the highest as well as the most northerly of Oregon's volcanoes), in his company. Here we found we had different interests as Wayne settled down in the lounge with a case of beer whilst I had a huge meal in the plush restaurant. We bivvied a few hundred yards away from the lodge ready to return for breakfast. Here at 5,940 feet and just on the timberline, ski-ing is possible all year round though avalanche danger means that in summer the runs are closed by midday.

The traverse round Mount Hood was enjoyable though arduous as the trail, which here is part of one that completely encircles the peak, makes many steep ascents and descents in and out of glacial stream canyons. Unlike the PCT in the volcanic areas further south where it rarely rises above timberline, on Mount Hood the trail really is on the mountain itself and I liked the feel of that. This close I could see the details of the superb ice falls, cliffs, hanging valleys and glaciers. The Washington state volcanoes, Mounts Adams (12,276 feet), St. Helens (complete with steam plume) and the mighty 14,410-foot Rainier, came into view during the open stony traverse round Indian Mountain the following day. On Wayne's recommendation (this was, after all, his home terrain) I forsook the PCT to join the Eagle Creek Trail for the descent to the Columbia River where I left, after 27 days and 450 miles, the state of Oregon.

The descent began with a very steep jarring jog down the unmaintained Indian Springs Trail to a junction with the Eagle Creek Trail. On reaching Eagle Creek itself the hitherto pleasant character of the wooded descent changed dramatically. A succession of beautiful waterfalls and pools led down to the Columbia River with stupendous Tunnel Falls bringing the East Fork Eagle Creek down to the main river as the centrepiece. Here the narrow, exhilarating trail is blasted into the side of a vertical cliff 75 feet above the river, passing behind the 150-foot drop of Tunnel Falls in a spray-drenched rock passageway — a superb and imaginative piece of trail building which I could have wandered up and down for many hours. Wayne and I met here in the late afternoon, as we had arranged, for only then does the sun shine on the falls, so that we could take photographs of each other on the brink, so to speak. The trail is naturally very popular and camping is restricted to certain areas. We stayed at Blue Ridge Camp. Only 1,120 feet high, this was the lowest camp on the walk so far but would not be for long as it lay just 8 miles from the PCT's low point of 150 feet at the crossing of the Columbia River. More waterfalls, rocks and narrow paths led down to the trailhead and dirt roads to the little town of Cascade Locks where I was treated to a sumptuous picnic by Wayne's parents who'd come out to meet him again.

Camp in Cascade Locks Marine Park was on an island in

the Columbia and here I met another PCT backpacker doing the Oregon and Washington sections called Robert, and finally Jay J. Johnson who I'd heard so much about. He admitted that after nearly nine months and nine thousand miles he was growing tired of the trail and looking forward to finishing. Southbound backpackers I met at the trailhead for the Eagle Creek Trail had said Larry was about a week in front of me but Scott and Dave only four days away and intent on averaging fifteen miles per day through Washington. I hoped to do twenty and some rough calculations showed me I might just catch them before Canada. The mystery of Jay's notes to Susie was explained. They'd been left when he'd been ahead of her on the trail and was worried she'd miss the route. Sadly she'd had to abandon her hike after catching a serious stomach infection, a major fear of all PCT backpackers, that had landed her in hospital in Ashland.

The walk across the Bridge of the Gods into Washington cost me fifty cents. I had just 480 miles and one state to go. For the first time I began the think that I would actually complete the walk. People I spoke to now instead of expressing astonishment that I was walking to Canada were astonished to hear I had walked from Mexico, now over 2,000 miles away. Along with my maps and food the post office in Stevenson on the Washington banks of the Columbia produced an edition of the Pacific Crest Club Quarterly sent to me by Warren and which contained the letters I'd sent him telling the story of the walk up to Bullfrog Lake in the High Sierra. Reading these was a very strange experience. Was I really still on the same journey? My shoes had a few seams coming apart so I visited a cobbler to have them stitched up as I reckoned they'd last another 480 miles with a little care. Jay Johnson had told me he walked in $25 work boots and only the weekenders seemed to wear traditional heavy, expensive mountain boots! Most of the long distance backpackers I met had changed to lightweight boots or shoes.

Two days of climbing saw me back up in the hills as I started the last month of my walk. The waterless 17 miles and 4,000 feet of ascent from Panther Creek to Sheep Lake (an unappealing muddy puddle), in stifling humidity was hard but mitigated by glimpses of the huge glacier-spread bulk of Mount Adams looming up ahead. Rain overnight at

Sheep Lake (whose dank waters I drank liberally laced with purifying tablets), continued into the next day accompanied by a white mist that dampened everything. I had passed the time and place for continuous sunny weather now. The Washington Cascades have a wet, variable climate anyway and in September, which was only three days away, the first snows of winter can fall and storms are likely. In the drizzle I met Jay, heading for the lower Cascade Crest Trail, his mind on the simplest, easiest and quickest way to reach Canada. Dense, wet, cloud-enshrouded forests were the scene for the next few days with camps by Big Mosquito Lake and the White Salmon River, which despite its name was a dry gully where the trail crossed it though a noise of falling water led me to a gushing spring in dense undergrowth fifty yards downstream.

The weather cleared at, scenically, just the right time as I emerged from the confines of the dripping woods to traverse at timberline below Mount Adams in the Wilderness Area. From here on, bar one or two days in logged areas, the whole PCT in Washington was a delight, a magnificent finish to the walk giving the most sustained area of mountain grandeur and wilderness apart from the High Sierra. Flowery meadows interspersed with groves of sub-alpine fir and mountain hemlock gave a soft foreground to the massive White Salmon Glacier and the steep, fractured, ice-fall-ridden Adams Glacier that poured down Mount Adams, a bulky, flat-topped mountain off whose sides the white ice flowed in great surges, split and cracked with crevasses. Wreaths of dirty cumulus drifted around distant peaks far to the north whilst snowless Mount St. Helens gave off a few wisps of steam. Just before my forest camp by Midway Creek I watched a rich russet pine marten dart across the trail with a small bundle in its mouth.

The sandy site was enveloped in thick mist at dawn but it had cleared by the time I set off on a long 22-mile day up into the Goat Rocks Wilderness where for once the PCT actually follows the crest of the hills. This area of jagged, narrow ridges, small glaciers and tiny peaks (the highest being Old Snowy Mountain at 7,930 feet) is the remains of a large volcano. I entered it with a curving ascent round the Walupt Lake Basin in mixed forest with the rugged vista really opening out on the above–timberline climb to the 6,460-foot Cispus Pass from where I looked across the deep

Klickikat River valley to the barren rock and talus wall of Gilbert Peak. A final 1,000-foot 2-mile climb up the slopes of Old Snowy through glacial run-off washes and dusty scree slopes interspersed with rich alpine meadows led to the tiny rough stone Dana May Yelverton Shelter at 7,040 feet surrounded by wind and frost-stunted four to ten foot high hemlocks and whitebark pine. I dumped my gear in the shelter then climbed up to the ridge just above it, a superb vantage point, to watch the sunset and the impressive panorama of Mounts Adams, St. Helens and Rainier. A bright moon rose as the sun set over the dark, permanently frozen, Goat Lake. After months in the forest I felt a sense of euphoria at being back high in the mountains again. The shelter kept the overnight wind off but the holes in the roof would have rendered it useless in rain, although I could have pitched the tent inside on the earth floor.

A pretty pink, red and orange dawn saw me off on a grand day of narrow, winding, mountain paths above deep, glaciated cirques, surrounded by jagged rock peaks and grey, debris-spattered glaciers. A saddle at 7,080 feet just above the shelter gave the highest point on the PCT in Washington as I crossed above the hard ice of the Packwood Glacier to wander around pinnacles on the knife-edge crest between Egg Butte and Elk Pass. A sign warned that there were no passing places for stock on this section of the trail. Then, down in the flat hanging valley of wooded McCall Basin, I lost the trail and my route completely. After a futile hour going round and round the basin trying to find a path out, I bushwhacked out on compass bearings and had a terrible mile of stumbling through dense forest, and clambering over fallen trees before finding the trail again at Lutz Lake. This tiring delay turned what should have been an easy day with plenty of time to reach the highway and store at White Pass, my next supply point, into an arduous push to reach the post office before it shut. I reached Lutz Lake at midday with 11 miles and 2,000 feet of ascent left. I expected the post office to shut at 5 pm. I hammered up the climb to pause above beautiful, pale blue Shoe Lake and then continued across the rough but scenic slopes of Hagback Ridge before racing down into the forest to reach Highway 12 and then White Pass at 4.45, hot, exhausted and very thirsty. I felt faint in the store and sat outside for a few minutes downing a couple of cans of Coke before examining my mail. It turned out I could have obtained it at any time during the evening, the running of the store/PO/gas station being a very friendly and relaxed affair. Reading the register, I discovered that Wayne had passed through that morning and Scott and Dave four days ago, intending, they wrote, to finish in 18 days time on the 20th September. The long day ended with a bivvy on the White Pass Campground beside dragonfly haunted Leech Lake.

I woke to the varied cries of camp-raiding gray and stellars jays and the steady drumming of hairy woodpeckers plus a leaden sky that soon led to heavy, steady rain. Without really thinking about it I had a rest day, my first since Ashland thirty days before when I'd bought my new pack which was now well-used and comfortable. The Cracker Barrel Grocery Store at White Pass had a small laundromat and allowed trailers to take showers so I spent the day alternating between there and the Continental Cafe across the road in the ski lodge where Jay turned up mid-morning. For the first time since those long-ago pre-Weldon, pre-High Sierra days I began to feel as though I was part of a community of backpackers on route for Canada. Offered space for sleeping above the store I shared it with three backpackers heading for Goat Rocks Wilderness for the Labor Day weekend that marks the end of the summer holiday season in the USA. The full moon that night was the last one of the walk though I never saw it as it poured with rain well into the morning. When the moon was full again I would be back home in England.

I sent on a postcard to Scott and Dave at Stehekin, the last supply point before Canada, in case I didn't catch them up and also one to a hiker calling himself the 'Doo-Dah Man' whose entries in the registers were annoying me. He had stated bluntly that going through the Sierras in the snow was impossible, that we couldn't have done it and therefore must have skipped them like he had. I was making no special claims for our journey but I didn't like the implication that I was a liar, so I wrote a few choice words in the register too. Before leaving White Pass I weighed my pack, and with six days' supplies in it, it came to 63lb.

I had a muddy, slippery, viewless hike out of the pass all the way to a camp at Twin Lakes on a trail badly mangled by horses. Being a holiday weekend I saw dozens of other backpackers, mostly heading south. The twenty miles and

2,700 feet of ascent in $7^1/_2$ hours to Twin Lakes put me on the edge of Mount Rainier National Park through which the PCT passes for a few miles and which gave excellent views of the mountain itself, the highest by far in the Washington Cascades, dominating the view for miles around. At Chinook Pass I crossed one of the access roads into the park and for six miles either side of this busy highway the trails and hillsides were packed with day-hikers — justifiably as the views are superb and the walking enjoyable as the trail winds around ridges, across meadows and past pretty pools with only a few groves of trees so that there are unimpeded vistas all the way back to the Goat Rocks Wilderness and Mount Adams. Every lake was surrounded by tents. By Sheep Lake, I met a backpacker walking from Snoqualmie Pass, where I was heading; he had done the whole PCT in 1975 — no snow in the Sierras in May then he told me. He'd seen Scott and Dave and said they were having a rest day in Snoqualmie the next Monday which was only two days before I hoped to reach the pass. I might catch them yet!

The hikers I met were all friendly though describing my journey time after time did take up much of the afternoon. One woman said 'you must be hungry after walking all that way!' and gave me some fresh plums, cucumber, tomatoes and a beef sandwich which was more that I could eat but she wouldn't let me refuse. The excellent walking continued through the narrow notch of Sourdough Gap and along the narrow crest to Big Crow Basin where I camped next to the trail.

The hills were becoming more rounded and wooded as I left Rainier and its environs behind and I had a lengthy descent along this dwindling Cascade crest before climbing up to a camp on a bench below Blowout Mountain, a climb nourished by handfuls of succulent huckleberries plucked from the bushes along the way. Views of cloud-swathed Rainier, to the south now, were good but more exciting were the peaks ahead, the rugged cluster of steep-sided summits that made up the enticingly named Alpine Lakes Wilderness across Snoqualmie Pass, my next supply point. A thick mist, gusty wind and flurries of rain were the start of a long day that was one of the worst, if not *the* worst, of the whole walk. Not that it was hard or exhausting or dangerous. It wasn't, it was just soul destroying because of what had been done to the land. Virtually all the forest had been cleared but the trail was a muddy, snagged mess. The sound of chainsaws and bulldozers echoed all around. The area was a huge tree slaughterhouse. There were roads everywhere, and there was too much hot sweaty uphill work, I just wanted to escape the blasted terrain. Near Snowshoe Butte I was amazed to see a backpacker coming towards me. Who else, I wondered, would choose to walk through this desolation? Paul turned out to be a PCT hiker of course, no-one else would walk here. But rather than a through hiker he was walking a section of the trail for a week each summer. So far it had taken him four years to walk this far from Canada. At that rate it would take him another 28 years to reach Mexico! Ahead of me, Paul said, were an Australian PCT walker called Ron Ellis and Greg Poiner, a hiker I'd last heard of at Weldon where I'd been told he'd set off to attempt the Sierras solo in early May.

Only a few hours later I caught up with Greg and walked the rest of the day with him. He'd left Mexico on March 12th, three weeks before me, and had started through the Sierras but descended once he realised how much snow there was left. Wanting to do a continuous walk but not wanting to trudge up the road in Owens valley he'd headed east to travel up the White Mountains, the desert range that reaches 14,000 feet and lies between the Sierras and the Rockies. They are also the range Colin Fletcher describes in his book *The Thousand Mile Summer*, an account of a six-month, 1,000-mile backpacking trip up the length of California that had been an inspiration both to me and to Greg. I enjoyed talking to him, feeling I'd met an imaginative and adventurous backpacker after my own heart, in complete contrast to all those I'd met who weren't prepared to leave their designated routes or take any risks. Meeting him restored my morale on a day when it fell very low — a day when even camping was a problem due to the logging operations. We were unable to reach the lake we'd hoped to camp by as the trail had been destroyed and a vast giant latticework of felled but uncleared trees blocked the way. Eventually just as dark was falling we found two bumpy spots either side of the trail just big enough for the tents. Mosquitos and midges ended an unsatisfactory day.

The sound of heavy logging operations starting up nearby woke us early and had us on our way. This was the only section of the trail I tried to run away from. The vandalised scenery continued but we distracted ourselves with conversation and fast walking and at 1.30 pm we were descending by the ski tows to Snoqualmie Pass where Interstate 90 roars across the Cascades and there is the usual collection of a ski lodge, cafe, store and Post Office that are found at most of the road crossings along the Washington PCT. The Commonwealth Campground harboured Ron Ellis, the Australian, who complained that people kept asking him if he was the English PCT hiker! I was often asked in the last few weeks whether I was the Australian or English backpacker by people who assured me, as they did Ron, that to them our accents sounded identical. Ron was doing the PCT in bits. He'd done Campo to Acton, only starting on May 13th, but had then travelled up to Belden and was hoping to do the Sierras and the Mohave sections after reaching Canada though he knew the first winter snows might stop him. He'd been distracted he said by the volcanoes and had taken days off to climb every one of them since Lassen Peak! A message in the trail register from Scott and Dave said they hoped to finish on the 24th. Seeing them again was becoming more probable. I hoped to finish by the 24th too.

However a delay ensued as a savage storm swept in, wreathing the pass and campground in swirling mist and sheets of rain and bringing tales of snow with the weekenders as they retreated from the higher trails. I spent the day in the cafe writing letters and talking to the PCT walkers as they drifted in during the day. As at the beginning, the end was producing a confluence of through hikers. By evening there were seven of us there including Ron DiBaccio who I'd last seen in Cabazon with his girlfriend Cheryl and who, alone now, was still on the trail after a summer spent between it and the coast. He'd been behind me since rejoining the trail in northern California, determined to catch me up and only managing to do so because he'd injured his ankle in Big Crow Basin and had had to be rescued. He was brought down on horseback and caught a lift round here to rest for a few days before continuing again. Ron arrived with Robert who I'd met in Cascade Locks with Jay, who also turned up later. The storm continuing, I had most of the next day off as well, finally leaving at three in the afternoon in cloud and with snow dusting the lower hillsides.

At 5,000 feet, 2,000 feet above Snoqualmie Pass, I found slippery wet snow lying on top of slippery wet mud that required care in its negotiation, especially as the route wound round steep slopes above deep valleys. Even in the cloud this was a dramatic section of the PCT. Camp was made after only 7½ miles by Gravel Lake and I went to sleep hoping for better weather. But it was not to be, at least not yet. I woke to find a fresh fall of snow several inches deep covering the tent. It was not raining and the snow on the ground was thawing, leaving me camped in a rapidly spreading puddle. The humidity made everything damp, and the air was harshly cold. I walked in all my clothes and still felt chilled and wet. My feet were sodden, there being several holes in the tattered uppers of my shoes. I vowed to push on as hard as possible on every clear day from now on and prayed that the onset of winter wouldn't prevent the successful completion of my walk in its last stages. I used and was glad of the ice axe as the snow was up to six inches deep on the higher sections of the trail which were often narrow, cut into the steep, rocky hillsides. I left the snow to descend to Park Lakes Basin then down sixty-six switch-backs to Lemah Creek where I camped on a very wet site. I had seen nothing all day.

Jay and Robert who'd been camped only a quarter of a mile away passed my camp as I was dawdling over breakfast on a day that looked as though it could go either way. I caught them up at the top of the long climb up Escondido Ridge by which time the storm, after three days of continuous rain and snow, had finally abated. The clearing weather made me realise that I was in the middle of some spectacular and rugged mountain country. Across the deep Lemah Valley the hanging glaciers of Lemah Peak glistened in the sunshine. I was entering the North Cascades, an area of steep rocky peaks densely packed together above deep valleys that is undoubtedly the wildest and most rugged country the PCT passes through. Following Jay's example I spread out my wet gear on the warm rocks to dry whilst I had lunch. An excellent scenic walk followed across the upper Escondido Ridge and I could finally appreciate the grandeur of this area. Then long, easy angled but seemingly interminable switchbacks led down to a camp beside the Waptus River. This was to be the pattern throughout the North Cascades: long climbs to ridges and high passes followed by long steep descents into deep wooded valleys then immediately another climb. Along with the Yosemite section the PCT here had the most feet of ascent and descent per mile of anywhere along its length.

The superb tower of Cathedral Rock (6,724 feet) and the snowy slopes of Mount Daniel (7,899 feet) were highlights of the trek over Cathedral and Deception Passes though the really spectacular view was from Surprise Pass, a wonderful view of shining white Glacier Peak (10,541 feet), the next in line of the strato-volcanoes. However, unlike in northern California, Oregon and Washington to Snoqualmie Pass, the Cascades here are not a range of wooded hills only occasionally rising above timberline, but a rugged mountain range with glaciers and cliffs and rock peaks amongst which there are also occasional volcanoes. For the first time since the Sierras I felt as though I was walking continuously day after day in real mountain country and this continued for the rest of the walk, making the last fortnight a grand finale indeed. Here in the Alpine Lakes Wilderness the final glory of the PCT was beginning.

September 14th dawned beautifully clear. It was my 33rd birthday. The clarity of the views was excellent all day as a cold, east wind blew preventing any heat haze from forming. I travelled 23 miles over Trap Pass which gave a good view of Thunder Mountain and down to Stevens Pass and Highway 2 where for once there was no ski resort or store. I ended the day at the rather decrepit wooden shelter called Janice Cabin where I found Jay and Ron Ellis and also plenty of mice. A brilliant starry sky gave a hard frost that felt like autumn. The changing colours gave the lie to the sun's illusion that summer was still here: reds and browns were beginning to predominate amongst the undergrowth and along the stream banks. I spent a day walking with Ron, a day that gave views of Glacier Peak ahead, Mount Stuart to the south-east and especially of Mount Rainier, large, white and seemingly floating above the forest to the south. On the shoulder of Skykomish Peak we found the best blueberries of the walk so far and spent half an hour eating them before descending to camp with Jay at pretty timberline Sally Ann Lake. A beautiful soft dawn had me awake early looking south to the dark edges of rose-tinted peaks. Again the clarity of the light was superb as a cold north-east breeze gave a sharp, etched look to the mountains; it was the best light since the High Sierras. A great walk ensued across open, almost treeless autumn green hillsides dotted with patches of red and purple berry bushes.

Ahead stood the glaring, almost painful, white of Glacier Peak then from Red Pass we had a stupendous view of the rugged glacier-covered peaks of the North Cascades. The 756 glaciers of the North Cascades make up nearly half the glaciers in the USA outside of Alaska and from Red Pass it looked like it with splashes of white everywhere. Here I left Ron, whose company I'd appreciated, as he was taking time off from the PCT to climb Glacier. I wanted to reach Canada so I pressed on, entering the Glacier Peak Wilderness and camping by Glacier Creek. The last days of summer continued as I crossed Fire Creek Pass and passed by lovely, half-frozen Mica Lake set in a rugged alpine cirque. Unfortunately beyond the deep canyon of Milk Creek I could see the trail switchbacking up the 1,900 feet east wall for $2^1/2$ miles. Worse though was the leg-pounding, switch-backing descent down to the canyon bottom. In the dim distance I could just make out the white cone of Mount Baker, the last volcano before Canada. Camp was down in the woods by the Suiattle River near a group of hunters and their horses. I'd met a few hunters over the past few days and heard the occasional shot as the season was just starting and that night as I sat in the tent doorway one popped up suddenly waving his rifle to ask me the time! The only thing I felt like hunting were the mice which were becoming increasingly bold causing me to hang my food from branches after they'd gnawed into some trail mix. At this camp one mouse entered the tent and ran all over my shoes, rubbish, pans and pack coming within a few inches of me, apparently unalarmed by the torchlight. It seemed to have an unhealthy fascination for my socks.

During the night I woke with a sharp pain in my head. The mouse was chewing my hair! I zipped the tent door shut and rubbed my head ruefully. I'd survived rattlesnake country and bear country only to be molested by a mouse! Presumably these rodents were fattening themselves up for the rapidly approaching winter. Autumn tints of red, brown, yellow and green coated the hillsides as the PCT wound by the rugged stratified face of Fortress Mountain. The metamorphic rocks of the Cascades in northern

Washington give a distinctive appearance to the mountains that is unlike that anywhere else along the PCT, an appearance more akin to that of the Canadian Rockies than the rest of the Pacific Coast ranges. Around the rock-girt cirques below, Plummer and Sitting Bull Mountains the trail is magnificent, traversing high above the forest which lies below, stretching into the distance along the perfect u-shaped valley.

I was heading for a backcountry campsite called Five Mile Camp, recommended in the guidebook, that lay down in the forest near Pass Creek. As I approached I could see shapes and hear voices. The figures turned towards me and we all let out shouts of glee. After 12 weeks and 1,400 miles I'd met up again with Scott and Dave, just 100 miles from the Canadian border. We had a grand reunion, all trying to tell our tales at once. Too tired to pitch the tent I slept outside. Instead of mice a deer disturbed my night continually approaching me noisily then backing off when I shone my torch at it.

A few miles away lay a roadhead from where a bus took us down by Lake Chelan to the little hamlet of Stehekin, which is only accessible by boat or plane, (the road does not leave the valley). Here I collected my last food parcel, last set of maps and last mail. I spent a day watching the sea planes land and take off and planning my supplies for the last six days. Back at the trailhead I left the others after a night in the shelter eager to reach the border. They were planning on taking six days to the finish but I hoped to walk it in four. Suddenly the realisation that I was going to make it to Canada had hit me and I couldn't rest but was urged on by excitement and a nagging fear that something might go wrong at the last minute. Also I felt I wanted to finish alone, to be able to take it all in and experience whatever emotions came.

Ascending back up into the Cascades for the last time by Bridge Creek I rounded a wooded bend in the trail to come face to face with a black bear. It was only about thirty feet away and walking towards me. For a second or two we both froze then the bear ran off, uphill, rippling through the undergrowth and brushing aside bushes as though they did not exist. I was surprised by the fluidity and grace of movement of such an apparently bulky and ponderous animal and I knew then why one is always advised not to run

153

away from a bear. This was the closest I'd come to one of these prime symbols of wilderness and I was glad to have had such a close encounter. The North Cascades Highway, the last cross-mountain road before the border, was crossed at Rainy Pass. I left the North Cascades National Park which I'd been in for only a few miles, before I camped by Porcupine Creek. The final seventy miles were accomplished in three days. Days of glorious scenery and a fitting end to a magnificent wilderness walk. From the narrow notch of Cutthroat Pass I had a long traverse past arid-looking rock peaks, across scree and talus slopes, and long trails lined with the reds and yellow of autumn. The feeling that summer was ending was amplified by the groves of alpine larches whose needles were turning a bright yellow that matched that of the Golden Horn granodiorite rocks of Tower Mountain and Mount Hardy. The PCT here lies well to the east of most of the Cascade range and is in the rain shadow of the higher mountains to the west, hence its dryness.

I relished these last days and particularly the final high camps. Backpacking is essentially about living in the wilderness and the quality of the camp sites used is central to the activity. The Pacific Crest Trail gives site after site of the highest excellence and this is maintained right to the finish. After a long switch-backing climb straight up the canyon wall from Glacier Pass I enjoyed my penultimate camp by a tiny trickling creeklet amongst alpine larch and sub-alpine fir at 6,600 feet just below Tatie Peak. A crescent moon hung over the bare rocks of the hillsides above me. An overnight frost heralded a fine day that had me traversing at timberline between a series of passes with magnificent views all around and the vivid splashes of autumn closer to hand. A few maples, a startling scarlet in colour, hinted at the closeness of Canada. My final high-level camp was by a barely flowing spring on a small shelf a mile or so before Rock Pass, with the dry rock summits of the Pasayten Wilderness above me.

September 24th, my 174th day since leaving Campo on the Mexican border, dawned with thin cloud stretched over the peaks which the early sun turned a dark, sombre red. Soon it began to rain and a cold wind blew. So I completed the PCT bundled up against the weather as I passed rugged Three Fools Peak and pretty Hopkins Lake before descending to reach Monument 78 on the international frontier at 12.45 pm. I took some photographs, despite the torrential rain, of the 4^1/$_2$-foot bronze monument that stands in a small clearing in the forest. After 2,600 miles I wanted some record of my arrival in Canada. The pillar opens up and inside I found messages from previous PCT hikers to which I added a few comments of my own. Then it was back on with my pack for the last time for the final seven-mile walk to Manning Park and Highway 3 and a wet camp on Cold Springs Campground. The Pacific Crest Trail walk was over. I felt pleased, of course, but also very, very sad. A part of my life was over too.

6

USA

THE CONTINENTAL DIVIDE
3,000 MILES DOWN THE ROCKIES
FROM CANADA TO MEXICO

During the Pacific Crest Trail walk I learnt of a proposed trail down the length of the Rocky Mountains from Canada to Mexico, to be called the Continental Divide Trail. Warren Rogers told me that his counterpart on the CDT was one Jim Wolf who had already written a number of guidebooks to suggested routes for the trail. This information ticked away in the back of my mind and by the time I finished the PCT I knew what my next major backpacking project would be: an attempt on a complete border to border Continental Divide walk.

The Continental Divide is so called because it is the watershed of America: the line that separates water that runs into the Atlantic Ocean from that which runs into the Pacific. In North America this watershed, which in its entirety runs from the Bering Sea to Tierra del Fuego, is to be found in the Rocky Mountains which are actually a series of very different mountain ranges rather than just the one the name implies. My intention was to follow the Divide as closely as possible from Canada to Mexico. The distance is about 3,000 miles and I hoped to complete the walk in five to six months.

Although officially designated as a National Scenic Trail by the US Congress in 1978 the Continental Divide Trail does not yet exist so I had to plan my own route linking sections of cross-country travel, existing trails, dirt roads, old stockways, miners' tracks and, as infrequently as possible, paved highways. This lack of a trail made the walk a much tougher challenge than the Pacific Crest Trail had been. Jim Wolf's four guidebooks to the northern half of the Divide (for Northern Montana, Southern Montana and Idaho, Wyoming and Northern Colorado) provided me with ideas for routes for the first 1,600 miles and Jim also sent me route suggestions for the rest of the trail (in

Southern Colorado and New Mexico). He and the Continental Divide Trail Society were very helpful and I bought all the back numbers of the society's bi-annual newsletter *Dividends* to read all I could about previous through hikers, and to glean information and ideas about possible routes. Although several backpackers had set out each year planning on border to border routes I noted that very few actually finished. In fact only four parties completed CD routes between 1980 when *Dividends* was first published, and 1985 when I set out, and of those, two had two members and one four, leaving the third as the only successful solo trek I could find. Amazingly it was carried out by the only other British walker, Stephen Pern. (John Merrill set out on a CD trek in 1982 but abandoned it after 250 miles.) Obviously completing my trek would require good planning, determination and, probably, a lot of luck.

Scott Steiner, one of my companions on the High Sierra epic during the PCT walk, offered further help as he had walked part of the CD in 1984: from Silver City in southern New Mexico to Rawlins in southern Wyoming, and had kept me informed as to his progress. Some of his advice was not conducive to planning a through trek, though. Most of the route in New Mexico, he wrote to me from Chama in the north of that state, is 'a complete and total drag'. He suggested I should 'a) skip New Mexico; b) begin 100 miles to the east in the mountains near Santa Fe; c) hike New Mexico as fast as you can!' Determined on a complete border to border route I decided to adopt the last idea. Hiking from Canada to the New Mexico – Colorado border didn't sound right somehow even though such a journey would make more geographical sense as the Rocky Mountains dwindle away in northern New Mexico leaving the Divide to cross a flat, semi-desert 7,000-foot high plateau. Scott also offered to accompany me through northern Montana for the first month of the trip, a section where, if I went north to south and traversed it in late spring/early summer, I would need skis or snowshoes, ice axe, crampons and a rope. Clearly an experienced companion would be a great help on this part of the walk.

Scott's offer helped me resolve one of my major planning dilemmas, namely which way to go: Mexico–Canada or Canada–Mexico? I had spent months deliberating over this. Jim Wolf advised north–south as easier for logistical and

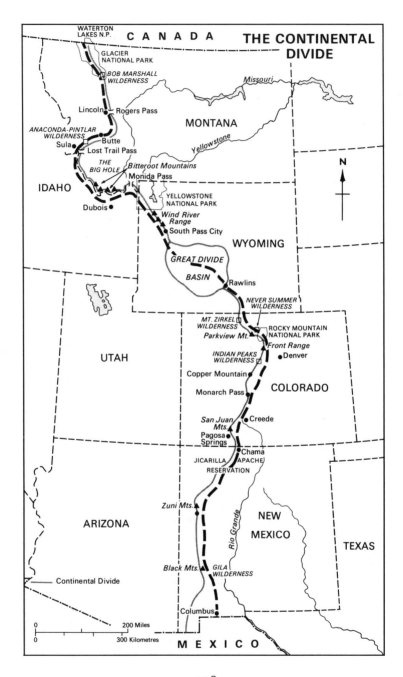

climatic reasons. Ned Tibbetts, an outdoor pursuits instructor in California who I'd written to for advice as he'd done the southern half of the Divide, advised south–north as did Scott, in order, he said, to get New Mexico over with and not have the 7-800 miles in that state to face at the end. This aesthetic argument was a very important one but eventually more practical reasons prevailed. The main one was that I hoped to have less trouble with snow by going south. Once out of the last of the previous winter's snow in the north I had a good chance of reaching the lower, easier terrain of New Mexico before the next winter's snow began. If I went north I would have to start in March or April in order to reach Canada before the end of September when progress in northern Montana would almost certainly become impossible. This would mean dealing with snow in southern Colorado and perhaps having to miss some of the spectacular mountains there and take a lower route. Going south I wouldn't be able to start until late May/early June due to snow but I could expect snow-free travel in Colorado in September and in New Mexico in October and November. Also on the Divide I would face the possibility of problems with grizzly bears for the first time and would have to hang up my food overnight and cook away from my tent and sleeping bag. These magnificent creatures occur along the northern half of the Divide in several locations and the thought of trying to keep my gear free of food smells until I reached there if I went south–north seemed fairly daunting so I decided it would be nice to deal with grizzly country first. Then I would be able to go back to my British backpacking habits of meals in bed, especially breakfast! The least important factor in my decision was the thought that as I'd already walked from Mexico to Canada it would be nice to now walk the other way. So finally I decided on Canada–Mexico and a late May departure.

Did I make the correct decision? In retrospect, no. But I doubt that if I'd gone south–north I would have finished! The early snows in the north would certainly have stopped me as they did the only two northbound hikers I met. Aesthetically, though, New Mexico made for a flat, uninspiring ending. How much better it would have been to end amongst the magnificent alpine scenery of Glacier National Park instead of at a tawdry, minor border customs post.

Unlike on the PCT where the guidebooks had had adequate maps in them and the trail was mostly easy to follow, I needed a full set of detailed maps for the Divide Walk so I ordered 300 topographic maps from the United States' Geological Survey in Denver whose staff were very helpful and agreed, via a phone call, to post batches of the maps to me at selected places. This solved the problem of logistics and the cost of shipping them to Britain and then back to myself in the USA — but did mean that for some areas I only had a hazy idea of a route, compiled from 1-inch to 16-mile scale state maps. I would work out the detail when I arrived at the start of each section and picked up my maps. As well as map parcels I would need food drops too and this time I used Alpineaire, whose wholefood meals I'd enjoyed most of those I'd eaten on the PCT. I sent them long lists of foodstuffs ranging from complete dried meals to compressed fruit and nut bars, to send to fourteen designated points (mostly Post Offices). I had periods of between five and fourteen days between these supply points so the weight of food would be an important consideration. From home I sent out guidebooks and the planemetric Forest Service maps I'd used for some of the outline route planning (not all the Divide lies in National Forests, especially in New Mexico). Gear was selected carefully with the generous help of several companies. As on the PCT, durability and strength had to be considered as well as weight and bulk and I ended up with a basic pack of 45lb including camera gear. With fourteen days of supplies as well (maps, fuel and books to read as well as food) the weight would creep up to 85lb on occasion.

The difference in latitude of the areas along the Divide (nearly 50 degrees north at the Canadian border and just over 30 degrees north at the Mexican one) is so great that there is a big variation in ecological zones with regard to the altitude at which they occur. The upper tree line in Montana lies at 8,500 feet but in New Mexico it's at 11,500 feet. The highest sections of the Divide are in Colorado where it is over 11,000 feet for many miles but the terrain here is similar to that occurring much lower down further north. Most of my route was over 6,000 feet, the lowest point being in fact the start at 4,000 feet. The Rocky Mountains are really two totally separate chains, with firstly the Northern Rockies running down from Canada to central

Wyoming where they fade away into the flat desert of the Great Divide Basin (whose edges I would follow for 200 miles) then, starting just north of the Colorado border, the highest part of the Rocky Mountains which run right through the state of Colorado to fade out just south of the border in northern New Mexico and which are therefore often referred to as the Colorado Rockies. For the first 800 miles, the wildest and most remote section of the route, I planned five food drops. Then four food drops would see me through the 500 miles of Wyoming but I could only find three convenient ones for the 800 miles of Colorado which seemed to be (and was) cutting it a bit fine. The most problematical section of all was New Mexico where my route was sketchy to say the least. I thought it would probably work out at about 800 miles and again I only had three food drops planned here. My hope was to average twenty miles a day though I was only planning on twelve for the first snowbound section. The food drops were chosen on the basis of being either on the trail or within twenty miles of it. I decided, wrongly as it turned out, that I'd rather carry very heavy loads than have to go far off my route for supplies.

Research into weather conditions revealed that the general nature of the Rockies' climate was wetter than that of the Sierras though not the Cascades. I expected to encounter several storms especially during the first month, June, which is usually wet, and again in the Colorado Rockies where summer thunderstorms are common. However in New Mexico I knew I'd probably be praying for rain as the area was very arid anyway and water in the autumn would be scarce, many sources having dried up over the summer. I planned on carrying a gallon or more at times relying also on ranches and wells.

The last weeks before the trek were, as always, hectic and seemingly disorganised as I tried to sort all the last minute logistics. Phone calls to the USGS and Alpineaire confirmed my drop arrangements; plane tickets and travellers' cheques were purchased, my flat was abandoned and my belongings put into storage courtesy of friends. Lists of where I hoped to be and when, were given to everybody I could think of: my mother (she was to send me the guidebooks and other odds and ends), Peter Lumley and Kate Spencer at *Footloose* who were to provide me with batches of film during the trip and to whom I was to send trail reports for publication in the magazine as I walked, various of the companies who'd supplied gear and several friends who'd offered to write to me. It was all very chaotic and tiring and I never thought all the arrangements would be finalised but they were, of course, and suddenly it was the end of May and I was on my way to Heathrow and a flight to New York.

As I would be crossing into the USA via Canada and not at a customs' post I needed to obtain my six months entry permit before I started the walk and the only way I could do this was to enter the USA, obtain my permit, then leave for Canada to re-enter the USA a few days later. Due to this complication I couldn't fly direct to the nearest city to the start of the walk (Calgary in Canada), but had to go via New York where I entered the USA and persuaded a doubting official to give me a permit before crossing the city and leaving on a flight to Toronto. Then a final flight took me to Calgary from where buses and taxis got me, exhausted, to Waterton Town Site and the first camp of the trip on the 29th May. The journey, involving three taxis, three buses and three planes, had taken $1^1/2$ days. I was a day early as intended so as to have a day's rest before meeting Scott but, as I was admiring the bighorn sheep that wandered round the streets of the little town, Scott turned up, also a day early! We decided, foolishly on my part, to start there and then. I hadn't seen Scott for three years and somehow he looked different. It was a while before I realised he'd shaved off his beard.

So at 4.30 pm on May 30th I set off on my Continental Divide Walk, my mind on avalanches, grizzly bears and the weight of my pack. We had eight days' supplies, cross-country skis, ice axes, crampons, avalanche transceivers and a rope. My tent and cooking gear would do for both of us but even so our packs were huge and unwieldly. During the first ten days we covered just 95 miles yet I remember them as the hardest miles I've ever done due to the weather and the snow. After just $4^1/2$ miles we crossed the international boundary, marked by a small monument, and left Waterton Lakes National Park and Canada for Glacier National Park and the USA. Dusk saw us at the Waterton Ranger Station where we had to persuade the ranger to give us a camping permit for our trek. He finally did so, after going over our plans in detail with us, though he wrote 'Not Recommended' across it and warned us of avalanche danger. Foolishly we didn't heed his advice. He also told us of a party of fourteen who had set off the day before heading for Mexico though they had taken a lower route. A maximum of six backcountry camps are allowed in Glacier on any one trip, so we had seven days to reach the little town of East Glacier on the south-east edge of the park.

Walking along the Divide itself is impossible in Glacier as it follows a jagged, rocky crest made up of loose sedimentary rock. Even our lower route proved difficult and dangerous so early in the season. The ranger was right to think it wasn't feasible. The very first full day saw us up in the snow skiing in bright sunshine surrounded by marvellous peaks but by late afternoon we were dashing for the shelter of the forest as a storm roared in in a matter of minutes. Snow fell and the wind blew for most of the night. Supper comprised handfuls of lunch food hastily eaten whilst sheltering under a tree, for due to the potential grizzly problem we didn't want food near the tent. I'd had to protect my food from black bears in places along the PCT of course but grizzlies are a far more serious hazard. Both can become addicted to human foods and are therefore a menace around camp sites but grizzlies are more likely to actually attack you than the smaller black bears. Once a bear loses its fear of people and starts raiding camp sites it has to be tranquillised and moved to a remote area or even in extreme cases killed. As there are only a few hundred grizzlies left in the 48 contiguous states, mainly in Glacier and Yellowstone National Parks, it is important that visitors to their homes, which is what backpackers in these National Parks are, should take great care not to attract these animals and further threaten their existence. This is an important reason for carrying out bear avoidance practices as well as the obvious one of personal safety. Grizzlies can be a threat if you come upon them suddenly and they feel you are threatening them and one way to avoid this in dense vegetation where they can't be seen is to make a noise, so, not wanting to annoy everyone with my attempts at singing, I attached a bundle of small bells to my pack to jangle as I walked. This proved infuriating at times but whenever I thought of silencing the bells I thought of meeting a bear round the next corner and let them jingle on. To keep away bears at night, and they are mainly nocturnal creatures, it is necessary to hang one's food from a tree so that it is at least ten feet above the ground and four feet away from the trunk of the tree and to sleep upwind and about a hundred yards from one's cooking and food storage area. Bears have an excellent sense of smell so freeze dried and dehydrated foods are better than fresh food.

Despite all the warnings I'd received, in guidebooks and leaflets, on rather garish trail signs and from the ranger we'd talked to, I knew that I would be very lucky to even see a grizzly bear and very unlikely indeed to have any problems with one. Even so, just the knowledge that these creatures, which can weigh up to 1,000lb and run much faster than a human being, lived in the country I was passing through, ensured that I stuck religiously to all the precautions, which is why that first night we were huddled disconsolately under a tree in the blizzard munching trail food for dinner. We didn't bother cooking because we had to melt snow for water and we were too tired and cold to want to stay outside for very long.

The storm blown to tatters by the wind, we skied along the Highline Trail (or at least where we thought it probably was) under Mount Kipp, admiring the superb mountains around us as we went, to cross the Continental Divide itself for the first time at a saddle. Then, just as we felt we were progressing well, we made an error. Instead of dropping down to the forest's edge to round a spur and begin the circuit of the large Cattle Queen Creek basin (as the map showed the trail doing), we went straight over the spur on the basis that as we couldn't see the actual trail anyway we might as well take the direct route and not be faced with an arduous ascent. However from the top of the spur we could see why the trail went round it: steep, broken cliffs fell away below us for over a thousand feet to the creek. For some reason I still don't understand we decided to descend this cliff and there followed a desperate and dangerous scramble made worse by being done in cross-country ski boots, with skis on our packs, during which I was not at all sure I was going to survive. At one point Scott became stuck and had to remove his pack to continue. He'd hoped to drop it a short distance to the next ledge but it bounced and we watched, horrified, as it crashed several hundred feet over a couple of small crags to come to rest by a stunted pine.

Amazingly his skis survived the fall and nothing was seriously damaged. If we'd lost the pack and all the gear in it so far from a road or any form of help we would have had a serious problem and if one of us had slipped and been injured the situation would have been grim indeed. But slowly and painfully we crept down the loose rocks to the safety of the valley below. I arrived there exhausted but relieved to still be alive. I was I think still suffering from jetlag, otherwise I'm sure I would never have agreed to such a hazardous descent. Several steep sections of hard avalanche snow had then to be crossed, using ice axes with the skis on our backs, as there were too many snow-free gaps to make skiing practical. We crossed Cattle Queen Creek then climbed up to a wide bench where we camped in a grove of sub-alpine fir. Our kitchen was on a rock outcrop with fine views across the deep valley of Mineral Creek. The six miles we had progressed had taken us nine hours.

Our attempt at a high-level route close to the Divide collapsed the next day. We followed fresh grizzly tracks through the snow as we continued on the Highline Trail to Ahern Creek. We'd picked up these tracks very close to our camp, a camp at which we'd simply left our food a few hundred yards downwind of the tent as the stunted trees were only six feet or so high. What we'd do if we turned a corner and met the bear we were following on these steep, treeless slopes we had no idea but luckily that did not happen and we parted company with the tracks at the creek where they headed up towards a high pass on the Divide. We continued round this huge bowl towards the notorious Ahern Drift where the snow remains the year round. An inspection through my binoculars showed that where the trail wound across the face of a steep cliff it was banked up with snow and corniced. After the previous day's experience we decided not to risk trying to cross this and descended the scree below the drift to pass under the cliff and then climb very steep soft snow back to the trail, a climb aided by the trees sticking out of the snow which we were able to pull up on. This quarter-mile section took us a couple of hours and more steep snow followed to a shoulder where, feeling relatively secure, we stopped for lunch. Although stormy, the weather had been warm with no frosts at night and the spring thaw was well under way making this crossing of steep-sided avalanche-prone cirques dangerous. How dangerous we saw when, from our lunch spot, we heard and saw two huge, wet, slab avalanches slide slowly and relentlessly across the next section of our route. Discussion was unnecessary. Hoisting our packs we set off down the spur to the Mineral Creek valley below, 'a desperate thrash down very steep, thickly vegetated slopes with the occasional rock step'. Rain poured down during this exhausting retreat and I was near collapse when we reached the creek and set up camp. It was a nightmarish experience that left us facing a long trailless trek out to the road through dense forest, not a pleasant walk to look forward to with skis on our packs.

A strenuous bushwhack through thick forest brought us out on the Going-To-The-Sun Highway the next day and we then slogged up this road and over Logan Pass to rejoin the trail through the park. This highway is the only road over the Divide in Glacier National Park and, as such, is very popular giving, as it does, magnificent views of the surrounding mountains. The weather for once was hot and sunny, making the climb hot work. My frame of mind was not improved by the car-borne tourists many of whom slowed down for a closer look. Indeed one car slowed to a crawl whilst one of the occupants leaned out to take a photograph of me from only a few feet away without a word of greeting or indeed any other acknowledgement of my existence. Further on though a truck swerved to a halt and the driver called me over. 'What the hell you doing, boy?' said a slurred voice. I explained, briefly. 'Hell, man, you're sure crazy. You need a shot of good ol' Tennessee bourbon.' A bottle was thrust at me and, prepared at this stage for anything that might ease the ascent, I took a deep, throat-searing swig.

At the car park at Logan Pass another curious car traveller approached us, this one sober. Conversation revealed he was local and had both skied and walked the Divide in this area. Keen to help us he offered to take our ski gear and mail it to Scott's home in Vermont. This was a great help and we accepted with relief. Without the swaying burden and extra weight of our now useless skis and poles, our progress was a lot easier. As we knew there would still be some snow to deal with plus, undoubtedly, snowmelt river crossings we kept the ice axes, ski boots and one ski pole plus of course the rope. Five miles and 1,300 feet down the road from the 6,650-foot pass we left the tarmac to camp a few miles into the woods near Deadwood Falls. We were one day behind schedule.

However the initial extreme difficulties were over now and the walk became more like a normal backpacking trip. Two snowbound passes, Triple Divide and Pitamakin, were crossed before we descended to the campground at Two Medicine Lake. One of our two camp sites en route was at popular Red Eagle Lake where for the first time we camped with other people. In fact there were three other parties there consisting of one, two and three people. Quite a crowd, it seemed! We'd picked up a heavy, six battery torch on the trail and found it belonged to two fishermen from Indiana who had massive packs weighing well over 100lb each, weights easily explained when we saw what they contained: amongst other things a week's supply of tinned food, an axe, household pans and a complete frame tent. A steel cable was provided for bearbagging our food and it took all of us to haul the Indiana people's packs, full of tins, up in the air. On our first attempt I stood under the pack to give it a heave up as the others tugged on the line the owners had brought with them. As I pushed the pack up it swung wildly before the line broke and the pack crashed to the ground and I leapt out of the way. A second try broke the line again though this time I stood well clear and only after a stronger cord was borrowed did we have success in hanging the load. Then, ironically, the lone hiker left a fish he'd caught lying on a rock overnight, a clear invitation for bears but, luckily, not taken up.

Approaching Two Medicine Campground we saw a number of lightweight tents pitched and on arrival found that they belonged to the large 14-strong group who had set off the day before us who were called the Connecticut Continental Divide Expedition. The weather being very wet and windy we huddled under one, of their large communal tarps to talk of our trips so far and our plans for the future. They had a back-up van and support team ferrying round spare gear and collecting food and mail for them and were exploring alternative routes as well as doing Jim Wolf's one by splitting up into smaller groups. So far they had stayed together, and although on a lower route than ours had still had problems with snow and also a few serious river crossings. Six or seven of them intended going all the way to Mexico but the others were only doing sections of the whole route. Other walkers would be joining the trip for short sections along the way too. They felt that seven months were needed to complete the walk and that without a support vehicle it would be almost impossible which made my plans for a five and a half month, unsupported, mainly solo trip seem very ambitious. I could only hope they were wrong.

A snow-free crossing of Mount Henry on the drier eastern edge of Glacier showed us the flat plains to the east for the first time as well as glimpses of the snow-capped tops of the Bob Marshall Wilderness, our next destination. Rich flower meadows and green aspen groves made for a relaxing finish to our crossing of Glacier as we arrived at the village of East Glacier and our first day off, a day spent, as so many days off were to be, eating, writing, washing, sorting maps and gear and preparing for the next stage of the walk. Glacier we felt had been worth all the danger and hardship. We were left with memories of beautiful lake-filled cirques backed by golden cliffs and a strong sense of wilderness. Signs of grizzly bears had been everywhere, including ripped up signs at a camp site where we later learnt a grizzly had been seen the day before we camped there. Although we hadn't yet seen a grizzly, we had seen bighorn sheep, mule deer, elk, marmots, ground squirrels and white mountain goats whose climbing ability was quite extraordinary.

Lowry's Diner in East Glacier became base for our stay as the weather continued wet and windy. I was there at 6.30 am to write my first trail report for *Footloose* over a stack of hot cakes with maple syrup and endless cups of fresh hot coffee. Our pack weight was reduced somewhat by sending off our crampons as all the snow we'd encountered since Logan Pass had been soft and we were hoping it would remain so. However my first food parcel from Alpineaire and 24 USGS maps soon made up for the weight disposed of.

Leaving East Glacier on June 9th also meant leaving winter for summer. It was to rain only once during the next 19 days and 250 miles and after that the rain was due to summer thunderstorms. A short final stretch in Glacier National Park took us to US Route 2, a major highway, and the Burlington Northern Railroad where we watched a mile-long goods train with six engines climbing up slowly to cross the Divide at Marias Pass. Once over these trans-Rocky Mountain routes we had 170 miles to travel before we met another east–west crossing. Most of this vast untouched country is made up of the 950,000-acre Bob Marshall Wilderness and the 240,000-acre Scapegoat Wilderness. The first of these is named in honour of a legendary figure in the American wilderness movement, Bob Marshall, who worked for the Forest Service and made great efforts to have roadless areas designated as wilderness or primitive areas in order to preserve them. He was also a keen and prodigious hiker with a record of many long, tough solo walks.

Trails through deep forested canyons took us back up to the Continental Divide, a three-day trek of constant creek crossings and permanently wet feet. Kip Creek, North Badger Creek, Pentagon Creek, Open Creek and Strawberry Creek were just a few of those forded, mostly with ease in knee-deep water. Strawberry Creek, though, was hip deep with a strong swirling current and slippery stones underfoot but even here we did not need to use Scott's 180-foot 8-mm rope. Worse than any of the fords though was the bridge over the south fork of the Two Medicine River. This consisted of planks about 18 inches long nailed through the centre to a single log, with just a slack rope for a handrail and the river roaring through a narrow rocky chasm thirty or so feet below. It took three attempts before I managed to cross. The first two times I tried to balance with both feet on each plank which immediately started it swaying unnervingly from side to side. The way to do it, as Scott showed, was to cross with one's feet in the dead centre of each plank to avoid it moving. A difficult balancing act with a 75-lb pack nevertheless.

Our days of muddy trails in the forest were rewarded when we climbed up steep snow slopes to the Divide itself (with ice axes but in running shoes!) below 8,412-foot Kevan Mountain. Here we found the best views of the trek so far: a vista of snow-dappled mountains stretching as far as the eye could see. I climbed up snow-free Kevan Mountain for an even better view. North lay the peaks of Glacier National Park, already part of the past, still brooding under heavy, dark clouds. To the south ran the long limestone cliffs that characterise the Bob Marshall Wilderness or 'The Bob', as it is known to afficionados. After the days in the canyon bottoms I found this sudden space exhilarating, a feeling not dimmed even when we lost the trail during the

3,500-foot descent to the Spotted Bear River, for I knew that the next day we would climb back up to hike along the base of 'The Bob's' showpiece, the Chinese Wall, a 1,000-foot high limestone cliff that stretches for mile after mile, towering above the forest. After losing the trail again in soft snow we reached the Wall after a climb over 8,183-foot Larch Hill and followed its base for five miles or so. It was a magnificent walk, despite the treacherous knee-deep snow, with the Wall rising high above us and to either side, whilst on our left lay wave after wave of green forested gentle hills.

On the eighth day out from East Glacier we dropped down to a roadhead at Benchmark where we found the CCDE party again. We'd followed their tracks in the snow with occasional puzzlement when they disappeared only to reappear several miles further on. Different groups of them had taken a variety of routes so we'd actually followed the tracks of separate ones not just one party as we'd thought. During those eight days we saw no-one except for one solo woman backpacker heading in the opposite direction. The CCDE's support party gave us a lift down to the Benchmark Wilderness Ranch where we had sent food parcels to be held for us for a fee of $20 each by proprietors Bud and Bev Heckman. Although outfitters and very knowledgeable about the surrounding area these folks were definitely not walkers but horse travellers and they looked the part with denim jeans, studded western shirts, stack-heeled cowboy boots, and brightly coloured bandanas. We spent some time chatting with them and were told that grizzlies were no problem in 'The Bob' because as hunting went on there (though not for grizzlies themselves which are protected) they were frightened of people. They scorned our attempts at bear bagging, pointing out that on their hunting trips they had large store tents and hung dead game in camp as well.

Restocked with food and having left the rope and our cross-country ski boots with the CCDE support people who'd offered to ferry them to our (and their) next supply point (the town of Lincoln), we left Benchmark for the Scapegoat Wilderness, a drier more arid region than either Glacier or 'The Bob'. It wasn't dry enough to prevent mosquitos being a problem though they had been a problem since East Glacier where they forced us to use the tent at night even though the weather was clear and the sites spectacular. After two days of crossing and recrossing the Divide we began a partly cross-country walk along the crest of it that was to last for nearly 100 miles as the gentler more rolling terrain meant the walking was relatively easy. Route-finding was not that simple though as in the cols and passes were deep forests where taking the wrong turning was all too easy. Close attention to map and compass was essential as we found after one incorrect descent which luckily ended with us taking the right direction eventually. Every so often we met up with various members of the CCDE, occasionally hiking or camping with them and I was surprised to learn that many of them had abandoned their tents to save weight. We ventured our first bivouac of the route on a nameless 8,150-foot summit with a wonderful view where the breeze kept the mosquitos away.

Four days in the Scapegoat Wilderness saw us at Rogers Pass and the first trans-mountain road since US 2, 12 days previously. With another week-long section ahead, resupplying was necessary so we hitch-hiked down to Lincoln. It took three long, hot, frustrating hours before anyone offered us a lift and then it was someone going to join the CCDE support team. Perhaps this was due to our appearance after 12 days in the back country! We arrived at the Lincoln Campground in an incredible 70-mph windstorm that was snapping branches off the lodgepole pines and we had a struggle erecting the tent, especially as some of the ferrules had snapped off the flexible alloy poles. I made a note to write to the manufacturers for a replacement set. The campground, which was quite small, had been totally taken over by the CCDE and we spent our day off with them. My mail from home including films and a pair of boots had arrived but not my food parcel, probably because I was now five days ahead of schedule due to our rapid progress in the snow-free hills. I notified everyone of this and restocked from the supermarket. I mailed home my ice axe, ski pole, cross-country ski boots, gaiters and other items; 14lb worth in all. I also bought a pocket knife ($4 and made in Ireland, the US ones were far more expensive!) to replace the two I'd managed to lose so far.

The next week was my last with Scott whose month on the trail was nearing its end. This segment of the route lay in the Helena National Forest mostly along the Divide itself, high above any water sources so that at times we had to carry three gallons between us. On the first steep 1,300-foot climb out of Rogers Pass I strapped my full water bag to the top of my pack only to discover that it had sprung a slow leak giving me an unwelcome cold shower, especially as there was a cold wind blowing. Days were planned carefully to take advantage of water sources but many of these had dried up in what I learnt was a very serious drought that had been afflicting Montana for several years, causing many farmers to lose their livelihoods. Helena is a commercial forest and our biggest problem was navigating through freshly logged areas, unmarked on our maps, where the trail just disappeared. In one area the loggers told us that 6,000,000 feet of board timber was being cut. Generally though the walking was easy, often on jeep trails through gentle, pastoral scenery with flower-rich meadows and shady lodgepole pine forest. Our nights were spent out on hill tops watching the sun set and the black starry sky. It was too dry for mosquitos so the tent stayed in the pack. During the day the main interest was in the flora and fauna. The flowers were out in full now, purple lupins and shaggy white bear grass lining the route whilst amongst the birds were killdeer (a type of plover), red-tailed hawks and great blue herons.

The little town of Basin, where Scott was to depart, was a shock. Due to the construction of a freeway past it, the town is dying. All the shops were shut with just the post office and one bar (catering for the construction workers) left open and many of the houses were boarded up. Luckily my food parcel for Lincoln had been forwarded here. I wouldn't starve! After a farewell drink Scott set off to hitch-hike to Colorado and I wandered off into the woods to search for my first pitch alone on the walk. We'd travelled 350 miles together and the partnership had worked well. It was going to be strange being on my own.

South of Basin, the Divide curves round the copper mining city of Butte at low elevations and my route followed dirt roads and jeep trails through dense lodgepole pine forest with occasional open meadows and lakes. Arriving on the freeway north east of Butte I met up yet again with the CCDE support team, Steve, Chris and Andrea, plus one of the walkers, P.J. They offered me a lift into Butte later in the day which I accepted as I'd been suffering from toothache for the past few days and needed to see a dentist.

First though they took me bouldering on the huge granite rocks that littered the woods here. Chris and Steve were climbers rather than walkers and lent me a pair of 'sticky' soled climbing shoes called Firés which I hadn't used before. I was astonished by them, they really did stick to the warm rock and I managed many traverses and short climbs I'm sure I could not have done without them, my limits being my lack of arm and finger strength. This was a fun way to spend half a day and I really enjoyed it.

In Butte I checked into the Thrift Inn Motel then, the next day, located a dentist who could see me at short notice and solve my toothache. I was in his chair one and a quarter hours whilst he lanced an abscess and removed a nerve for a charge of $57. At least I would now be able to sleep at night, something I had not done for several days. I had a second day in Butte shopping and managed to spend $150 on groceries and bits of camping gear (a 7 by 9-foot tarp in case the tent, whose poles were now dropping to bits, failed completely, a couple of stuffsacs and other odds and ends). Some food I sent on to my next supply point, Sula, where I hoped to be in eight or nine days time and where I knew there was only a small store. In the afternoon the CCDE started to trickle in — Kirk Sinclair, the group's leader, Cindy, Jim, Steve and more — and we took over an all-you-can-eat pizza place. They'd come through the ranges west of the Divide rather than on my closer to the Divide, but less interesting, route. A Greyhound bound for Chicago, a day and a half away, took me the ten miles back to Homestake Pass where I'd left my route.

The continuing walk round Butte was not very inspiring (I'm being polite!) and I hiked it quickly, doing 25 miles a day, drawn on by the enticing peaks of the Anaconda-Pintlar Wilderness. This is a superb region of rugged mountains and cliff-ringed cirques. From my trek through it I remember most the many timberline lakes, perfect settings for high level camps. At one, Upper Twin Lake, I had the privilege in the early dawn of watching from the tent a moose cow and calf wander through the mist-wreathed marshes at the lake's edge. However the Anaconda-Pintlar is not large and after three days I came down from the alpine scenery to lower forested hills as the Divide wound its way to the next road crossing at Lost Trail Pass.

On entering the Anaconda-Pintlar I'd turned west as the

Divide begins here its huge loop around the vast hollow known as the Big Hole, the westernmost valley of the Mississippi-Missouri Basin. Rounding it meant travelling west for 130 miles before returning to a southerly direction and then heading east to the border of Wyoming and Yellowstone National Park at Mack's Inn. This is remote and lonely country and during my 450-mile walk from Homestake Pass to Mack's Inn I met just one other backpacker and only half a dozen people in total, mostly in the valleys, apart from those in the few tiny villages I went down to for supplies. Often I went for four or five days without seeing another person. Logistics were difficult too, and twice I had to hitch-hike 20 or 30 miles to resupply points. On one occasion I was offered a lift within minutes but on the other I had to wait for five hours.

Through the Anaconda-Pintlar I had good weather and walked on well-maintained trails. South of there all that changed. The trails, where they existed, were neglected and often hard to follow, overgrown with dense vegetation in the meadows and covered with fallen trees in the forests. There was no sign that anyone ever came here. The weather changed too and afternoon thunderstorms became the norm though without much actual rain. The air was hot, humid and sticky; debilitating conditions to walk in. Biting flies and mosquitos added to the discomfort.

I'd read in the papers at Butte about the epidemic of forest fires caused by lightning that were raging through the western USA and as I lay in the tent on the night of July 7th whilst a huge thunderstorm raged all around I hoped I wouldn't run into one — little knowing that the storm was starting a fire right in my path. Two days later after a hard twenty-mile day I began a descent to Hogan Creek where I hoped to camp. Thunderclouds had been around all day but something didn't seem right about the purple-red dense clouds billowing up ahead of me. A faint acrid smell swept by me and I realised I was walking into a forest fire. A rapid retreat led to a dirt road and a felled area from where I had a view over the valley ahead. It was full of smoke and I could see trees burning on its edges. A quick map consultation showed a possible way round the blaze and I set off wearily to try and circle round it. I had no water and anyway didn't dare camp so close to the conflagration. An hour later as I appeared to be heading towards the fire again a Forest

Service truck pulled up. They didn't give me any choice: 'jump in the back, you can't walk through this. We'll drive you out.' I scrambled into the open back of the pickup and was given a hardhat to wear before being driven out to Lost Trail Pass straight through the fire. For half a mile or more the fire raged on either side of the road, trees bursting into flames like huge fireworks and spitting burning lumps of pine tar. Branches burnt black and glowing red at the edges crashed down all around; at one point the truck had to be driven over one. Isolated fires flared up here and there in patches of deadfall and dense underbrush. The heat was overwhelming and it was quite clear I could never have walked through such an inferno. If I hadn't been picked up by the fire crew I'd have been in a serious situation. They dropped me off at Lost Trail Pass where a temporary fire fighting camp had been established with over four hundred people, some from as far away as Michigan. I was told that the fire covered 1,200 acres and with the wind changing direction several times a day it was unpredictable and out of control. Several fire crews had had to run for their lives when the fire suddenly raced towards them.

From Lost Trail Pass I hitch-hiked down to the tiny hamlet of Sula, my next supply point, to camp behind the store. With a store, Post Office, campground, showers and laundromat all Sula lacked was a cafe. Even so I had a day off waiting for the fire to either burn out or to be able to move on as I wanted to return to the trail where I'd left it. I rang my cousin Kris Gravette who was living in Idaho at the time and she drove up to meet me and accompany me for a few days. The combination of two English people walking together in the hills produced the required effect. It rained heavily for two days! So I was able to make my link back to where I'd abandoned my route before heading south into the wild, rugged and unvisited Beaverhead Mountains. From Lost Trail Pass it was 200 miles to the next paved road, the Interstate at Monida Pass. I had food for fourteen days for this section so started with a very heavy pack. Originally I'd planned on going right through to Mack's Inn, another 70 miles, but, realising how much I'd have to carry if I tried to do so, I'd sent some food on to Dubois, Idaho, thirty miles from Monida Pass intending to hitch-hike there.

The next 200 miles was over almost trackless mountains,

and after Kris left on the second day out from Lost Trail
Pass, I had ten days of the toughest walking I've ever done.
The worst day was July 14th when I went from the south
fork of Sheep Creek to Upper Slag-a-Melt Lake, a journey
of 12 miles and 4,500 feet of ascent that took me ten hours. I
ended the walk completely exhausted. Most of the day
consisted of a steep bushwhack by a creek through dense
forest, full of huge tangles of fallen trees and dense
undergrowth, large rocks, side creeks, marshes and masses
of flies. Even the few descents went slowly as they were on
steep, loose, stony slopes covered with shiny, slippery
clumps of beargrass. I crossed four high saddles that day.
But the rewards of such days, as I noted in my journal, were
'pristine cirques . . . no campsites, no trails, no fire rings, no
cut trees . . . immaculate scenery.' Genuine untouched
wilderness in fact. The row of 10,000-foot jagged rock peaks
along the Divide, the Bitteroot Mountains, held the eye and
caused me to stop and stare in awe on many occasions. The
great pyramid of Homer Youngs Peak was particularly
dominant. But also attractive were the flower meadows and
the crystal clear timberline tarns with their shining stones
and silver flashing trout. The absence of the usual signs of
humanity gave an unreal air of innocence and perfection to
this region that made it especially memorable. I also
climbed my highest peak (10,200-foot Elk Mountain) so far
in this section.

In places where the terrain was exceptionally rugged,
such as round the 12,000-foot Italian Peaks, I dropped
down to side valleys to follow dirt roads across vast
sagebrush plains before climbing back up to the woods and
hills. Such short-cuts were the only way I could complete
this section without running out of food. As it was I reached
Interstate 15 at Monida Pass on July 22nd with no food at all
and then had to wait five hours in the blazing sun for a lift to
Dubois and a night in the Crossroads Motel. Kris came out
to pick me up from here and drive me back to the pass which
was a relief as I didn't fancy another long wait for a lift.

Around Monida Pass (elevation 6,800 feet) the terrain
changes from forest to grassland and miles of rolling grassy
hills where the walking, usually on jeep tracks, was easy.
This is cattle country and I passed vast herds. Cows meant
dirty water and so the Potable Aqua iodine tablets came into
regular use. Foul tasting but preferable to dysentery! After

a few days in the grasslands where I saw many of the fast moving dainty antelope, a contrast to the bigger, heavier elk and mule deer of the forests that I'd become used to, the route followed the Divide up into the Centennial Mountains, a sloping tableland of sedimentary rock cliffs, flower-filled meadows and forest groves. Some of the trails are still maintained here and I came across a one-man trail maintenance crew, Tim Thomas (whose ancestors, unsurprisingly, came from Wales), blazing and clearing the trail. I camped with him at Rock Spring near a flock of 2,000 sheep whose shepherd I'd met earlier. He came up here with his flocks every summer and met most backpackers who visited the area; 54 came through in 1977 he told me but I was the first of 1985. The camp with Tim at Rock Spring was the first I'd shared with anyone apart from the two with Kris since Scott had left at Basin, a month ago.

A long descent from the Centennials brought me to Mack's Inn, a tiny fishing resort on the banks of the wide but shallow Henry's Fork, Snake River. I was 815 miles from the Canadian border and on the edge of Wyoming and Yellowstone National Park though actually in Idaho whose border with Montana I'd been following for days. Montana was finally behind me now. I was now back on schedule, all the days I'd gained having been lost with the delays for teeth and fires in Butte and Sula and the diversion to Dubois plus the unexpected toughness of the Beaverhead Mountains. However I had to have a day off at Mack's Inn as I needed a camping permit for Yellowstone and the only way to obtain one was by hitch-hiking to West Yellowstone where there was a Ranger Station. This took several hours and two lifts, the second from the Dubois postmistress who remembered me. West Yellowstone is a typical tourist town, crowded and full of trinket shops, and the harassed ranger was unsympathetic and told me brusquely that I had to go to Old Faithful for a permit even though a written enquiry had given this place as the permit issuing station. I came close to losing my temper, especially as Old Faithful, forty miles from Mack's Inn, was my next destination on foot but I restrained myself and hitch-hiked back to Mack's Inn in heavy rain, permitless and cursing the National Park bureaucracy.

The CCDE rolled in again in ones and twos, the last time I was to see them and we had a pleasant evening drinking beer and playing pool in the bar the end result of which was that I didn't get to bed until 1.30 am, and didn't leave till well past midday. As well as socialising with the CCDE people I'd written my thirdtrail report for *Footloose*, sent home my longjohns and thermal shirt as I hadn't worn them for weeks and picked up and sorted my mail. I also bought some more glue for my boots, whosesoles had started to fall off after only 200 miles and which I'd been sticking back together every couple of days, a procedure I was becoming fed up with.

The exceptionally hot and dry weather I'd had throughout the months of June and July in Montana and Idaho came to an end as I left Mack's Inn for Wyoming and Yellowstone, the world's first national park, created in 1,872 'as a public park or pleasuring ground for the benefit and enjoyment of the people' in which its 'curiosities or wonders' would be retained in their natural condition. As I climbed the 1,800 feet up from Henry's Fork Snake River valley to the western boundary of the park, what seemed beforehand to be nothing more than a trudge on dirt roads through logged forests became an exhausting struggle against the weather as three massive thunderstorms in succession hammered down on me. At first I simply donned my Goretex jacket over my T-shirt and shorts and walked on. Then, to my surprise, as the torrential rain turned to wind driven hail I realised I was shivering and rapidly becoming severely chilled. Protected by the slight shelter of a pine tree I quickly changed into my insulated jacket, overtrousers, two hats and two pairs of gloves. Even with these on I still felt cold as I continued up hill as fast as I could walk. The storm raged as I pitched camp on the Yellowstone boundary and, as I was now in grizzly country again, I erected my separate groundsheet (carried for bivouacs), as a lean-to shelter several hundred feet from the tent and cowered under it, sitting on my pack, whilst I cooked and ate my dinner. I then bearbagged my food high in a tree, a procedure I would now follow every night for the next week. During this time the weather remained cool with afternoon rain and thunderstorms nearly every day and night, and temperatures averaging 5°C rather than the 12°C they had been. On several nights there were frosts with temperatures inside the tent a degree or two below freezing. I cursed myself for having sent home my thermal shirt and longjohns from Mack's Inn but was relieved I'd kept my insulated vest which I'd considered sending home as it too had been unworn for two months.

The day after the first storms I reached the crowded resort of Old Faithful, home of the world's most famous geyser which you can watch spout every hour from the comforts of a bar! I'd rented a cabin here whilst in West Yellowstone as camping is not allowed and this was a supply pick-up point for me. I was glad of this as it gave me the opportunity to dry out my damp gear. The resort boasted a grocery and showers amongst the knick-knack shops and the cafes, but not a laundrette. At the Ranger Station I obtained a permit for the rest of my stay in Yellowstone which involved convincing the ranger that I really was going to walk twenty miles a day rather than the eight or so she said were normal for backpackers. I had, as in Glacier, to specify which selected camp sites I would use each night. I also of course went to look at the geyser. The great, gushing white fountain is spectacular but the concrete benches, walkways, hotels, coaches and other tourist paraphernalia rather detracted from it though I could see that it must have been an awesome sight for the first people who came across it when it was still in the wilderness. I learnt quickly that the time to shop and eat in the cafes was when the geyser blew as then everyone else went off to watch it!

I preferred, though, the quieter backcountry thermal areas I went past, such as the Shoshone Geyser Basin and the Heart Lake Basin with their bubbling hot pools, small geysers, steaming creeks and sulphur-coloured rocks. My first night out from Old Faithful I camped at the Lone Star campsite where I was joined at my camp fire by a party of four, all summer workers at the resort taking advantage of a couple of days off. They weren't prepared for the bad weather though and, having only T-shirts, sweatshirts, jeans and thin windbreakers and no warm or waterproof clothing, they returned to their 'tourons' (as they called the tourists — a cross between tourists and morons!) the next day when it dawned cold and windy with dark clouds and hints of rain.

Apart from the thermal areas the walking in Yellowstone was generally unspectacular as most of the southern section of the park that I traversed consists of a vast lodgepole pine forested plateau broken by several large lakes. The walking was easy though for which I was thankful as I had a very

179

heavy pack (around 85lb) as it was 270 miles from Old
Faithful to my next supply point, South Pass City. I saw few
people and had most of the designated sites to myself.
Asking the ranger at Heart Lake Ranger Station about this I
was told 'you're fifteen miles from a road, most people don't
like to go that far.' She also told me that bears had raided
and stolen food from the site a couple of weeks previously. I
saw no sign of bears but was particularly careful there.

From Yellowstone I entered the Teton Wilderness, a
region of deep, glaciated river valleys rimmed by massive
brightly coloured cliffs. As I left Yellowstone I met a
backpacker heading the other way who was singing loudly.
He'd just seen two grizzlies, a mother and cub, on the trail
though they'd crossed the river as he approached. I went on
rattling my bear bells loudly but although I saw fresh tracks
and droppings on the trail, I saw no sign of them. My route
in the Teton Wilderness weaved in and out of the canyons,
climbing to cross high meadows and broad passes with
superb views of the surrounding peaks including the Tetons
themselves, unbelievably pointed and steep, away to the
west then decending rapidly back into the dense forest. I
took a higher route closer to the Divide than that
recommended in the guidebook and made several river
fords including that of Soda Fork which was strong and
deep. At one point I crossed the Divide on a 10,000-foot
plateau where the views were superlative but from which I
was driven by a violent thunderstorm which actually had me
running for cover despite the weight of the pack. I also
crossed the unique Parting of the Waters where North Two
Ocean Creek splits, one branch travelling 3,488 miles to the
Atlantic, the other 1,353 miles to the Pacific. Cow parsley,
mountain bluebell, red monkey flower, yellow columbine
and other flowers decorated the creekside. I saw few
backpackers but several horse parties and the wide, churned
up trails showed the popularity of this area with horse-
packers.

I also encountered bears twice in this area, the only time I
saw any during the whole walk. The first occasion was
whilst I was camped by the twenty-foot-wide North Buffalo
Fork creek. Late in the evening I heard a noise and, on
looking out of the tent, saw a small black bear foraging along
the opposite bank, apparently oblivious to my presence.
Eventually it wandered off into the trees. I was glad I was

still hanging my food, a practice I continued through the Teton Wilderness on the advice of a ranger I'd met who told me grizzlies roamed this far. Two days later as I approached Bear Cub Pass (appropriately named as it turned out) on the southern edge of the wilderness I topped a rise on the trail to see a bear and two cubs a few feet in front of me. They were going away from me but must have heard or smelt me for the she-bear began to turn round as I backed away out of sight. Retreating several hundred yards I left the pack and circled round to try and see where they had gone. As I approached the trail I heard a loud crashing noise that I soon saw was the bear cubs climbing rapidly up two adjacent trees again only a few feet away. I nearly joined them! Instead I moved away very, very quickly, collected the pack and made a wide sweep around the bears making as much noise as I could whilst doing so.

South of the Teton Wilderness I entered the Bridger-Teton National Forest which also had churned up trails though from a different source: cattle. During my fifty-mile crossing of this area I disturbed herd after herd of cattle which crashed off heavily through the forest. Although I had to purify my drinking water again I was glad they were here for it was obviously only due to them that the trails were still visible. I met no-one else in this featureless region of forest and meadow and there was little sign that anyone ever came here.

In total contrast was the Bridger Wilderness, a magnificent alpine region along the west slopes of the Wind River Range. My route took me for nearly a hundred miles through this wonderful country and I met thirty or forty people nearly every day, enough to make it seem crowded! The approach towards the Green River with the massive bulk of aptly named Squaretop Mountain ahead was one of the best parts of the whole trek. Despite the people about I had every camp site in the wilderness to myself and every one was a superb timberline site, the kind every backpacker dreams about. The weather was cold, windy and wet for much of my time in the Bridger Wilderness. Indeed whilst talking to a party of eight Boy Scouts at Upper Jean Lake, it even snowed a little. Despite the unpromising conditions I again took a higher, more mountainous route than that suggested in the guidebook with three camps at over 10,000 feet, the highest being 10,500 feet, for the first time on the walk. The popularity of this region is well deserved and it's one I'd like to return to as its inspiring cirques, glaciers and peaks require more than a cursory five-day visit. My final day in this region, after I'd dropped down to stay in a log cabin and eat some real food at friendly Big Sandy Lodge, took me across a rugged cliff-hemmed 11,500-foot pass between the dramatic rock spires of East Temple Peak and Temple Peak and above the dark waters of Clear, Deep and Temple Lakes. This pass was the highest point I'd reached on my Divide walk and made a fitting climax to my traverse of the Northern Rocky Mountains, for south of the Bridger Wilderness the great chain of the Rockies is interrupted by the arid wastes of the Great Divide Basin.

Here the Continental Divide splits into two as water that runs into the basin does not run out again but is lost in its two million sandy sagebrush and grassland acres. The Divide runs round the edges of this vast flatland. Lack of water makes crossing the centre of the basin through the Red Desert very difficult so I followed the side of the Atlantic drainage and went round the northern and eastern rims. Even here I often went twenty or more miles between water sources, which were usually cattle-populated trickling creeks or springs, in temperatures reaching 30°C in the shade. On my route through the sand and sagebrush there was rarely any shade. Ironically sudden thunderstorms at night with brief but heavy rain had me pitching the flysheet in the dark on four occasions. The Great Divide Basin is not uninhabited though and I came into contact with more roads and industry than I had in the mountains for the land here contains oil, coal and uranium and small towns like Jeffrey City and Sinclair have sprung up around these deposits. I also passed through the restored frontier town of South Pass City, a historic relic now as the goldrush that created it died out long ago, where I had a food and map pick-up at the tiny Post Office and where Bill Lowe who runs the only cafe let me sleep in his porch. The register for Divide walkers he keeps I found interesting. It was the first one I'd seen since Lincoln. There were no entries for 1985. Many westward-bound pioneers came this way too as it provided an easy way through the barrier of the Rockies to the rich lands of the Pacific coast.

I spent nine days on the 175-mile crossing of this dry country and the most interesting feature was the many herds of antelope I saw. The hot and hard terrain gave me sore, blistered feet even though I walked in just my liner socks and training shoes and twenty or so miles a day was quite enough. Private land around the North Platte River where I couldn't camp resulted in one 28-mile day which I finished by staggering along the road in the dusk to the oil town of Sinclair. Here though I found the Pasco Inn whose new proprietors welcomed me and restored my morale. The place itself, built in a grandiose Spanish style, has a character and atmosphere totally lacking in the featureless motels I usually stayed in in towns.

From Sinclair it was just two hours' walk on the highway with an Interstate and railway alongside to Rawlins, the largest town on the whole of my route, where I stayed for $8 a night on the Western Hills Campground. I had another mail drop here and I also needed to use the laundromat, the first I'd found since Sula 46 days previously! My clothes needed a wash! At the Post Office I picked up a huge bundle of mail including seven letters, a card from a friend on holiday in China, maps, food and a new pair of boots sent via Scott. I had another 250-mile section coming up so I spent a day eating and stocking up with supplies. Now after 1,300 miles of walking I was about half way between Canada and Mexico.

When I left Rawlins on August 27th for a last 50-mile walk across the Great Divide Basin before starting the climb up into the Southern Rocky Mountains, a heatwave was forecast and I little knew that I was leaving summer for winter. Four days later and I was camped on the Continental Divide in dense forest having left behind the arid wastes of the basin. The change came abruptly: as soon as the land began to rise the trees appeared.

During my last days in the semi-desert basin lands I spent an evening in the tiny covered wagon of a Basque sheep herder named Eloy Tuyville hearing stories of a lifetime spent with his flocks in the hills. It was four months since he had been down to a town, supplies being brought up by his employer every couple of weeks. On his horse with a rifle at hand (for coyotes) and wearing chaps and a denim shirt he looked more like a cowboy than a shepherd. His current flock was 2,500 strong. I thoroughly enjoyed talking with him and eating my supper of fried potatoes, tortillas and beans with chilli, cooked by Eloy in his neat, organised little home.

I also met two backpackers, the first I'd seen in nearly three weeks. Inevitably Lisa Wolf and Tom Mortenson were Continental Divide walkers, heading north after having left the Mexican border in March. We stood by the side of the dirt road for three hours in the hot sun swapping stories and advice. Talking to other long distance backpackers was very enjoyable.

Returning to higher mountains in the Sierra Madre, an uplift that stretches into Colorado, meant I no longer had to carry several quarts of water at a time. This was a relief as I'd left Rawlins with 14 days' supplies, enough I hoped to take me to Grand Lake on the edge of Rocky Mountain National Park 250 miles away. I was surprised to find on returning to the woods that the aspens were already coming into their autumn colours, their leaves turning from green to yellow and deep gold, a month earlier than usual. After the dry wastes of the Great Divide Basin I took great delight in the clean creeks clattering over their rocky beds, the grassy meadows and the green vegetation plus the varied land-scapes where each turn in the trail brought new vistas of rock outcrops and forested hills instead of just more sagebrush flats stretching to infinity.

In the Sierra Madre I again took a higher route than that outlined in the guidebook and followed the Divide itself, usually on old stock driveways, wide swathes in the forest where thousands of sheep were, and in places still are, driven to and from their summer upland pastures. High point in the Sierra Madre is 11,007-foot Bridger Park from whose summit I had my first sight of the ranges of the Colorado Rockies stretching away to the south, a grand view of peaks I would soon reach. The weather was still unsettled, as it was to remain, with occasional showers and afternoon thunderstorms. I soon abandoned any thoughts of sleeping out under the stars and used the tent every night.

On September 1st I left Wyoming for Colorado during a period of rain and strong winds. One day later I climbed up to the higher peaks of the Park Range and the Mount Zirkel Wilderness where I camped above Mica Lake, at 10,500 feet, a superb site surrounded by the jagged Sawtooth Range and Big Agnes Mountain. It was one of the finest pitches of the whole walk in fact, but also one where I had a tremendous thunderstorm that kept me shut in the tent all evening whilst it flashed and boomed overhead. More storms stopped me early the next day, for climbing the exposed 11,900-foot Lost Ranger Peak seemed unwise with lightning around so I camped at 3 pm in a small grove of trees. The day to my camp site though was the best complete day's walking I'd had since the Bridger Wilderness. Views ahead of the southern Mount Zirkel Wilderness tops, Lost Ranger Peak and The Dome, plus ones back to the cirque around Mica Lake were the backdrop to the beautiful timberline scenery I travelled through. I passed perfect Gilpin Lake and went in and out of deep canyons and cirques topped by knife-edge crests towards the tundra-like open plateau of the southern wilderness regions.

The early halt proved worthwhile as it meant I was able to enjoy the eight-mile high-level walk over Lost Ranger Peak and the slopes of Mount Ethel without any fear of storms. I was away at 7.50 am for a 9-hour, 24-mile day. Lost Ranger, the highest peak on the walk so far, gave excellent views of Mount Zirkel and Big Agnes Mountain and the rounded bump of The Dome; the summit lay right on the edge of steep, broken cliffs that fell away abruptly to tiny Prairie Lake, a blue dot below my feet. Snow patches showed that winter is never very far away at this altitude. The rest of the high-level walk was glorious too and I met three backpackers heading south here. By the time the usual afternoon storm set in I was safely down in dense forest by placid Percy Lake where I just managed to pitch the tent before the deluge began and the huge black clouds rolled in.

After an hour or so the storm cleared and I went for an evening stroll round the calm lake, a relaxing end to a good mountain day and one rewarded by a close-up view of a golden brown pine marten staring down at me from a tree trunk. There was absolute calm, a peaceful contrast to the fury of the storm, and the lake was beautiful and mysterious with waves of mist from the drying woods drifting across its surface. All was silent except for the gentle dripping of water from the trees, the swish of a fish rising and, just once, the skittering splashes of a duck taking off. All was lit by a magical golden light and I felt completely at peace with the world and myself.

From the Park Range the Continental Divide turns eastwards across the Rabbit Ears Range to the Never Summer Range where it travels northwards for a few miles before making a hairpin bend to return southwards again. This quirk in its Mexico-bound line means that in the Never Summers, water flowing down the west slope of the Divide is bound for the Atlantic Ocean whilst that flowing down the east slope is headed for the Pacific. It also means that for ten or so miles the Mexico-bound walker is headed towards Canada. Before reaching the glories of the Never Summer Wilderness though I had to cross the lower, mostly wooded, hills of the Rabbit Ears Range (named after Rabbit Ears Peak, a wooded hill with two pillars of stone on top, supposedly resembling rabbit's ears). One peak, Parkview Mountain, towers above the rest of the range at an elevation of 12,300 feet and it was my intention to spend a night in the tiny summit shelter here.

After a day spent crossing low-level forests and pasture land by means of paved and dirt roads I camped by beaver dam and willow-lined Middle Fork, Arapaho Creek — 17^1/$_2$ miles but 5,350 feet of ascent from Parkview Mountain. I woke to a sharp frost (-1°C in the tent) and a clear sky. There was no water on Parkview and the last source was 6 miles and 3,000 feet from the summit so I planned to haul 3 quarts to the top, have an evening meal (Alpineaire Potato & Cheddar with Chives) that only needed three quarters of a pint of water for rehydration and a dry breakfast. Beyond the peak it would be five or six miles before I could hope to find more water. The whole day took 8^1/$_2$ hours with the final 3,000-foot climb up steep trailless slopes taking 3^1/$_4$ hours, luckily there was a cold wind that kept me cool and stopped me from becoming too thirsty. The Forest Service hut on the summit was a tiny stone one with a wood floor, concrete roof, and large shuttered glass windows on all sides. I opened some of the shutters for the view and to let in light. The summit slopes fell away steeply in long grassy ridges and stony slopes on all sides. Stuck in the frames of the windows were the business cards of previous visitors which ranged from computer manufacturers to local outfitters. I added my *Footloose* card to the collection. A skittering sound revealed a mouse on the floor so I hung my food bags from the roof. Further evidence of animal inhabitation lay in the chewed pages of the hut book which reminded me of the bothy books of home, and in which the entries proved very interesting. Jim Wolf had been here on July 22nd 1981 'Scouting Continental Divide

Trail' and on July 29th 1983 Stephen Pern, my British predecessor on the Divide, heading north, had written 'best views so far on my journey from the Mexican border'. Most of the entries were not from Divide hikers of course. The most intriguing was from Floyd Shiery of Baton Rouge, Louisiana (August 22nd 1985), who had inserted a quote from the Anglo-Saxon poem 'The Wanderer':

Oft him anhaga are gelide þ
Metodes mildse theah-the he'mod-cearig
Geord lagu-lade lange scolde
Hreran mid handum hrim-ceals sae
Wyrd biþ ful araed.

So I finished my 100th day of the walk with 1,500 miles behind me, actually on the Continental Divide, at my highest camp ever. Outside the tiny hut the sun shone but the wind roared. There was a stack of firewood but I was not going out to light a fire. At 10°C it was not very cold anyway. The views when I did step out of the door to appreciate the sunset were comprehensive but distant — the Park Range, the Snowy Range and Elk Mountain in Wyoming, the Rawah Range, the Never Summers, the Front Range, the Vasquez Mountains, the Gore Range and the Flattops — all the mountains of the northern half of the Colorado Rockies were visible, stretching away to the horizon in every direction. I had the pleasure of watching both sunset and sunrise, red in each case but a dubious beauty with regard to the dawn.

And the old adage about a red sky in the morning being a warning turned out, on this occasion, to be true. My last comment in my journal before I left that morning reads 'Looks like another nice day'. The first comment of that evening, written on the same line, reads 'How wrong I was!'. A steep, knee-jarring 2,700-foot descent took me down a narrow ridge to the forest and then to a highway at Willow Creek Pass. Complex route finding in the dense forest, most of it cross-country or else on old, unmaintained trails that kept vanishing, occupied me as far as the maze of logging roads at Illinois Pass so that I did not notice the build-up of clouds that led to thunder and rain as I began the climb up into the Never Summers (and never was a mountain range more appropriately named!). On reaching timberline I was facing hail and snow so I took shelter in a small grove of trees whilst I donned all my clothes and decided whether to go on or not. I could camp in reasonable shelter where I was but if the weather stayed bad I would be on the wrong side of the mountains in relation to my next food drop and also a day behind schedule, a delay for which I had very little in the way of food. But if I continued I would have to cross the shoulder of Farview Mountain at a height of over 12,000 feet and then find a way down to Parika Lake, the first place a camp would be possible.

I opted to go on, found a staff in lieu of an ice axe and set off into the blizzard. My feet, in running shoes, (the boots Scott had forwarded to me at Rawlins had turned out to be too small), were soon soaked and cold as there was now several inches of snow on the trail. I pushed on for 2 miles or so and about 800 feet of ascent to enter the Never Summer Wilderness in driving snow, high winds and thick mist. At a barely visible trail junction at 12,126 feet I began the descent to the col at Farview Pass at 11,900 feet where I cleared the snow off the sign to check where I was before dropping down another 600 feet to Parika Lake where I camped in the slight shelter of some stunted spruce bushes. The wind and my frozen hands made pitching the tent quite difficult, as was keeping the inside moderately dry, especially as the inner was still damp from the frost of two nights previously. I threw the contents of the pack into the tent then left it outside as it was plastered with snow. I lay my bivouac groundsheet over the tent groundsheet to give me a dry surface to put things on then scrambled in, put dry socks on my frozen feet and crawled into the sleeping bag. The temperature inside the tent was 4°C. Several cups of hot, sweet coffee followed by a large curry helped me warm up as the storm blew itself out. By early evening the snow had ceased, leaving a covering of several inches on the ground and I ventured outside in a bitter wind to beautiful surroundings and a marvellous crystal-clear light with all round the snow-covered mountains washed in the gold of the evening sun.

This had been the first serious snowfall since the beginning in Glacier National Park, over three months ago. The 7th September was early for snow but I realised that making it through Colorado without more of the same was unlikely; the changing colours of the aspens had already shown me that winter was arriving early, and this snow confirmed it. Given this I would need some extra gear, in particular some boots, gaiters and an ice axe whilst a thermal shirt and longjohns would be useful too.

The day after, the storm dawned cold and clear, so clear the intensity of the light reflecting off the snow was painful. Clouds over the 14,000-foot Long's Peak in Rocky Mountain National Park turned red then pink as the sun rose. A red sky . . .? I had a difficult decision to make. I needed to be in Grand Lake, the next supply point, by tomorrow at the latest as I had barely a day's worth of food left. By the most direct route the town was only sixteen miles away yet by the most interesting and challenging route, and the one closest to the Divide, it was 36 miles, via the hairpin bend. I still hadn't decided whether to go for safety or adventure as I packed up but the clearing sky decided for me. I went for the long route. After all, I reasoned, if I wanted to travel from Canada to Mexico by the shortest route I'd have caught a plane! Also, I'd already done the highest section of my route in the Never Summers, during the previous day's storm.

My reward for taking the harder way was one of the most satisfying and splendid mountain days I have ever had. The results of the storm made the scenery truly spectacular. Crisp snow lay underfoot as I crossed Baker Pass and Red Dog Pass and traversed high above the forest across the slopes of the Cloud Peaks whilst the summits, Mounts Nimbus, Stratus and Cumulus, rose above me. The line of the trail was barely visible but the snow melted off very fast once the sun was high which I was glad about as the traverse round the hairpin, as the Divide turned from north to south between Seven Utes Pass and Agnes Lake, was on very steep, slippery, grassy slopes with no trail. There were good views north to the Rawah Range from here and to the west Parkview Mountain, white with snow, showed that the storm had been extensive in its range. People were fishing in the superb timberline mountain tarn of Agnes Lake, nestled under the steep screes and cliffs of Nokku Crags and towering Mount Richthofen. Heading south again I finally left the high country at Thunder Pass and entered Rocky Mountain National Park with a 2,000-foot descent down into the forest and the valley of the upper Colorado River. Camp, after a 25-mile and 11-hour day, was on the crowded

Timber Creek Campground as I did not have a permit· forbackcountry camping in the park. I was just six miles from where I'd been the night before!

Grand Lake, a 'gateway' resort just outside the National Park, was only a twelve-mile valley walk away and I was there early the next day to book into the Shadowcliff Mountain Lodge, a combined guest house, youth hostel and religious retreat. It had taken 14 days to travel the 257 miles from Rawlins, the longest section between supply points of the whole trek. Grand Lake has many stores and in one of them, a small outdoor shop called Never Summer, I bought a pair of Italian made Pivetta 5 boots for $129. Expensive, but they were the only ones that fitted my wide feet and after the storm I knew I had to have a pair of boots. However the other items I needed were not available. After all, they were winter items and, as I was told, 'it's still summer'.

Summer it might have been but the weather forecast was not promising. With 520 miles of high mountain country in Colorado to cross before I would reach the lower, flatter elevations of New Mexico I felt under pressure to push on, so I left Grand Lake as soon as my chores were done, to walk along the edge of the reservoirs that fill the valley here, and camp on another official site, Big Rock Campground. This time, though, I had the place to myself. A notice said that that very day the water supply would be turned off until the next spring. It was September 10th and the season was coming to an end.

From Big Rock I entered the Indian Peaks Wilderness, an area so near to Denver and other heavily populated places that a permit is required for backcountry camping, one of the few wilderness areas where this is so, because it is so popular. I obtained my permit from the ranger which required listing on a form the 'zones' in which I intended to camp though I was not, as in National Parks, obliged to state exactly where I would camp and only use official backcountry sites. Bureaucracy out of the way I climbed back up to timberline along the deep, narrow, densely forested canyon of Arapaho Creek only to be met by another savage storm below Arapaho Pass that caused me to stop early and camp at Caribou Lake in the slight shelter of a clump of stunted limber pine. As I set up camp the rain turned to hail then snow. By the time I was organised and inside the tent I felt quite chilled and it took an hour or so of huddling in the sleeping bag plus the consumption in rapid succession of hot coffee, onion soup, and cheese and biscuits before I warmed up again.

As I lay in the tent listening to the roar of the wind I thought that I could hear a voice calling but on looking, very briefly, out of the door on a couple of occasions I could see no-one in the dense cloud and swirling snow. I decided I must be imagining it, translating the tortured shrieking of the pine branches into a human voice. By 5 pm the storm had abated so I ventured outside to look at the magnificent snow-covered peaks and to stroll round the lake. And there across the other side of the cirque was a hiker with two dogs coming towards me. He was looking for his brother, Joel, who was hiking the Divide through this area and was due to camp here today and for whom he'd brought supplies, humping them up to Arapaho Pass in the storm. I promised that if I saw Joel I'd tell him his food cache was at the pass in a black garbage bag. The hiker, his two dogs bounding after him, strode back up and over the pass. I envied his light day pack. But then he'd envied me my long journey and my stay in this beautiful cirque surrounded by the jagged ridges and peaks of Mount Achonee, Navajo Peak and Santanta Peak.

By 9 pm a steady rain was falling and at some point it turned to snow for at 3.35 am I woke to find the tent sagging badly and covered in snow which I knocked off before returning to sleep. Awake again at 7 pm I found 2 inches of fresh snow on the ground. The flysheet, frozen inside and out, cracked and snapped as I forced it with difficulty into its stuffsac. Above, shreds of cloud sped across the blue sky and the sun glinted on a high cliff. The wind was bitterly cold and I set off wearing several layers of clothes. Joel had not arrived and when I crossed Arapaho Pass the black plastic bag was still there. As I travelled through a classic alpine area of rock-girt, tarn-filled cirques and steep-sided rugged peaks above beautiful meadow and grove-dotted basins replete with tumbling, sparkling creeks I could see why the Indian Peaks Wilderness is so popular though I met no other walkers. Passing through the wilderness via the Diamond Lake and Devil's Thumb Trails I reached 12,000 feet at Devil's Thumb Pass from where I could look south along the single crest of the Front Range stretching ahead of me linking the complex area of ranges in Northern Colorado with those in central Colorado.

I followed the Divide along this crest above deep forested canyons and steep-sided tarn-filled cirques over Rollins Pass where a few cars were parked, as a gravel road crosses the mountains here, to take the narrow Ute Trail from Rogers Pass below the now knife-edged ridge towards the great white wedge of 13,294-foot James Peak. I camped on the northern slopes of this mountain at 12,550 feet, the highest camp of the trek and one of the most glorious with wide-ranging views over all the Colorado Rockies. The pitch was a small, barely-level stony one above a tiny smear of a creek. A low, crudely built stone wall showed it had been used before and indeed Jim Wolf in his guidebook recommends it. I was glad the weather was settled as the site is very exposed and I could only force the pegs a few inches into the ground. The golden evening light gave a wonderful depth to the black-shadowed canyons and later as the stars appeared in the vast endless blackness of the sky, lights of towns appeared far below in the farther valleys and out on the plains. A huge slash of light must have been the city of Boulder. Moving lights revealed vehicles and roads. It all seemed so far, far away and I felt totally isolated from it all, alone up here with just my little tent, my candle, the stones and the cold, cold night. A week previously I had been on the summit of Parkview Mountain whose bulk I could see clearly away to the north-west.

I'd worried a little about climbing the steep, icy slopes of James Peak but there was no real difficulty in the ascent to this the first of five 13,000-foot-plus peaks I traversed the next day, the highest day's walking of the trek. From James Peak eight miles of glorious, cross-country ridge-walking took me over these mountains, Parry Peak at 13,391 feet being the highest and therefore the highest point reached on the whole trek from Canada to Mexico. Virtually all the snow had gone and it was wonderful to be able to stride out unhampered by the weather for a change. After crossing US40 at Berthoud Pass where the cafe was shut but a soft drinks machine provided several Cokes and the gift shop road maps of Colorado and New Mexico, I climbed back up to the Divide and followed the crest for a short way before descending to camp at 11,500 feet below Vasquez Peak, just on timberline in a well-watered basin.

September 14th, the following day, was my 36th birthday

so I took it easy, climbing 6,300 feet and walking 19$^1/_2$ miles in 9$^3/_4$ hours! For this region this type of day was not unusual. In his guidebook Jim Wolf describes the 55-mile section between Berthoud Pass and Copper Mountain as having 'more up and down per mile than any other on the entire length of the Continental Divide Trail'. The day was clear and with the fear of more winter storms over my head I wanted to go as far as possible every day there was good weather. For the first time in over a week I wore shorts and t-shirt as I climbed 12,947-foot Vasquez Peak and then set off for Jones Pass on another high-level ridge walk over tundra-like terrain with excellent views, especially of the rugged Gore Range, my next mountains. Further ahead I could see the snow-capped Sawatch Range. The hardest part of the day was actually a descent, the jarring 3,000 feet of steep jeep road leading down from Jones Pass to the attractive Bobtail Creek valley. My legs felt like jelly by the bottom of the descent and my thigh muscles really hurt. The hunting season was just starting and I'd met a heavily camouflaged ptarmigan hunter with a shotgun near Jones Pass. Later on, I met two bow hunters, also clothed in camouflage (even their packs!). From Bobtail Creek I switch-backed up the side wall of the canyon with views of the steep rock walls of Pettingell Peak and Hagar Mountain before dropping down to the South Fork William Creek where I met two women on a two-day backpack round 'The Loop', a popular 20-mile circuit of the creek. The arduous day ended with a 1,500-foot climb back up a steep trail to camp below Ptarmigan Pass, again just on timberline at 11,600 feet. I couldn't imagine any better way to spend my birthday.

Rain came in during the evening and the next morning saw me descending to the town of Silverthorne in dull, showery conditions which turned to torrential rain as I entered the town so I spent a few hours in the cafes and stores of the shopping centre. Apart from food the stores produced a headtorch (a Pampa one for $20 to replace my handtorch, an 'unbreakable' Teknalite one, which had broken), a long-sleeved thermal vest and some candles. But again there were no gaiters, ice axes or longjohns for sale. 'Still summer', they said in the stores. The *Sunday Denver Post* told a different tale. Three climbers had died of exposure in a blizzard on the Grand Teton in Wyoming on the day I'd had the storm at Caribou Lake. They'd had no bivvy gear, no warm clothes and no waterproofs. I finally left Silverthorne, after three cafe meals and several long conversations about my trek, at 5 pm, in now dry weather, to climb up by South Willow Creek, camping beside the water at dusk in thick forest.

A scenic if strenuous (4,500 feet of ascent) walk of 16^1/$_2$ miles through the Eagles Nest Wilderness brought me to my next supply point, the chic, expensive purpose-built ski resort of Copper Mountain. On discovering the price of a night in a bed here ($68!) I camped 1^1/$_2$ miles out of town, hidden in the woods above Guller Creek, to return for breakfast and to write and post my mail. A bookshop here had Edward Abbey's *Desert Solitaire,* recommended to me by Scott. Abbey's breadth of vision, his love of wilderness and freedom and his militant, angry environmentalism, all forcefully expressed in lucid, crystal clear writing, was to have a profound effect on me over the next few weeks.

The weather remained uncertain with flurries of snow as I crossed two more 12,000-foot passes, Searle and Kokomo, and then followed winding trails mostly in forest for three days around the slopes of Mounts Massive and Elbert, at 14,421 and 14,433 feet the two highest peaks in the USA Rockies and ones which, although they do not lie on the Divide, I had hoped to climb. However the snow already lying at higher levels and my desire to press on before more snow fell meant I had to abandon this plan. As I passed below them visibility was minimal due to low cloud and heavy rain showers, high up it was probably snowing. The one day I had of sunny weather in this section, spent passing through the Holy Cross and Mount Massive Wildernesses on the Main Range Trail, was in dense viewless forest almost the whole time. The weather could only worsen though and sure enough it did.

The final four days' walking to the tiny ski resort of Garfield, my next supply point, took place in snow and hail as a cold front swept down over the Rockies from Canada. The first two of these days were reasonable with merely dense mist, hail and light snow, compared with the third when a full-scale blizzard that dumped six inches of snow on the ground swept in. A stick was procured for use in lieu of an ice axe again as I battled over several high passes at the height of the storm. I met several hunters in the woods, all off them commenting on how unusual it was to have such weather so early in the year. Crossing 12,154-foot Tincup Pass on a barely visible dirt road was the hardest section. High winds blasted the snow at me and I could hardly see as I staggered up the road. A four-wheel-drive vehicle passed me and offered a lift which I turned down though I did accept a candy bar. 'You'll need the extra energy!' Near the top I came upon the car again, stuck in a drift, but the driver freed it as I approached and hurtled off down the other side. To make matters worse I had no map for about ten miles of this section and was working on compass bearings, trail signs, advice from hunters and guesswork! Once over Tincup the storm abated and I camped by Chalk Creek under clear skies. The tent, soaked from the storms and condensation of the previous days, froze solid overnight as the temperature inside fell to −4°C.

Crossing 12,200-foot Chalk Creek Pass to Garfield the next day was hard as the strong winds had created deep snow drifts and above timberline the rocks and grass were slick with rime and ice. Visually I was in an arctic world of white and black tundra with half frozen tarns and clouds of snow trailing from the peaks. Bleak and desolate but coldly beautiful also. In contrast the warm colours of the aspens in the valleys as I descended to Garfield seemed like another world. Garfield is a tiny ski resort, still closed for the summer when I arrived, though with a post office inside the ski lodge and a cafe and gas station/store nearby. I only stayed for half a day despite the many chores I had to do as I still had 300 miles of high mountains to traverse and the forecast was for more snow. The date was September 24th and another problem now was the growing lack of daylight. Daybreak was at 6.30 am and darkness fell by 7.30 pm leaving no time for drying the tent and airing the sleeping bag if I was to walk 20 miles per day, especially as the sun was not high enough in the sky to warm anything before 9 am. By then I was usually already walking.

Arriving at Monarch Pass, above Garfield, I could see that the snow already lying was going to present problems enough and that more snow could well force me down to lower elevations. The cafe at the pass gave me mixed predictions as to what weather to expect. The optimistic forecast came from a long distance cyclist I met here named Burt who was on a 3,800-mile ride from San Francisco to

North Carolina. With a load of only 30lb he was doing 100 miles a day. Using motels most nights, he carried only a plastic tube tent, a cartridge stove, vapour barrier clothing and a synthetic filled sleeping bag. Of course he only camped at sheltered low elevations and he admitted that even so the tube tent was not ideal as it was both draughty and prone to condensation. Over lunch we had an interesting discussion on tent design, trying to match the weather protection and roominess of my tent with the lack of weight and bulk of his. We came up with a few ideas but neither of us is likely to go into production just yet! The long-range weather forecast that Burt had obtained was for a fortnight of fair weather but the staff in the cafe said that another cold front was sweeping down from Canada bringing more snow.

From Monarch Pass I had a scenic, above timberline walk to 10,800-foot Marshall Pass where I camped. The going was slow however as the trail was covered in ankle to thigh-deep soft snow with a breakable crust. I met two bighorn sheep hunters on horses whose tracks made the second half of the day's walk much easier but I realised that if there was this much snow above timberline further south, then progress would be very slow.

South of Marshall Pass the Divide swings west for 150 miles then back east for the same distance before returning to a southerly route. This loop takes the backpacker west round the San Luis Valley and the headwaters of the famous Rio Grande, the third longest river in the USA. Initially the Divide runs west along the relatively low and gentle Cochetopa Hills (elevations from 10,500 feet to 11,500 feet: below timberline here) and I had many miles of pleasant walking in dense, undulating forest reminiscent of the terrain in central Montana though there was generally a good trail. At one point I descended for the first time in weeks to below 10,000 feet to cross the edge of the open, sagebrush rangeland of Cochetopa Park, whose low hills were resplendent with the golds and yellows of the aspens. Down here there was no snow visible anywhere and I encountered a few of the magnificent ponderosa or yellow pines that I remembered well from my Pacific Crest Trail journey.

This late summer idyll was over in a few days though, and as I ascended beside willow-thicketed and beaver-dammed

Cochetopa Creek towards snowy heights, I was soon back in the reality of 1985's early winter. Characteristic of the south-west of the USA are the steep-sided, flat-topped hills known as mesas and I was entering this area now, an area known for its aridity and its desert scenery but one that also contains high mountain ranges. Spread through the states of New Mexico, Arizona and Utah and encroaching on southern California, southern Colorado and parts of Nevada, the South-West is a distinct geographical area conjured up superbly in the books and articles of Edward Abbey whose *Desert Solitaire* I was now avidly reading. One phrase stuck in my mind throughout my travails in the southern Colorado mountains: 'When traces of blood begin to mark your trail you'll see something, maybe.'

Immediately though I was still in the High Rockies with the plateau of Flat Table Mountain rising above to show me the type of scenery to come. As I climbed beside Cochetopa snow patches appeared and a cold rain began to fall. Just beyond the boundary of the La Garita Wilderness I met two more bighorn sheep hunters using llamas as pack animals, a growing practice in the USA. They told me of a horse party turned back by deep snow when trying to reach San Luis Pass, where I was headed, a few days previously.

That night it snowed and I soon found out why the horse riders had had difficulties. En route to San Luis Pass the trail crosses a 12,700-foot unnamed pass over a side spur then contours round the western slopes of a steep bowl before reaching another pass. There was a bitter wind blowing as I struggled through knee-deep snow up to the first pass to be greeted by a view of totally snow covered terrain with no sign of the trail. Examination of the route ahead through my binoculars showed that the rim of the next pass was corniced. I started across the steep slopes anyway, using a stick for support again, but soon found I could make no progress on the deep soft snow with its breakable crust. With no gaiters my boots were full of snow and my feet numb with cold whilst the wind made standing upright difficult. I consulted my maps and found I could reach San Luis Pass by descending one valley and ascending the next so I did this, plunging down the snow slopes to Spring Creek then climbing back up laboriously beside Cascade Creek to reach the snowbound pass and the Divide at 5 pm. Exhausted and knowing I needed both gaiters and an ice axe for safe travel in the snow I decided to descend to the little mining town of Creede, which was on my list as an 'emergency' supply point.

Most of the descent was done in the dark including the passage through the narrow, deep and spectacular gorge above Creede where many of the mines lie. Here the river and the dirt road compete for space under the overhanging cliffs and it felt quite eerie crossing and re-crossing the unseen but noisy torrent with high above a slash of sky resplendent with stars. I staggered into Creede and fell into the nearest motel, as tired as I'd been since the first days in Glacier so long ago.

Creede was a good spot for a day off and I felt I needed to recoup my strength, my last complete day off having been 33 days previously in Rawlins. San Juan Sports provided me with gaiters (ex-hire ones, $5) and some Lifa longjohns plus a rental ice ace, to be sent back from New Mexico. Advised by the Forest Service to wear something bright so that hunters could tell I wasn't a deer I also bought a bright orange acrylic bob hat which I designated my 'anti-hunter' hat. As a precaution, wise as it turned out, I also purchased a backpackers' trail guide to the Weminuche Wilderness, where I was headed next, so that I could work out lower alternatives to my planned route along the Divide itself if necessary.

Disaster struck the next day as I was trying to find a way through the maze of dirt roads that criss-cross the hillsides above Creede. Suddenly one of the shoulder straps of my pack snapped in two. Close examination showed that it had probably frayed on the plastic stiffener in the hipbelt which on that side had worn through the upper edge of the belt. I'd patched it but it was still obviously rubbing on the shoulder strap. Whatever the cause my pack was now useless. Grimly I headed back into Creede. A delay was the last thing I could afford just now, though I was thankful that if such a thing was going to happen it had occurred only a mile or so from a town and not high in the mountains in deep snow, miles from anywhere.

San Juan Sports brought out their largest pack, an external frame model, and I attempted to repack my gear in it. The result was laughable as less than half my equipment went into the pack. Phone calls to the company whose packs the store stocked drew a blank, how long it would take to provide a larger pack was unknown as their computer was 'down', a state normal for business computers in my experience, and mightn't be 'up' for days. Until then they could do nothing. Continuing her helpfulness Dana of San Juan Sports phoned a store called Pine Needle Mountaineering in the nearest big town, and ordered for me a 104 litre capacity Gregory Cassin pack. These packs, I knew, were reputedly the best made in the USA.

For three days of, naturally, glorious weather I waited impatiently in Creede for my new pack. Two bow hunters (yes, bow and arrows) from Texas called Chelsea and Jay were in town on their annual two weeks' elk hunting trip and I spent some time in their company as they were in the next motel room to me. Their friendliness helped me through those frustrating days. We had much in common, especially a love for the wilderness, but I still failed to understand why they wanted to kill animals they obviously liked and respected. They explained to me how difficult bow hunting was and how much of a greater chance it gave to the animal than rifle hunting, making it 'fairer'. Ironically they never even saw an elk despite going out at dawn and dusk every day, clad in their non-rustle camouflage outfits, whilst I saw several the day I finally left Creede.

Eventually my new pack arrived, in kit form, and I spent some hours putting it together and fitting the harness and frame before setting off. It felt strange of course, as my old pack, after 2,000 miles and four months, had just about moulded itself to my back, but I was glad to be back on the move again. Once above timberline on the willow-covered Snow and Jarosa Mesas I encountered deep snow and soon lost the indistinct trail. When, after two days of slow yet energy sapping progress, a storm came in from the south west I decided, not without some mental protest, to take a lower route. I was in 'The Bend' where the Divide swings round the head of the San Luis Valley to turn back east and I hoped that if I cut the corner of this loop I would find less snow in the San Juan Mountains to the south. My descent took me down to the knee-deep Rio Grande which I had to ford. Even here at only 10,000 feet it was snowing. My first attempt to return to the peaks ended in failure. From a 10,900-foot camp at Black Lake I tried to reach the Divide at Twin Lakes. After progressing 4 miles in $2^1/_2$ hours into the strengthening storm I realised I couldn't make it as the snow was becoming deeper and the wind stronger. Reluctantly I turned back and descended to ford the Rio Grande again and to camp where I'd been at noon the previous day.

Waking there the next morning to a snow-covered tent and a grey, windswept sky with sheets of sleet slashing across the river, I finally accepted that a high-level route along the Divide was no longer feasible. The storm I was in had been raging for three days and showed no sign of abating. In fact it was to last for another five days. Consulting my maps I found I had two alternatives. I could return to Creede via a 40-mile road walk then continue on roads for another 100 or so miles to Chama in New Mexico or else I could try and find a way across the Divide and down to the town of Pagosa Springs from where 50 miles of highway would take me to Chama.

The 140-mile road walk was to be avoided if at all possible so I decided on one more try at crossing the mountains, this time via Weminuche Pass, at 10,600 feet the lowest point on the Divide in the San Juans. The terrain was fairly flat too, with easy gradients which were climbable despite the snow cover. In reasonable weather I began the ascent, following horse tracks for the first three miles, glad of the flat trail they'd broken in the snow. But soon I was trail breaking myself in ankle to knee-deep snow as I crossed the pass itself, a $2^1/_2$-mile-long meadow surrounded by mountains. The scene was very impressive but a little eerie as I went through in total silence and stillness watching huge black clouds gathering ahead. Above the Rincon La Vaca the rock peaks of The Window and the Rio Grande Pyramid stood out, stark and cold with an apparent hostility that made me shiver. Camp after a long, arduous $14^1/_4$ miles was by the Pine River in the shelter of a spruce grove. For the fourth night in a row it snowed and at dawn I went through the now usual chores of packing up freezing equipment in the half-light. Worst was taking down and packing the tent. Frozen condensation meant the pole sections had to be thawed out before I could dismantle them by running my hands up and down the ferrules. Stuffing the flysheet, frozen solid inside and out, into its bag, removed any remaining feeling and warmth from my hands. I was beginning to hate mornings.

Descent was via the Pine River, Divide Lakes and Piedra

Stockway Trails. I was glad I'd bought the trail guide to the Weminuche Wilderness as I didn't have maps for this area south of the Divide. It was the weekend when the rifle hunting season began and I passed many hunter's camps and heavily laden packtrains, 10 of the latter in one 7-mile section, trapped at the lower elevations by the snow. All asked me if I'd seen any elk. 'No, only hunters' I'd reply. With so much bright orange around I'm sure the elk were miles away. To cut down the number of hunters who shoot each other, rifle hunters in Colorado must wear orange garments and hats. Orange camouflage clothing is even available!

At Williams Creek Campground near the trail head I was entertained by a party of hunters from Denver who were very interested in my trek and especially in the fact that I wasn't carrying a gun which they felt was very remiss of me. In fact whilst we were sitting in their campavan having a drink, the owner, a pleasant, mild, middle-aged, middle-class man, pulled open a drawer to reveal a small arsenal and handed me a small handgun. I'd given, weakly, my reasons for not having a gun as being that they were too heavy and anyway I wouldn't know what to do with one. 'There, that's not heavy and it's very easy to use' I was told. The lethal bit of metal lay on the palm of my hand. I didn't dare move in case it went off! Gingerly I handed it back. If I can't travel without having to carry one of those, I thought, I'll stay at home. Returning to my tent later on I noticed the sticker on the back window of their pickup truck: Freedom means God, Guns and Guts. I realised that I didn't understand these people.

The storm continued but down here it took the form of heavy rain rather than snow. Trudging into Pagosa Springs in the downpour a car stopped and the driver offered me a lift. I gave the now automatic polite refusal but as I did so the man's accent registered. He was from Liverpool! I accepted the offered hospitality and spent an evening with him and his American wife, sleeping the night on their living room floor. After eight days of wet snow, sleet and rain all my gear was damp so it was nice to have the opportunuty to dry everything out. Alan and Charlotte Shaw suggested, gently, to me that I looked as though I could do with a day off. I realised they were right when, after accepting, I felt a great wave of relief sweep over me.

Anyway, they told me that the following Monday, when I would hope to reach Chama if I pushed on without a break, the post office would be shut as it was an official holiday. The Shaws were going shopping in Durango the next day so I went with them and their two sons to spend the day window shopping and reflecting on how I'd never have expected that a day spent wandering round shopping malls and stores could be so relaxing! My only purchase was of two more Edward Abbey books, *Down the River* and *Abbey's Road*.

This welcome break and the Shaw's friendliness set me on the road to Chama with dry gear, clean clothes and feeling quite revived after the rigours of the snow. Two days of fairly dull highway walking during which I read five books saw me in New Mexico and the little town of Chama, two weeks behind schedule. I pitched camp on the Twin Rivers Campground and set off for the post office. I was then surprised, not to say startled, to be stopped by a policeman, a typical US policeman in a large car and armed with a gun and dark glasses, who addressed me by name. 'You called Townsend?', he drawled. 'Message for you from England'. When I'd recovered from the shock I found he had a message for me from Peter Lumley who had rung that morning and was ringing again. I hurried on to the post office to receive the same message and directions to the local police switchboard which lay in the front room of the home of Mrs Vicki Lazell. As I walked up her path she called to me out of the window. Peter had just rung again. She told me that he'd sent a message to Chama asking me to phone him and then as the days went by and I didn't phone, he and his wife Kate had begun to worry until that very day they'd decided to phone the police and, if I didn't turn up, ask for a search to be mounted. I was glad to know I was being looked after and even gladder that I hadn't been a day later! Mrs Lazell was thrilled to be involved, this was the first time she'd had a call from outside the state, never mind outside the USA! Peter had rung originally to offer me the editorship of *Footloose*. 'Do you want it?' he asked. 'Yes' I replied firmly. I now had something to think about as I plodded through New Mexico.

After a day of chores and re-stocking in Chama I prepared to set off on the last 700 miles to the Mexican border. I picked up my heavy (75-80lb) pack and stared at it in disbelief as the velcro-attached shoulder harness ripped out of the back. I spent some time trying to make it hold but eventually had to concede that it wouldn't. So here I was again, after just 12 days with my 'best pack on the planet', with another broken rucksack. I phoned Gregory. Send it back, they said, and we'll mend or replace it. How long? Oh, not more than ten or so days. I phoned Peter. Help, I said. He arranged for Karrimor to send me the biggest rucksack they had in the USA poste restante. Their US distributors, based in Minneapolis, rang me on receiving a telex instructing them to do this. Where's poste restante? they asked. I explained. Thought it was a restaurant, they said. But they sent the pack and it only took five days. I'd now spent ten days in the last twenty waiting for new packs. My finances were sinking rapidly into the red and my weight was going up as I spent the mostly rainy days in an assortment of cafes eating an assortment of Mexican meals. I even took up road running to get some exercise!

South of Chama my route lay across a 7-8,000-foot arid plateau for 300 or so miles, all the way to the Gila Wilderness and the 9-10,000-foot peaks of the Mogollon Mountains and the Black Range. In New Mexico 65 per cent of the Continental Divide lies on private or Indian land and only for fifty miles in the Gila Wilderness is there actually a trail so my plan was to parallel the Divide on dirt roads for much of the way, travelling cross-country where possible. Information from the Bureau of Land Management, which owns much land in New Mexico including 15 per cent of that along the Divide, told me that: 'the Divide in this state is merely a low ridge running north east to south west through the western one half of the state' and that 'most of the Divide crosses open, shrub country. Pinon-juniper will be the predominant tree cover, with the southern 100 miles mostly mesquite and creosote bush'.

Across northern New Mexico my route, running south then west, was mostly on dirt roads in flat, featureless, semi-desert terrain. Hot, hard walking under a baking sun. Endless expanses of scrub-dotted sand stretched out on all sides, the monotony relieved by occasional clumps of small, gnarled pinon pines. I could see for miles, not a good feature of the landscape as it meant that hours of walking led to very little visible progress. The Divide itself lay in the Jicarilla Apache Indian Reservation, closed to backpackers for the first 100 miles south of Chama. I parallelled it on minor highways before rejoining it south of the reservation. Certain places broke the sameness, remaining etched in the mind, oases of difference in the vast plateau separating the Rocky Mountains to the north from the desert ranges further south. A short section of trail, a luxury in this land of rutted, hard baked roads, ran above the deep, impressive canyon of the Rio Chama before the river lost itself in the waters of El Vado Reservoir, its untrammelled and wild nature trapped, like so many rivers in the South-West USA, by the need for water of those settled in this arid and inhospitable land. On the north slopes of the canyon, exposed to the full heat of the sun, a sparse covering of desert shrubs, pinon pine and a few ponderosa pine lay on the golden rocky slopes. To the south however was a dense covering of true forest dominated by Douglas fir and various types of oak. Mule deer could be seen briefly as they flicked out of sight amongst the vegetation.

Water, or rather lack of it, was a problem. I carried a gallon most days, filling up at every available source. Windmills provided fresh water but all too often filthy cattle ponds were all there was and the iodine tablets were in frequent use. Even so I had several nights out with a minimum of water, one when I failed to find a lake marked on the map (by autumn many of these shallow lakes have dried up) with only a quart left and many miles to go the following day before the next source, in this instance a roadside puddle. Small villages like Regina provided relief from the heat and thirst (Coke, coffee and conversation) and were looked forward to avidly. At Regina in fact Virginia Randall's hospitality was such that I ended up staying the night, sleeping on the floor of a huge shed, and enjoying another half day of talk before moving on. Much of the way I walked reading a book to pass the time.

Once back on the Divide I found myself in Navajo land (another branch of the Apache) and these people were very friendly, constantly stopping in their pick-up trucks to offer me a lift. Towards the end of a long, hot day it was often difficult to refuse but I always did. A week out from Chama brought me to Chaco Mesa, a vast and complex plateau lined in the south by mile after mile of steep cliffs. An hour was spent in the involved but intriguing task of finding a way down through the marvellous cirques, walls, ledges and coves. I wandered along terraces looking for descent routes, often being forced back up by sheer rock walls. Eventually I saw what looked like a continuous arete from top to bottom that didn't look too steep. I worked my way round to it and once there, was down in minutes and back to slogging across the flat, sandy, sagebrush-dotted soil.

South of Chaco Mesa though, the terrain was a little more interesting, with smaller mesas abounding and, slowly appearing in the distance, 11,000-foot Mount Taylor and the long green ridges of the Zuni Mountains. Most memorable in this spacious land were not the hills though but the skies, huge and blue with vast white clouds spreading up from distant horizons. And at dusk orange and red then purple, blue and grey. The best sunsets I've seen anywhere. The dawns were spectacular too, the sun a huge orange ball turning the cliffs of the mesas, cold and grey in the first frost-tinged light, gold and warm as a pale purple suffused the landscape. An hour later and the flat, dull daylight had reduced all to normality.

In sight of the Zuni Mountains I reached the tiny, tourist hamlet called Continental Divide that sits at 7,275 feet on the Divide itself astride Interstate 40 and its roaring, rushing cargo. Here I stayed for five days waiting for yet another pack to arrive. The one Karrimor had supplied me at Chama was simply too small (no fault of theirs, they'd sent me the largest pack they had in the USA at the time) and would carry neither the weight nor the bulk of my load comfortably. Since Chama I'd been obliged to stop every hour to take the pack off and relieve my bruised hips and sore shoulders. I knew I could not go on like this so I rang Gregory and then waited until a replacement Cassin pack was sent out to me, my fourth rucksack in five weeks! I'd walked 200 miles from Chama in 11 days but still had at least 400 miles left to Mexico. With just three weeks of my entry permit remaining it was going to be a dash for the border.

Beyond Continental Divide I found the Zunis to be pleasant wooded ridges, not really mountains but a welcome relief from the open plateaus. Then came El Morro National Monument to provide more interest and I spared half a day to look round this sandstone cliff in which generations of travellers, starting with the first European explorers, the Spanish, in the 1500s, have carved their names and left

205

messages, giving it its other name of Inscription Rock. Far older than the carvings are the remains of a pueblo, an ancient Indian village, which lie on top of the rock. The reason for all this attention is a basic one: water. A permanent pool lies at the base of the cliff shaded from the sun, the only guaranteed water supply for miles. The Indians had a path leading down from their village round the back of the rock but the more daring climbed down the cliff face, and small steps and handholds can still be seen, cut in the soft rock.

South of El Morro symmetrical hills dotted the landscape, cinder cones left by volcanic activity. Beyond them a faint blue haze marked the mountain ranges of the Gila National Forest where I was headed. A pass I'd come through in the Zuni Mountains, prosaically called Big Notch, could still be seen from forty miles away. Quemado, a small town, was passed through and here I felt the first twinge of realisation that the walk was nearing an end when I picked up my last food parcel and packet of maps. Bored with the semi-desert terrain, for the only time on the walk I deviated from the Divide to pass through the Mogollon Mountains, a more interesting and challenging area than the flat plateaus. As I climbed slowly up into the hills of Apache National Forest the weather changed. Hitherto in New Mexico it had been like summer but now a cold wind blew and with it came rain; great grey sheets sweeping across the barren slopes. I arrived at the store in Apache Creek in a torrential downpour and thick mist. The storekeeper was enjoying it, so different, he said, from the usual weather here.

I'd hoped to save time by taking a direct cross-country route from Apache Creek but two difficult days of winding my way through steep terrain, up and down crag-lined mesas in dense, spiny desert vegetation on Gallo and Apache Mountains soon ended that plan. However, the trails, neglected, overgrown and often impossible to follow, were hardly any better. My planned 20–25 miles a day became in actuality 12–15. In the river canyons trails marked on the map simply didn't exist, washed away by the frequent floods when rain or snow falling on the mountain tops swept down these deep defiles. Following the San Francisco River I crossed 14 fords in 4 miles, in bitterly cold water for the sun, low in the sky, never gained enough strength to heat up the bottomlands of these cliff-lined, narrow canyons. Whitewater Creek was worse with endless fords, ice on the rocks and frost on the ground. My sodden feet were soon frozen and the day there ended with a steep climb in the dusk on a snow-covered trail to Hummingbird Saddle, at 10,400 feet my last high-level camp. I had climbed up into the Mogollon Mountains and the Gila Wilderness, the last high mountains before the border. The next day I climbed to the 10,770-foot summit of Mogollon Baldy, the last peak of the walk, before descending in a snowstorm to camp in the shelter of tall ponderosa pines whilst the wind roared overhead.

Descending from that camp to the Gila cliff dwellings I realised that my plan of climbing back up to the Divide in the Black Range would have to be abandoned. I was running out of time. Reluctantly I accepted that I would have to road walk, or march rather, the remaining 125 miles to the border. I did pause for a quick look round the cliff dwellings, fascinating networks of houses built half way up a high cliff by Indians, yet only inhabited for about 40 years, then abandoned over 500 years ago.

This final slog along the tarmac took six days. On the 20th November I crossed the Continental Divide for the last time at 6,599 feet just before leaving the Gila National Forest. I didn't notice much along the way during this last section, my eyes were on the distant horizon. Several people offered hospitality along the road and this eased the effort but during those last days I just wanted to finish. My last camp, though, was a peaceful bivouac well away from the road on the desert floor under the stars. An owl watched over me from a nearby yucca plant. Then it was the last plod to the border 3 miles beyond the little town of Columbus, a nondescript border with a few ugly concrete customs' buildings and a chain link fence. It was November 27th. The journey from the Canadian border had taken 179 days. I had 2 days of my permit remaining.

I touched the border fence and turned away. I felt, well, nothing much. A little sad perhaps, a little triumphant but really it hadn't sunk in that the adventure was over, that I'd walked the Continental Divide from Canada to Mexico.

7

Iceland

ALMOST A CIRCUIT OF THE MARKARFLJOT

Six months passed rapidly following my return from the Continental Divide Walk. I had a new job, editing *Footloose* magazine, a new home to create and a mass of correspondence to catch up with as well as over 3,000 colour transparencies to sort through. I still found time for the hills however; New Year 1986 was spent in the Lake District and weekend's throughout the winter were spent skiing with Tyneside Loipers in the Cheviots and the Cairngorms. Occasionally I had a weekend's backpacking in the local hills and I made one solo four-day ski tour of the Cairngorms. The lengthy winter stretched the ski season into May but as spring finally developed I found myself longing for a longer trip and developing the familiar symptoms of a need to slip away into the wilderness — symptoms such as poring over maps and staring vacantly into space.

Circumstances precluded any trip of more than a week or so which meant the opportunity was there for one of those many journeys I'd planned but never carried out as the time needed never seemed to be available. Another Scottish trek? North to south through Wales? On considering and rejecting these and other possibilities I realised by my lack of real enthusiasm, that I wanted to travel further afield. Scanning through a pile of outdoor holiday brochures in the *Footloose* office I came across Dick Phillips' *On Foot in Iceland* and began to read a little more closely. An hour later I was on the phone to Dick, making notes, ordering maps and feeling excited. Iceland it was to be. Initially Alain Kahan was to come with me but we failed to co-ordinate our free time so I ended up going alone. I had no set route, no long trail to follow, just a 1:100,000 scale map of the Landmannalaugar/Thorsmork region of southern Iceland and the words of Dick Phillips ringing in my ears: 'there will still be much snow, river crossings could be difficult, the summer bus services will not be running', plus more advice on those lines for I intended visiting Iceland in June, very early in the season. Given Dick's warnings and knowing his depth of experience of backpacking in Iceland (he has run a travel service for independent-minded travellers to Iceland for over twenty years), I planned a few tentative routes into the interior on the basis of going in one way then after three days turning back to reach the coast road by another route. A there-and-back again ploy but the 'there' would be wherever I reached in the time available.

Iceland had been on my list of countries to visit ever since I'd first seen pictures of the country. A rugged mountainous country (average altitude 1,640 feet, only 25% of the country is below 650 feet), Iceland is often called the 'Land of Ice and Fire' because of the combination of vast ice caps (Vatnajökull is, at 3,243 square miles, the largest ice-cap in the world outside of Greenland and Antarctica and 11% of the country lies under the ice) and the many active volcanoes and their associated phenomena (geysers, hot springs, boiling mud pits and similar). Despite being 39,750 square miles in area, making it the second largest island in Europe, the uncompromising nature of the terrain (only 25% of the land has continuous plant coverage) has kept settlement to the coastal regions only and despite 1,100 years of habitation the population is only about 240,000. All of these people live around the coast (which is more hospitable than the interior) where they can carry out fishing, one of Iceland's most important industries, leaving the interior uninhabited.

Conditions I knew would be rugged and the weather possibly stormy so although only out for a week it was with a 50-lb pack that I boarded the Icelandair flight to Keflavik on 11th June. Clouds prevented much of a view on the approach to the airport but from the coach to Reykjavik I could see barren lava plains and, rising into the clouds, stark snow-splashed mountains. After a night in Reykjavik I caught an early morning bus along the coast road (which encircles the island) to the small village of Hvollsvollur near the south coast. Low cloud again prevented a clear view of the mountains but the sight of great, grey slopes rising into the murk was exciting with its hints of hidden glories. The backpacking began on the dirt road out of the village heading east along the rich valley of Flotjsdalur past many farms. Ahead and to the south lay the wide estuary and flood plain of the Markarfljot river. My rough plan was to follow this river into the mountains on its northern (true right) side then return along the other.

The walk along the road took place in wind and drizzle

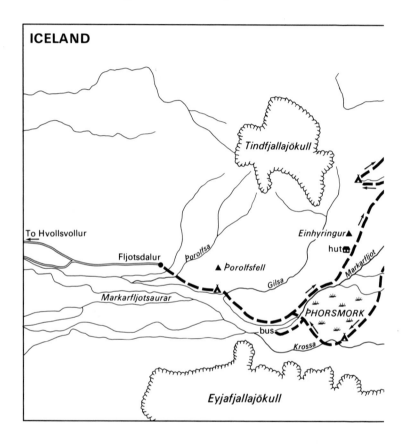

and I did take a lift part of the way as I wanted to leave the road as soon as possible. However neither the road nor the weather lessened the feeling that an adventure was beginning and that I was approaching exciting and challenging country. Across the river valley I could see the lower slopes of the Eyjafallajökull and Myrdalsjökull ice-caps. Standing alone out on the mudflats was the huge rock of Stora-Dimon. Cliffs soon hemmed in the road to the north and down them tumbled a series of crashing waterfalls. Small trees dotted the base of the cliffs which in places were made from columnar basalt, miniature versions of the Devil's Postpile in Yosemite National Park on the

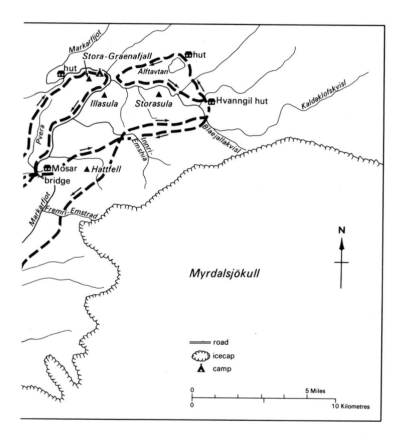

Pacific Crest Trail. Eventually I reached the youth hostel at Fljotsdalur, set up by Dick Phillips, and the base for the summer treks he organises, and the end of the dirt road.

I wanted to go beyond habitations and roads as soon as possible though so I passed the hostel by as heavy rain began to fall and had my first camp on a piece of green sward a few miles further on, on the lowest slopes of Thorolfsfell and above the gravel banks of the Markarfljot. Already I had wet feet from fording side streams running down into the main river. Birds were everywhere; terns swooped and dived over the rivers, groups of waders (oystercatcher, redshank, curlew and others) dive-bombed me shrieking angrily, swans, ducks and geese dotted the gravel banks and mudflats whilst on the cliffs fulmars were nesting. Above them ravens soared and croaked. Being this close to the Arctic Circle in June means that darkness never falls so one can forget the concepts of day and night. Even though I was only in Iceland for eight days I adapted to this, setting off whenever I liked and sleeping when tired, regardless of the time. Wind and rain buffeted the tent that night, not for the last time on this trek, and the temperature fell to 10°C. The dampness made it seem colder.

As Friday the thirteenth began the storm increased in force and I woke several times to lashing rain and high winds, returning to sleep immediately each time. Unable finally to sleep anymore I lingered over breakfast, noting in my journal '8.50 am — storm still blasting on ... 10.10 am — storm worse with much stronger gusts of wind shaking the tent.' Eventually I left at 11 am and struggled into the gale, which was hammering straight down the valley, for an hour and a half before taking shelter in a small cave on the banks of the Markarfljot. The effort of forcing a passage against the storm with a heavy pack required vast amounts of energy and the resultant sweat output proved too much for my 'breathable' waterproofs. On removing them in the cave I found my clothing underneath soaked. As usual though I was wearing synthetic clothes (a Dunova T-shirt and polycotton windshirt) and I added polypropylene long johns under my polycotton trousers and a long-sleeved Capilene shirt in place of the T-shirt as well as a synthetic filled sweater and a hat. The temperature in the cave was 8°C. For the first time ever on a backpacking trip I was carrying a tripod, which I'd borrowed from Peter Lumley, and I set this up in the cave to take a few self-portraits. An unusual place to start using a new photographic tool! The rock in the cave was rotten. Each time I brushed the roof a shower of dirt and pebbles fell on me. But I couldn't stay in the cave for ever and the photographic possibilities were somewhat limited so after half an hour or so back out into the storm I went.

A tributary called the Gilsa provided me with a first taste of the major difficulties I was to encounter during the trek as I spent some time finding safe ways across its many knee-deep, fast-moving channels. Across the Markarfljot I could see the greenery of Thorsmork, my ultimate destination for from there I would be able to catch a summer service bus back to Reykjavik as these began running on the fifteenth. For the moment though I was following the river upstream. The wide flood plain became narrower as I pushed on, forming a broad gorge with low cliffs running along the sides, the bed consisting of sand and gravel, soft and wet and hard to walk through. Above towered the twisted rock peak of Einhyrningur its two side summits curving upwards from the main rock pyramid like horns on a Viking helmet. I was roughly following a yellow line marked on the map and described in the map legend as a 'Mountain track with unbridged rivers only passable for four-wheel-drive vehicles during the summer.' Old wheel marks could be made out but it was certainly impassable to any vehicle in mid-June.

A bright orange roofed building came into view. 'Roundup shelter' read the map legend. I looked inside. Stalls and hay gave the visual clues to its use; more convincing was the smell. What I didn't know though was that such farmer's buildings are used by backpackers and skiers for shelter and that if I'd ventured further in I'd have found habitable bothy accommodation. Again Dick Phillips (who is both a voluntary area and maintenance organiser for the Mountain Bothies Association in Britain) was responsible for this. Not knowing about such shelter yet poised on the doorstep I continued in the rain leaving the main valley for a diversion along the Siki over several snow patches (I was now about 1,650 feet up) before descending to the Markarfljot again at Mosar where a sturdy bridge crossed the torrent above a spectacular waterfall. On the far side stood a hut but this was a private one, locked and boarded up. Occasional clear patches in the cloud cover gave good if brief views of the really wild surroundings; snowfield-slashed sharp rock peaks soared skywards out of the grey and black of the lava and sand valley in which the river roared and crashed its way towards the sea. The feeling of a world in the making, of the power of the elements in shaping the earth, was very strong.

I followed the track away from the main river to where it disappeared into the torrent of a tributary, the Thvera, to re-emerge further upstream. A few yards out into the deep powerful stream and I turned back. The force of the water when only knee deep made it difficult to stay on my feet and I could see it became deeper. Being washed downstream would land me in Markarfljot and over that waterfall ... no, discretion seemed wisest here. So I decided to follow the Thvera upstream in the hope of an easier crossing. But first I had to cross an unnamed side stream. This lay in a deep, steep-sided gorge into which I could find no way down until I'd followed it a mile or so upstream and the steepness eased off. A good, reasonably sheltered camp site on dryish ground lay on the far bank so I pitched the tent as it was starting to rain and the wind was strengthening. Despite the pack cover I was using and the stuffsacks and plastic bags into which my gear was packed, much of it was damp including my sleeping bag. I was glad it was a pile one, especially as the high humidity made drying it out unlikely. With a temperature of 7°C I was none too warm anyway and quickly donned my thermal underwear which I would sleep in. From the tent doorway I had a good view of the impressive cone of Hattfell, whose distinctive shape was to dominate most of the rest of my trek.

I spent the wet evening playing with logistics and possible plans for the next few days; a favourite occupation in camp when the weather confines me to the tent. I estimated I'd walked 12 miles that day and had 27 more to go to Landmannalaugar, the farthest I thought I could reach before I'd have to turn back, and from where it was 31 to Thorsmork. The bus back to Reykjavik from there left at 3.30 pm in five days' time. With conditions as they'd been so far, soft soil, soft snow, deep rivers and heavy rain, I realised I couldn't really hope to walk another 60 miles. But in an optimistic mood I made no definite decisions and wrote in my notebook: 'See how tomorrow goes'.

The heavy rain continued through the night and into the morning, turning to hail before I moved on. 'Unbelievable weather, worse than yesterday' I noted tersely. Once I'd clambered out of the stream gully I realised just what a sheltered camp site I'd had as a howling wind and lashing rain had me leaning into it to stay on my feet. I had all my clothes on; three layers on my legs plus gaiters and four layers on my top plus two hats and I was barely warm enough. I kept close to the Thvera as the visibility was bad but was forced eventually to climb high above it where it cut a deep gorge into the rock. From here, near the head of the stream, I crossed a col to descend to the Krokagil, a major tributary of the Markarfljot, my eyes fixed firmly on the hut visible on the far bank — in vain though as again I was turned back by the force of the snowmelt and rain swollen waters. A third of the way across I was hip deep and swaying. Not knowing how deep it would get I staggered back to the bank, cursing myself for not thinking to bring a ski stick or staff for crossings such as these. I went upstream but it became quickly obvious that I would have to go a very long way in the wrong direction before I'd have a chance of crossing.

I perused the map. Here the Krokagil river, coming from the south west, runs into the Markarfljot as the latter makes a loop and turns north-east before returning to its south-westerly flow forming a bend in which lies the 910-foot Stora-Graenafjall, its summit towering over the bend in that river. The most obvious thing to do was to return to Mosar and the bridge, but I hate retracing my steps and I didn't relish heading directly into the storm, so instead I decided to follow the Krokagil to the Markarfljot and then the river back to the bridge. This proved not to be an easy option. The banks were steep and cut with deep snow-filled gullies so I had a great deal of climbing to do on loose gravel and soft snow. Where there were terraces the remaining extensive patches of wet, heavy snow kept me to a slow pace. At one point I was faced with either a difficult scramble for at least several hundred feet up the steep bank (that was as far as I could see) or a wade in the river. I chose the latter and for several hundred metres I waded along through the thigh-deep water clinging onto the broken snowbanks that hung over the edge. When I climbed out my legs were numb with cold. I'd only travelled $7^1/2$ miles but when I found a flat site near the confluence of the Krokagil and the Markarfljot under the bulky Stora-Graenfjall and facing the impressive tower of Illasula I stopped for the day. I was too wet and tired to continue. Thankfully a brief break in the storm allowed me to set up camp in the dry but by the time I was settled inside the tent, snug in my sleeping bag and with water boiling on the stove, it was raining again.

Pink-footed geese flew by outside, honking loudly. I'd seen many of these during the day which was hardly surprising as Iceland is the main breeding area in the world for these birds. They brought back memories of home, for vast flocks of them overwinter on the flat farmland and mosses that lie inland of the Lancashire coast between Formby and Southport. I used to go out with the school Field Club to watch them, spending hours crawling along deep ditches trying to approach as close as possible before their 'sentries' saw us and the whole flock swept up into the sky with a rush of darkening wings to seek another stubble field to graze in.

'Fine country but dire weather' I wrote. Further replanning gave me a lake, Alftavatn, as my destination for the next day, partly chosen because, according to the map there was a hut there, which was owned by the Tourist Association of Iceland. I hoped this meant it would be open and that I could manage 15 miles in one day. In fact Alftavatn only lay 2¹/₂ miles from where I was — on the other side of the river.

The quiet woke me at 4.30 am. I unzipped the tent door and peered out. A light drizzle fell. There was no wind. I could hear the river and then a bird singing and saw a patch of blue sky, a small one admittedly but there in the grey sheet of the sky. 'The river' I noted over breakfast 'does look a little lower this morning, or am I only fooling myself?' I went to look. It was lower but even so I failed to ford it. At a bend where it was broken into channels by several shingle banks I managed, without the pack, to reach the first bank in strong, thigh deep water. But the next section was wider and faster, and, no doubt, deeper so yet again I retreated.

Below my camp the Markarfljot entered a steep-sided gorge. To round this I climbed steeply up the shoulder of Stora-Graenafjall to a height of about 2,000 feet from where I had good views of the surrounding extremely wild country: cloud-capped rock peaks above gravel and snow plains cut by deep river gorges in the foreground with, behind, the vague whiteness of the icecaps fading into the turbulent sky. A pleasant ridge led away from the shoulder and the summit above it to a contour well above the river and a descent to the Thvera, which I forded easily at the point where it had turned me back two days previously as it was much lower. As I crossed the bridge at Mosar the rain began. Head down I turned back northwards to cross a broad flat desert of lava and snow below the ramparts of Hattfell, the way marked by a series of yellow-topped wooden posts. Beyond the lava beds and Hattfell I met the track coming from Thorsmork in the middle of a vast snowfield. I slogged through this, variety being provided by short sections of ankle-deep mud and occasional knee-deep river fords. The weather worsened as I passed under Storasula. The bridge over the Innri-Emstrua provided shelter for me to don extra clothing. The river was covered by huge drifts here and although I could see no water I could hear it. Outside I was exposed to the full blast of the storm, a tiny staggering dot in this huge cold desert of snow and black sand. The rain turned to hail, then snow and sleet were blasted across the empty spaces by a ferocious wind. Visibility became nominal and I was glad of the yellow-capped posts.

The round-up shelter of Hvanngil was reached with relief, a feeling increased when I climbed the ladder inside to find bothy accommodation above the stable. There was even a bothy book and I found that Dick Phillips' parties used this place regularly. Comments on the weather showed that I was not experiencing anything at all unusual. I was tempted to stay but a mile or so away lay Alftavatn so I pushed on over several small hills and across a few more rivers. The large hut, situated on a flat mud plain near the frozen lake, and empty apart from iron bedsteads and mattresses, was far less welcoming than the bothy, but now I was here I was staying. I sat at the table with the sleeping bag pulled up around my shoulders cooking dinner. All my clothes were damp. The temperature was the usual 7-8°C. Rain lashed the hut and the wind whistled across the corrugated iron roof. Two and a half miles away lay my site of last night and every so often when the clouds lifted a little I could see Stora-Graenafjall beyond the end of the lake. For once though I was glad not to be in the tent.

With three days left and no sign of an improvement in the weather I decided I'd better head back towards the coast. I slept twelve long hours in the warmth of the hut, and woke to a calm, dry but overcast day. To avoid repeating my route of the previous day in reverse I followed the edge of the lake south westwards then crossed a low col to where the

Kaldaklofskvisl ran into the Markarfljot below Illasula and just across from my campsite of two nights ago. From here I intended to cross the black sand desert to the track for Thorsmork. There was just one problem: the river. The Kaldaklofskvisl roared down a gorge and was clearly unfordable. I'd had enough experience now not to need to wade out a little to find out. So I followed it upstream, all the way to the bothy at Hvanngil! But there was compensation in the form of clearing skies and good views, especially of the distinctive peak of Storasula. I actually had lunch sitting down and set up the tripod to take some pictures. To the south west I could see the serrated edge of the Tindfjallajokull ice cap.

At Hvanngil I discovered from the bothy book that another walker, Horace Gilkes, had arrived after me the previous evening. He expressed astonishment that I'd continued onto Alftavatn. He was, he wrote, checking on the condition of another bothy at Strutslaug and might return the same day. I wondered if he would and realised that I hadn't seen anyone at all since leaving the road five days previously. As it was 5.30 I decided to stay here, again only a mile or so from where I'd been the previous night. Partly I hoped that Horace would turn up. Some one to talk to, especially someone who knew the area well, as I guessed Horace did from his bothy book entry, would be quite pleasant. I hung up my wet tent in the stable and my wet clothes upstairs. The sloping-roofed, wood-panelled loft was surprisingly warm, 15°C! As I hung everything up I realised I hadn't worn my Goretex jacket for the first time on the trek.

The red-roofed hut of Hvanngil lies on the edge of the huge plain I'd crossed, just in the entrance of a narrow valley. Outside lie some long, low ridges. I climbed up onto one of these, making the most of the good weather whilst it lasted. From there I could see across the black sand to the distant Myrdralsjokull ice cap and down to the Kaldaklofsk-visl with its dramatic waterfalls edged with collapsing snow banks. Birds were everywhere; more geese flying lazily past in pairs honking loudly, a dusky, savage-billed arctic skua twisting overhead, a ringed plover running about on the gravel banks, and many more.

Back in the bothy I cooked dinner and gave my attention to the bothy book for a few hours. As well as Dick Phillips' parties many British walkers had found their way here as had many from abroad, though I noted that very few came before July and not many after August. Weather was a major topic of the visitors, sunshine in particular being obviously worth an ecstatic entry. Turning to my own journal I noted that if or when I came again I would bring warmer clothes and heavier, more robust, waterproof clothing. I wrote: 'I've been warm enough, just felt on the margins at times.'

At 10 pm I huddled down into my sleeping bag on a mattress for the second night running. It didn't look like Horace was going to return after all. But as is often the way with bothy life I'd just dozed off when I heard the door crash open. A figure climbed heavily up the stairs dumped a load on the floor then went down again. A few minutes later Horace returned upstairs and introduced himself, having divested most of his wet gear in the stable. He was, he announced, exhausted — the hut at Strutslaug had been partially damaged by an avalanche and was not habitable so he'd had to return here as he was not carrying a tent. In an effort to get warm, Horace lit two paraffin primus stoves, his own and an ancient one that lived in the bothy, and I joined him at the table and accepted a cup of tea. A tour leader for Dick Phillips, Horace was currently hauling in food dumps for parties to pick up as they came through and checking huts for damage they might have received over the winter. Used to Icelandic conditions he was better equipped than me with a warmer sleeping bag, far more clothes, including pile salopettes and a thick woollen Icelandic sweater, and an ice axe. His gear was strapped to a traditional army-style 'man-pack' frame. It looked highly uncomfortable but, said Horace, had only cost £4 and was very useful for bringing in awkward loads such as building materials that wouldn't fit in an internal frame pack. Eschewing the use of a pack bag he simply strapped his gear in a hefty kit bag to the frame. He wasn't surprised by the weather, more resigned really as he knew Iceland too well to expect better — but he did tell me that there had been more snow than usual this winter.

Steady rain greeted me on peering out of the window the next morning. It had been like this for three weeks, Horace informed me. His plan was to stay in the hut for the day and dry out whilst waiting for a tour party that should be arriving later on. Mine was to head for Thorsmork where I had to be the following afternoon. Horace reckoned it was a two-day walk in these conditions. Much snow had melted in the previous twenty-four hours and I was glad of the bridge over the Kaldaklofskvisl, the 'notorious KKK' as it was referred to in an entry in the Hvanngil hut book, and found several of the fords much deeper than before. The waterfalls were lined with toppling blocks of snow and the Blafjallakvisl was a rippling sheet of silver-green water running over the still solid snowfield. I had to follow this river upstream a short way before I could cross safely and it felt very precarious walking on snow-ice that lay a foot or more under a rushing stream. I was heading into the wind and rain as usual with low cloud shrouding the tops. The black sand desert dotted with the white splashes of the remaining snow faded away into the lower screes, cliffs and snow-filled gullies of the hidden hills and the greyness of the sky. All was pale and insubstantial, a world drained of colour and life. Trolls and goblins seemed likely rather than otherwise here.

On reaching the bridge over the Innri-Emstrua that I'd sheltered under during the storm of two days previously I saw that the then firm, flat bed of snow under it had cracked at the edges and tilted into the centre, to reveal rushing black waters below the jagged edges of white. Below the bridge two waterfalls crashed and spurted through the snow blocks covering the river above. Hattfell, the beacon of the walk, was passed by yet again and I was on new terrain as I passed to the south-east of it through a wide valley rimmed by low, long grey hills. Beyond this grim defile I entered an area of black sand and gravel hills through which I weaved my way to the bright orange blob of the Touring Association of Iceland's hut at Botnar. A truly blasted, inhospitable landscape surrounds this haven, a scene wild and inhumane, more lifeless and totally 'other worldish' than any place in any mountains I have ever passed through. I sheltered in the empty hut for a while, reading the hut book before continuing a winding descent through the black mounds that are the only natural phenomena I've ever encountered that rival in desolation the emptiness of abandoned industrial landscapes.

The descent took me to a bridge over the Fremri-Emstrua which poured down a boulder-strewn valley from the grey-white scarred snout of the Entujokull glacier which I could see just a few kilometres away. Flattish lightly vegetated terraces above the river looked to be possible campsites, the first I'd seen all day. I climbed out of the Fremri-Emstrua valley to another black sand plateau. This one, though, lay above the Markarfljot and I had superb views of this savage torrent as it roared through a narrow, twisted gorge down the sides of which poured thin streams of snowmelt water. Gently sloping sandy wastes led me slowly down towards Thorsmork, always with the sound of the river on my right. As I neared my destination the scenery softened and a green tinge began to creep over the slopes. Soon the patches of grass and moss grew and merged and then the first patches of stunted trees appeared, tiny groves of wind-stunted birches pale with the new leaves of summer. The sight of them, the first trees I'd seen for six days, made me feel quite light-hearted. A wave of relaxation swept over me and I realised just how keyed up to the struggle with the elements I'd become.

I wandered on, passing a small brown tent pitched out in the windy open landscape, the only other tent I'd seen. Up into the thicketed hills I went, weaving in and out of the woods with glimpses beyond them of the great icecap of Myrdalsjokull. On the banks of the Krossa I came upon a hut being prepared for the summer, whilst nearby, on neat green lawns divided up by smart gravel paths were pitched some tents, and cars were parked on gravel flats by the river. I had come out of the wilderness. I was not sure I really wanted to so I turned away from the people and the paths and the lawns, the cars and the hut, and climbed a small knoll to camp under the trees looking across to the sharp whiteness of the icecap. The evening was clear, calm and warm enough for me to sit at the open tent door, cooking and eating, whilst looking at the view for the first time on the trek.

I still had to find the bus though. There are three huts in Thorsmork; I visited two of them after a lengthy stroll that involved an unnecessary ford of the multi-channelled Krossa. Negotiating the maze of paths that lace the birch woods I was startled to hear voices, English voices! Around a turn in the path came a party of a half dozen or more walkers who asked me what lay over the next rise. I quickly realised that they must have arrived on the coach I was seeking — for the day trip to Reykjavik allowed for a two hours' stay in Thorsmork. And sure enough on the banks of the Markarfljot flood plain I came upon another hut and a tough looking coach. The journey was over.

At least the walking journey was over, for the coach ride across the Markarfljot plain to the coast was quite an adventure in itself as the driver negotiated many streams and river channels including some deep enough to bring the water up to near window level. A coach tour in Iceland is not quite like a coach tour anywhere else! Normally I regard coach journeys as merely ways to get to the mountains and I tend to spend them reading a book or studying maps. However, when the coach is churning through a swirling torrent and accelerating up a steep gravel bank there is actually a sense of travel, though I'd still rather walk. I knew I was really back in civilisation when I swapped to a 'real' coach on the main highway which even had a television. On it, live from Mexico, England were playing a football match in the World Cup. How small the world has become, I thought. Not twenty-four hours before I'd been in a remote, bleak and hostile wilderness where television does not penetrate and where anything more than a few miles away does not in real terms exist.

Despite only being a week long the Iceland trek gave me an intense experience, a challenging adventure tougher and more committing than I'd been expecting. For that week life again returned to the immediacy of living minute by minute, day by day in the mountains with only what might happen in the next few hours, what problems or glories might lie over the next ridge and across the next river, being of any importance. Usually it takes a week for me to feel that involved in a trek but the ferocity and intensity of the Iceland experience, the difficulties and dangers of travelling just a short distance in such dramatic and grand surroundings caused me to slip into that mood almost immediately. I returned from Iceland feeling scoured and shaken by my visit. Until then, despite the many short treks I'd made, the Continental Divide had been the last walk that really meant anything and I'd expected that to remain the case until I did another long walk. I was both surprised and pleased to find that just one week in Iceland in June during which I walked a mere 70 miles could be such a major adventure.

Postscript

When I walked from Land's End to John O'Groats in 1978
Tom Waghorn, writing in the *Manchester Evening News*
called the walk the 'dream of a lifetime'. I'm writing this in
July 1986 the day after giving a slide lecture on my
Continental Divide walk to a walking club in Lancaster. 'A
dream of a lifetime' one of the audience called it. This
turning of a particular walk, the 'dream', into something
separate from 'life' is, however, precisely what I am striving
to avoid. Travelling in the mountains, in the natural
landscape of the earth, the world which sustains us and
allows us life is not for me a 'dream', a tiny capsule totally
cut off from my 'real' life that I can take out and look at
every so often. Rather it is my life, it's what I do, what I
think about, what I live for. A time when I am not planning
or thinking about another backpacking trip does not exist.
And the next weekend's adventure is just as important and
exciting as the next six-month one. The day after returning
from Iceland I was in Keswick to take part in the annual
Lake District Four Three-Thousand Peaks Marathon
Walk, a 46-mile trek over the summits of Skiddaw, Scafell,
Scafell Pike and Helvellyn that starts at 2 in the morning. I
completed the round in 13 hours, 47 minutes and at the
present moment, this walk, a seventieth the length of the
Continental Divide, is the one I feel most pleased at having
completed.

But my first love is long distance mountain backpacking
and as my wilderness treks are not one-off 'dreams of a
lifetime' but a lifetime's occupation I am planning several
more. This summer I am planning a fortnight's backpacking
through Andorra in the Pyrenees with my companion from
previous treks Alain Kahan. Soon I would like to visit
Alaska and I'm currently collecting information on this vast
wilderness and trying to work out a feasible backpacking

trip. Iceland I intend visiting again, for longer this time, perhaps making a journey right across the island from south to north. And just at the tentative stage is another really big trek, a 3,000-mile backpack from the Iron Curtain to the Atlantic across the Alps and Pyrenees. This is just the start of a never-ending list of places I'd like to visit, wildernesses I'd like to explore if I have the time and the chance.

Being 'escapist', 'selfish' and 'unable to cope with the realities of everyday life' are some of the criticisms aimed at backpackers and other regular explorers of the natural world. Yet our modern detachment from nature, from the force of which we are a part, our futile attempt to prove ourselves separate from and superior to the ecological system that allows us to live, our view of the world as an enemy to be conquered, and a bottomless treasure chest to be exploited, are the very escapist and selfish attitudes that have led us to the brink of the abyss of annihilation on which we are poised. Re-establishing our place in the natural scheme of evolution and the real world is essential if we are to have a future. And this cannot be done intellectually, the process must go far deeper than the shallow streams of logical thought. An intuitive understanding of our oneness with the life of the earth and the forces of nature, with the rocks and rivers, mountains and deserts, with the other animals and the plants must be the starting point for a return to the earth from the remote ivory towers of the so-called reality we have imprisoned ourselves in.

Backpacking is my way of doing this. Every trek through a wilderness, every night in the mountains under the stars far from roads, cars, bright lights and the other trappings of civilisation releases the tensions and pressures of our false and stressful lifestyle. Of course I know that I carry the products of modern society on my back every time I venture into the back country but then I am not advocating a denial of tools. That would take me back beyond the Stone Age! Humanity is a tool-using species and tools are essential to our life but in modern society the balance has become such that it seems more as though humanity's purpose is to provide a market for tools rather than tools being produced to improve humanity's way of life.

So when the confusions become too much and I feel locked into an unnatural life of concrete, forms to fill in, and sterile logic, I pack up a rucksack and head off into the hills to pitch my tent, gaze at the sky, feel the wind and rain on my face, the rocks and earth under my feet and bring my life back to the only thing that exists, the present.